twitter is
not
a strategy

PREVIOUS TITLES BY TOM DOCTOROFF

Billions: Selling to the New Chinese Consumer

*What Chinese Want: Culture, Communism
and China's Modern Consumer*

twitter is

not

a strategy

Rediscovering the Art of Brand Marketing

Tom Doctoroff

palgrave
macmillan

First published in 2014 by PALGRAVE MACMILLAN® TRADE
in the United States—a division of St. Martin's Press LLC, 175 Fifth
Avenue, New York, NY 10010.

Where this book is distributed in the UK, Europe and the rest of
the world, this is by Palgrave Macmillan, a division of Macmillan
Publishers Limited, registered in England, company number 785998, of
Houndmills, Basingstoke, Hampshire RG21 6XS.

Palgrave® and Macmillan® are registered trademarks in the United
States, the United Kingdom, Europe and other countries.

ISBN 978-1-137-27930-9

Apple Jacks jingle © Kellogg Company. Used with permission.

Library of Congress Cataloging-in-Publication Data

Doctoroff, Tom.
   Twitter is not a strategy : rediscovering the art of brand marketing /
Tom Doctoroff.
      pages   cm
   Includes index.
   ISBN 978-1-137-27930-9 (hardback)
   1. Branding (Marketing) 2. Internet marketing. 3. Internet
advertising. 4. Brand name products. I. Title.
HF5415.1255.D63   2014
658.8'27—dc23

                                                          2014015232

A catalogue record of the book is available from the British Library.

Design by Letra Libre, Inc.

First edition: November 2014

10 9 8 7 6 5 4 3 2 1

Printed in the United States of America.

contents

Introduction   Back to the Future   1

1   New World Disorder   11

2   The Value of Strong Brands   37

3   Insight into Consumer Behavior   53

4   The Brand Idea   87

5   Engagement Ideas   153

6   Engagement Planning   189

7   Creativity 2.0: The Rules of
    Online Content   221

    Notes   243

    Index   253

introduction

back to the future

Business is in flux. We suffer from disorientation wrought by technological change. Convention has been upended, and the digital world—a universe of bits and bytes, atomistic fragmentation that mocks tradition—is all variables, no constants. The rise of search engines and e-commerce has changed the balance of power between marketers and consumers. In May 2013 the *Financial Times* warned, "Algorithms threaten to end 'Mad Men' era of TV ads."[1] Marketers, traditionally expert in product development and brand messaging, are now expected to decipher the meaning of statistics flowing from "machine-to-machine connectivity." And, given the dizzying pace of innovation occurring in cyberspace, reasonable people can ask: Across unsettled high-tech terrain, is the term *digital expert* an oxymoron?

CEOs look to the beast itself for salvation, intoxicated by the promise of new ways to maximize return on investment. A typical *Business Insider* headline: "Big Data Can Help Marketers Unlock up to $200 Billion."[2] Buzzwords abound: *CRM, cookies, digital ecosystems, experience optimization, platformization, algorithmic customization*. The advertising world is experiencing unprecedented tumult. In the midst of a digital big bang, the advertising giant TBWA advocates disruption to its clients—that is, the unsettling of category convention to achieve competitive differentiation—whereas Publicis Worldwide wants brands to "lead the change." But *what* change and how?

DIGITAL SALVATION?

Digital technology offers an infinite—and intimidating—range of ways for brands to engage with consumers. Connections can happen in real time. Brand communications can be transformed into brand journalism, with social network feeds providing consumers with relevant news as they go through their day. Branded apps—from Trailhead, The North Face's hiking path locator, to Allergycast, Johnson & Johnson's pollen index counter—transform passively received propositions into actual services. Brand promises flower into three-dimensional experiences.

The gamut of possibilities on this new commercial landscape is almost infinite, too broad for simplistic solutions. More important, the range of strategic imperatives confronted by various product categories is vast, and their needs are incompatible with a paint-by-numbers manual. One thing, however, is certain. Regardless of whether it is cola or computers being sold, the exploding array of digital channels presents increased opportunities to connect *and* confuse. Unless marketers master the timeless rules of brand building, they will get nowhere. In a hydra-headed digital world, the ultimate commandment of marketing still holds: Consistency is golden. Without long-term *ideas* behind it, the latest data-mining technique, augmented reality app, or search algorithm will be lost in the background buzz. Technological adventurism will never replace solid, coherent conceptual craftsmanship.

Ideas that stand the test of time are not quaint. Yes, the digital realm presents exciting challenges. But in that excitement it's

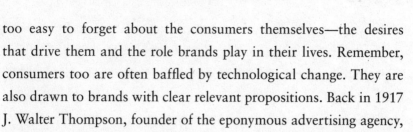

too easy to forget about the consumers themselves—the desires that drive them and the role brands play in their lives. Remember, consumers too are often baffled by technological change. They are also drawn to brands with clear relevant propositions. Back in 1917 J. Walter Thompson, founder of the eponymous advertising agency, a company that celebrated its 150th anniversary in 2014, uttered these enduring words: "Somewhere in your product, or in your business, there is a 'difference,' an idea that can be developed into a story so big, so vital, and so compelling to your public as to isolate your product from its competitors, and make your public think of it as a distinctly different kind of product."

The dazzling new kaleidoscope of choice and the pressures of a hyperconnected, "always on" digital lifestyle has left more than a few people unsettled. This includes many marketers charged with leading some of world's greatest brands. In an effort to avoid being branded traditional or obsolete, advertising and marketing professionals fall prey to technological temptation. We furtively deploy the latest or hottest digital innovation without fully considering the basics of brand strategy or message consistency. Consumers end up more confused and less loyal.

In the midst of this disorientation, order can be especially reassuring. The practice of marketing may be evolving, but the fundamentals of brand building are the same today as they were fifty years ago—the so-called golden age of advertising. Now more than ever, strong brands command price premiums. Now more than ever, strong brand ideas produce profit.

Only the brand idea—the long-term relationship between consumer and brand that remains steady yet evolves over time—can resolve the tension between traditional brand-building imperatives and the opportunities unleashed by technology and widespread consumer empowerment. Clearly defined yet dynamically interactive, it remains the sine qua non for both consistent messaging and engagement between consumers and brand. Traditional brand building is top-down, articulated by the manufacturer and fueled by message clarity and deep understanding of consumers' motivations. The new opportunities offered by technology are bottom-up, unpredictable, on the street—of, by, and for the people. Brand building has existed since the dawn of the industrial revolution; the new opportunities are entirely twenty-first century. Yet they need to coexist within the same discipline.

Plenty of qualified authorities are available to guide readers through the challenges of modern marketing. I am neither a so-called digital expert nor a creative guru. But, as CEO of JWT Asia Pacific, I have had the good fortune of partnering with dozens of clients, both multinational and local, many of whom have succeeded in establishing strong brands in the world's most dynamic commercial environments—and some who have not. If I have learned one valuable lesson, it is this: Anxiety is not productive. Brands can "lead the change" only when their marketing executives have the confidence to go back to the future and rededicate themselves to timeless marketing principles.

THIS BOOK'S CONTENT:
FREEDOM WITHIN A FRAMEWORK

It's time to take a deep breath. With the brand idea as its epicenter, *Twitter Is Not a Strategy* is designed to forge order from chaos for both marketers and consumers. I offer a four-part framework that unifies conceptual and executional essentials, demonstrating that the brands that address these issues most effectively will always reign supreme, boasting the highest margins and the most loyal consumers.

In the first two chapters I discuss the rise of brands and how digital technology impacts lives and consumer marketing. From video games to social networks that provide new platforms for self-expression to the Uber app that connects passengers with drivers for hire at the tap of a button, the digital world has yielded an explosion of lifestyle opportunities and consumer empowerment. Few people sit passively in front of the television waiting for commercials to interrupt them with information. New technology is two-way, and it enables ongoing dialog between brands and consumers who now demand a voice. They expect to be heard and join in on the fun—with brands whose advertising is as involving as any of their other entertainment options. And consumers want to be rewarded for loyalty. They don't want to be talked down to.

This is the essence of the new engagement—consumers want more than a messy short-term affair. Engagement is now more like marriage: long term (that is, consistent in message), enriched by dialog between consumers and manufacturers, and providing concrete benefits for both parties.

Engagement needs to be both authentic and constructed. Marketers must forge a paradigm that allows freedom within a framework, pulling off the trick of simultaneously permitting consumers to participate with brands while empowering marketers to manage the message and dialog. In *Twitter Is Not a Strategy* I outline a simple-yet-nuanced process to grab the holy grail of marketing: harmony between the clarity of top-down positioning and the dynamism of bottom-up consumer engagement; between long-term brand equity and short-term tactical messaging; and between emotional relevance and results elicited by data-driven technology. I address this in four interconnected modules, two conceptual and two executional, which build upon one another: consumer insight, the brand idea, engagement ideas, and the engagement plan.

Consumer Insights:
The Human Heart and Profit Margins

Technology is not changing humanity; rather, it's empowering people to satisfy their timeless urges in new ways. For this reason insight into consumer behavior—the secret sauce of power brands—has never been more important. Insights are more than observations; they explain the fundamental motivations behind behavior and preference. They answer the question "Why?"

The best insights spring from conflicts, or tensions, of the heart. Teenagers want to avoid alienation but also assert their individuality; adults want to maintain autonomy but avoid isolation. Tension can arise between competing human truths—aspirations that unify all of us. Or they can be between competing cultural truths, yearnings that differentiate clusters of people. (The desire for engagement with society is different in, say, Confucian China or Buddhist Thailand than in individualistic America.) Or the tension can be between competing human and cultural truths.

Consumers spend more time with brands that help *resolve* their conflicting desires. The role of such brands in their lives will be greater, and pricing can be adjusted accordingly. Insight into consumer motivations—for example, understanding why penny-pinched but status-conscious middle-class Chinese will pay a premium for goods used in public but not at home—is the font of robust profit margins. This truth is increasingly ignored as we dream of salvation through the latest app or data-mining technique.

The Brand Idea: From Chaos to Order

A beautiful brand idea is invisible yet possesses the gravitational force to unify messages across an exploding array of media, geography, and cultures. Far more than a theoretical abstraction, it remains the lynchpin of consumer loyalty, efficient media placement, and operational holism. It is the brand's life force.

On an untamed brandscape the brand idea ensures consistency across time and media. Nike lives and breathes a "Just do it" spirit. Everywhere. Axe deodorant promises "irresistible attraction" to

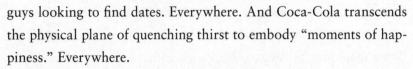

guys looking to find dates. Everywhere. And Coca-Cola transcends the physical plane of quenching thirst to embody "moments of happiness." Everywhere.

The brand idea is more than a positioning statement. It crystallizes the long-term relationship between consumer and brand that remains consistent yet evolves over time. It is inherently mutual and underpins subsequent engagement across both digital and analog media. Every brand needs a soul, etched with a carefully crafted concept. The brand idea is a fusion of insight into consumer behavior and unique brand offer (UBO)—one or more characteristics that differentiate a product from its competitors, on emotional or physical levels. The UBO can spring from a product truth, a differentiating characteristic of the product, or it can be a brand truth, equity accumulated over time by consistent communications. For example, Dove soap contains one-quarter moisturizing cream— that's a product truth; Johnson & Johnson has long been associated with tenderness—that's a brand truth.

Engagement Ideas: From Passive
Exposure to Active Participation

The best brands simplify life; they do not complicate it. That's why creative executions must be expressions of the brand idea. They can be short term, long term, thematic, or promotional, but all must be manifestations of the brand's soul. Each new thought must reinforce the existing relationship between people and the brands they love, lest confusion reign.

The modern business environment is ultracompetitive and hyperaccelerated, so content has to be more than interesting. It has to *do* more than break through clutter. Super Bowl Sunday notwithstanding, the days of sitting in front of the television waiting for cool TV ads to air are over. Creative executions must still be persuasive, and messages must be elegantly crafted, but we now measure success of communications by depth of engagement. As we say at JWT, we create ideas people want to spend time with.

In today's climate of technological liberation, creative executions should not only draw attention but also elicit active response. Great creative ideas are now participation platforms. They can be things people want to spend time with, or "opt in" to an exchange between consumers and brands. The more time people spend using, playing with, and spreading an idea, the deeper their involvement with a brand. For example:

- Axe deodorant's "sexy alarm," introduced in Japan, is a daily wake-up call. Delivered on smartphones by a different gorgeous girl every day, the call reminds young guys to maximize "score potential" by wearing Axe.
- Canon Australia's "EOS Photochains" transformed photography from solitary endeavor to group passion. Offline advertising invited photographers to contribute to a continually growing online chain of photos in which each shot inspired the next.
- Nike+ is a physical manifestation of the company's "Just do it" brand idea. A series of apps enables athletes to track their individual performances and then share results on social networks.

I also examine how engagement ideas are *defined* so they become medium neutral, bigger than individual communications channels. As media options proliferate, ideas should be equally expressible on everything from television to mobile phones to social media platforms to apps to video games, even to in-store shelf talkers.

I demonstrate how proper definition of the engagement idea can transform media consumption from passive to active. In the process I uncover how creative execution and media can be married to make any media vehicle pop, and how inspired selection of media can make the creative idea stronger.

Engagement Planning: Ideas Woven into the Fabric of Life

Although media have proliferated, every touch point remains an opportunity to both enhance the intimacy between consumer and brand as well as change consumer behavior in a way that increases likelihood of purchase. As a result media planning has entered a new era of melding engagement ideas with digital technology. Marketers need to deconstruct the artificial barriers between traditional (mass) and digital (one-to-one) media planning. New digital platforms—social networks, corporate sites, microsites, online communities, Facebook, Twitter, blogs by opinion leaders—can be aligned with how consumers always have, and always will, make decisions about which brands to buy. This "consumer engagement system," whether in the digital or analog world, can be broken down into six phases: trigger, consideration, comparison, preference, purchase, and experience.

The basics of brand building have not changed fundamentally, but the nature of engagement has. That's why I conclude this book by focusing on the new imperatives of online content—in other words, creative executions developed specifically for digital media. Nine guidelines are proposed to draw on both established wisdom and contemporary vision in illustrating how to optimize the power of online content in an era of consumer "pull":

- Let "people power" enhance authenticity.
- Let content create value exchange—that is, something useful in exchange for consumers' attention.
- For message amplification, wrap value in creative execution.
- Develop inherently social content.
- Produce "snackable" content to entice deeper engagement.
- Align content with the path to purchase.
- Reduce waste by targeting.

- Ensure content is discoverable.
- Use data to optimize creative execution.

Twitter Is Not a Strategy is not meant to be a breakthrough book. Indeed it might even be "antibreakthrough." It is a call for the entire industry to stand up and reclaim the conceptual high ground of marketing communications. Carefully crafted strategies and executions—adherence to the ABCs of brand building—will remain our lighthouse. As brand pioneers, we must explore the shoals of a new digital landscape. But let's not become stranded by anxiety and indecision. Timeless can be new.

one

new world disorder

Chaos has erupted in the communications industry. The digital revolution has intensified the clash between the top-down and bottom-up brand-building models: the former is fueled by clarity of message, which is articulated by the manufacturer; the latter is unpredictable, on the street, of and for the people. These opposing approaches must be reconciled. Marketers must permit consumers to participate with brands while retaining the ability to manage message and dialog.

Today brands are everywhere. A world without them is impossible to imagine. From the moment we wake up to the time we go to sleep, everything we wear, use, eat, or drink is branded: the Armani suit he puts on in the morning, the Starbucks coffee she drinks on the journey to work in her BMW, our smartphones, computers, even our toilet paper. Nothing is immune.

For companies brands are multibillion-dollar assets with the potential to make or break a business. These companies make huge investments every year to keep their brands alive and commercially viable. But it wasn't always this way.

A BRIEF HISTORY OF BRANDING

Branding as we understand it today is a relatively recent phenomenon. The original meaning of the term *brand* traces to ancient Egyptians who would burn marks into the flesh of cattle much as cowboys of the Wild West would thousands of years later. But branding in that context was more a mark of ownership than a way of visibly differentiating goods to customers.

For hundreds of years merchants sold products from anonymous jars, and goods were not always visibly differentiated. In the Middle Ages people would rarely see the same seller twice, and consumers often knew little about the quality of the products they were buying. In a broad parallel to the situation in China today, scams were common as manufacturers cut corners to save costs. In 2008 six infants died and nearly 300,000 were hospitalized when the toxic chemical melamine found its way into China's fragmented dairy supply chain. Local collection agents are paid based on the volume of milk delivered, and they were adding water to boost earnings. Melamine was used to compensate for the resulting drop in protein concentration. It was one of the country's biggest food safety scandals, and its impact can still be felt today because Chinese parents buy infant formula overseas. Similarly manufacturers in the Middle Ages would take advantage of consumers by using dyes that would later fade, or by adding less expensive lead to the alloys used to forge metal cups and utensils, resulting in the poisoning of the end users.

Then came the industrial revolution in the eighteenth and nineteenth centuries and the transformation of the agrarian economies of Great Britain, Europe, and the United States. This was an era of unprecedented change. The arrival of the steam engine facilitated mass production; factory lines churned out such goods as canned vegetables and toothpaste at wondrous speed.

Railway networks and new canal systems started to crisscross nations, linking major towns. Products spread, reaching consumers

Early advertising was born of the industrial revolution, which enabled mass distribution of products. It provided a stamp of reassurance, both literal and figurative. Well-known, consistent branding was also a means of discouraging consumers from buying locally or regionally produced copycats. (© Kellogg Company. Used with permission.)

thousands of miles from the products' points of origination. "Our market is the world," Henry J. Heinz said shortly after starting his eponymous food-processing company in the nineteenth century. Heinz possessed some of the more ambitious geographic aspirations of the time, but plenty of fledgling companies were beginning to eye the vast potential of globalization.

As products spread domestically and internationally, manufacturers realized they needed to find ways to differentiate their wares. They knew that turning a consumer into a repeat consumer required developing goods that were of consistent quality and easily identifiable as such. Stamping products with logos became the required guarantee of authenticity—branding was now a necessity.

Trademark legislation gave the branding movement greater impetus, providing companies with legal protection for their nascent assets. The iconic red triangle of the Bass Brewery was the first trademark registered in the United Kingdom, in 1876. The following year in America, Quaker Oats became the first breakfast cereal to be trademarked with the US Patent Office. It was registered simply as a "figure of a man in 'Quaker garb.'" More brands soon emerged. Procter & Gamble, Johnson & Johnson, Nestlé, Lipton Tea, and Heinz all were born during this time. Many still use the same logos that first helped differentiate their products more than a century ago. In 1886 Levi Strauss introduced the two-horse logo that still adorns the leather patch on its jeans. It depicts two horses pulling a pair of jeans in opposite directions, an immediate visual reminder of the superior durability of Levi products. The patch elevated a pair of jeans to a pair of Levis, each stamped with a guarantee of authenticity and promise of quality.

Products with new exciting monikers emerged as manufacturers realized naming their products could help drive sales. Companies like Procter & Gamble began replacing functional product names with more emotive labels. In 1879 Harley Thomas Procter officially named the company's white soap "Ivory" after a Sunday church reading from the Book of Psalms gave him a flash of inspiration: "All thy garments smell of myrrh and aloes and cassia, out of the ivory palaces where they have made thee glad." He thought the word *ivory* captured the soap's mild and long-lasting qualities. The new name appeared in mass-market print ads that focused on the soap's purity. The effort surely contributed to exceeding an impressive $3 million in annual sales by 1889.[1]

Manufacturers began to package their products in cardboard boxes, tins, and paper bags, which enabled further differentiation. Colorful eye-catching packaging displayed brand logos and provided information about where the product was made and by whom. Just like the trademark, packaging would become an asset. In 1915 Coca-Cola moved to protect itself against a tide of imitators by running a contest to create a distinctive new bottle shape so the genuine article could be recognized instantly, even in the dark or if it was broken.[2] The contour bottle was born, and nearly one hundred years later it remains one of the company's most iconic assets.

Coca-Cola's uniquely curved bottle is now an iconic tangible brand asset.
Since 1916, its contours have remained remarkably consistent and the source
from which small moments of happiness flow.

Gradually customers started to recognize and trust brands and asked for them by name. The value of branding quickly caught on. A Coca-Cola officer is said to have valued the company's trademark at $5 million by the early 20th century.[3] The multibillion-dollar industry of branding had been born.

TOP-DOWN VERSUS BOTTOM-UP COMMUNICATIONS

While branding began as a means to provide mass-market consumers with confidence that products had been standardized, branding evolved into something else entirely during the next century. Brands were built using a top-down communications model that spread a manufacturer's message to mass audiences. Commercials were broadcast across print, radio, and TV to drive awareness. But businesses also recognized the need to foster one-on-one engagement with consumers—the so-called bottom-up approach. For instance, in the 1950s marketers tried to talk directly to kids through entertaining content on the back of cereal boxes or by running competitions that required children to save a manufacturer's bottle caps.

The tension between different models—one rooted in message uniformity and the other in one-to-one engagement—has always existed. In the twenty-first century, perhaps the difference between conceptual (analog) and linear (digital) skill sets has exacerbated the gap between "new" and "traditional" marketers. The fundamental challenge of our industry lies in reconciling the gulf between these two paradigms.

Top-Down Communications

"A is for Apple, J is for Jacks. Cinnamon toasty Apple Jacks! You need a good breakfast, that's a fact. Start it off with Apple

Jacks. Apple Jacks! Apple Jacks! Apple Jacks! Ten vitamins and minerals—that's what it packs. Apple-tasty, crunchy, too! Kellogg's Apple Jacks!" This is an American TV jingle for Kellogg's Apple Jacks cereal from the 1970s. I was just a kid when it used to blast from the TV set in my living room. But almost 40 years later I can still remember it verbatim.

I was born in 1963—the era of television. I got home from school at 3 p.m., went to bed at 9 p.m., and spent the six hours in between sitting in front of the television. I would spend *hours* memorizing television commercials, not just because I wanted to but because I couldn't help it.

This was the era of top-down marketing. Tightly controlled messages were created in company boardrooms and pumped out through mass media. Brands developed clear, concise messages that viewers did not have to actively digest; they could passively receive and understand the information. Jingles, commercials, and brand messages quickly permeated the minds of children and adults alike.

Most people call this traditional advertising, but I prefer to refer to it as the timeless approach. It has been the standard model since advertising began to take off at the end of the nineteenth century. It first came to life through print (newspapers and magazines) and then radio. But the advent of the television really allowed this model to flourish.

Advertisers loved TV because people loved TV. This new box of imagination spread rapidly across the United States, revolutionizing everything, not just the advertising industry. According to Nielsen, a leading provider of information and insights into what people buy, fewer than 10 percent of American households had a TV in 1950. Within 15 years that figure had rocketed to more than 90 percent.[4] Advertisers could suddenly reach massive audiences, pushing product messages into every home in America. Furthermore they could convey brand promises in powerful ways. Messages were no longer static words on a page or disembodied voices on the radio. The magic of catchy jingles and aspirational images converged to sell a whole new level of dreams.

Advertisers pumped millions of dollars into television, and the industry exploded. American billings more than doubled during the 1950s, reaching $12 billion by 1960; the same was true all over the world.[5] During this period the goal was always the same: broadcast the message to as many people as the budget allowed. This was mass-marketing in the purest sense—it was about broad exposure leading to awareness, preference, and finally purchase.

During this era brands became established authorities. The Jolly Green Giant told mothers his corn was goodness itself; Pears soap left skin as soft as a baby's; only Bisto—a well-known British gravy brand—could make meat taste right. Advertisers controlled the messages. More often than not, consumers listened and did as they were told. And, boy, did it pay off. Children sang the Apple Jacks jingle, women bought the cream that made their skin soft so their husbands would love them more, and men bought cars that could and would change their social status. Life was simpler.

This model of advertising continues today, despite what you may hear. Reaching mass audiences is still a major goal for marketers across numerous categories, and TV continues to command the lion's share of advertising dollars. PricewaterhouseCoopers forecasts global TV advertising revenues will exceed $200 billion by 2017, up from $162 billion in 2012. America will continue to be the dominant market, accounting for 39 percent of total spending, but the fastest growth will take place in emerging markets.[6] For the foreseeable future, expenditures for TV advertising are expected to grow each year by 16 percent in Kenya, 15 percent in Indonesia, and 12 percent in India.[7]

Perhaps the most powerful remaining testament to the appeal of top-down advertising is the Super Bowl. According to Kantar Media, a firm specializing in media and marketing intelligence, this annual event generated $1.85 billion in network advertising sales between 2003 and 2012. The average rate for a 30-second advertisement also increased by more than 60 percent to reach a colossal $3.5 million in 2012. For advertisers the Super Bowl continues to be an important platform for spreading messages throughout the world. The morning after the 2013 Super Bowl, Volkswagen's "Get In, Get Happy" commercial, which debuted at the event, had clocked more than eight million views on YouTube. GoDaddy's "Perfect Match," an ad that showed fashion model Bar Refaeli kissing a geek, had racked up nearly six million views.[8]

To generate widespread awareness of a brand's message, digital platforms such as Google and YouTube, as well as online social networks, are also being used to capitalize on the popularity of the Super Bowl. This reminds us that traditional and new media do not exist in parallel universes. Advertisers are investing in seeding commercials on the Internet in advance of the game. Many advertisers budget $4 to $6 million to promote their ads through YouTube and Twitter during the weeks before the event.[9] To trigger deeper engagement, smart marketers also ensure that Google searches for their Super Bowl ads lead to a relevant page. This method neatly unifies top-down and bottom-up messages.

While TV advertising has changed significantly in the last 50 years—rousing emotive soundtracks have replaced jingles, and sophisticated minifilms have replaced cute animations—it remains the medium of choice for reaching mass audiences. TV is as relevant today as it ever was, and it will continue to be so for the next 50 years at least. Affordably forging clear brand propositions across broad swathes of people will always require mass media.

Handled incorrectly, the top-down model can be aggressive, thrusting, and unidirectional. It's no accident that marketing professionals often describe it in military language: *capturing* market share, *penetrating* the customer base, *defeating* competitors. It can be declarative, propagandistic, uninvolving. But in its best moments it can also encapsulate a belief, a set of values, even a religion. Nike's "Just do it" slogan expresses a spirit cherished by those who come

Nike's "Just do it" is more a near-religious belief than product proposition. Nike encourages all of us to challenge conventions and liberate our unique abilities. This poster shows iconoclastic Chinese tennis star Li Na. The headline reads, "Dare to aim higher than the sky." (Nike Greater China)

into contact with the organization. These three words, created by Wieden + Kennedy more than 25 years ago, have weathered decades of change and the explosion of digital technology to take root across the world. Adherents love and universally recognize the slogan. No one doubts that "Just do it" has powered Nike to become the multibillion-dollar corporation it is today. This is what a brand can achieve when top-down messages are conceptually clear and fueled by a deep understanding of consumers' motivations. This is what makes the model timeless. (Across all media, both traditional and digital, Nike's brand idea has been executed with great skill, as I describe in subsequent chapters.)

The Rise of Digital Technology

While TV remains a prominent medium, marketers must not consider it in isolation. The truth is that kids and adults today are not just sitting around waiting to memorize television commercials. People may not have changed much, but the world has. Technology has allowed people more control than ever of what they see, hear, and do.

When the world first shifted gears 20 years ago, *digital* meant websites, search engines, and chat rooms. But the matrix has grown and become infinitely more complex—and it's still constantly changing. It surrounds everyone now, transforming how people live their lives. As the media mogul Rupert Murdoch said a few years ago: "[The Internet] is a creative, destructive technology that is still in its infancy, yet breaking and remaking everything in its path. We are all on a journey, not just the privileged few, and technology will take us to a destination that is defined by the limits of our creativity, our confidence and our courage."[10] The journey from the conventions of the analog world, however, will be a bumpy ride. Murdoch's ill-fated acquisition of also-ran MySpace and his underwhelming efforts to monetize online news are stark reminders of the unsettling nature of digital technology.

Our smartphones are always with us, empowering and enabling us. These devices are intimate companions: They are the first things we see in the morning and the last things we see at night. They have become so prevalent in Japan that walking with a smartphone now has an official term: *aruki sumaho*. Advertising campaigns warning against aruki sumaho were plastered in subway stations after people became so engrossed by their smartphones they began falling onto train tracks. Who knows what more these devices will offer in five years' time? In Africa mobile banking is already coming of age. According to a report from the Pew Research Center, 56 percent of Kenya's nearly 44 million people make or receive mobile-phone payments.[11]

Through technology societies are becoming more connected, social, and liberated. Just 15 years ago social media did not exist. Now the combined number of Twitter and Facebook users is greater than the entire population of China—and that figure does not even consider Instagram, Pinterest, LinkedIn, and the plethora of other social networks. According to global conversation agency We Are Social, netizens in Asia collectively spend two million years on the Internet every month.[12] E-commerce provides new opportunities for price transparency. Consumers can get the best deal available; they are no longer stuck paying the inflated prices in their nearest store. The Internet allows previously isolated corners of the world to purchase otherwise out-of-reach products. Living in a lower-tier city in China, where flashy bricks-and-mortar stores might be in short supply, is no longer a barrier to conspicuous consumption. The Internet has opened the door for people to make the leap into consumer society.

Human relationships are changing, too. A whole generation is growing up without ever knowing what it is like not to be connected.

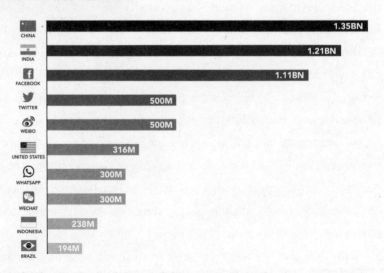

SOCIAL MEDIA USERS VS COUNTRY POPULATIONS

- CHINA — 1.35BN
- INDIA — 1.21BN
- FACEBOOK — 1.11BN
- TWITTER — 500M
- WEIBO — 500M
- UNITED STATES — 316M
- WHATSAPP — 300M
- WECHAT — 300M
- INDONESIA — 238M
- BRAZIL — 194M

It is misleading to think of the one billion users of Facebook as a "nation," but the sheer reach of the social media platform has upended the balance of power between manufacturers and people who buy their goods. The "little guy" now has the power to frame the debate.

The Internet is changing the way we choose our partners. More than one-third of US marriages are now said to begin online, while in China dating sites like Jiayuan.com and Baihe.com boast millions of users.[13] Pornography is no longer just a secretive item kept on the top shelf of a closet—the Internet caters to any desire at any time.

The living room, once used for passive escape, is now a site of liberation. The power of technology and digital games has transformed sofas into racing cars. People watch TV when they want; TV networks on the other side of the world cannot dictate when viewers watch programs. Gone are the days when Asia would wait months for a blockbuster Hollywood movie or TV show to reach its shores; favorite shows are just an illegal click away. In China, the world capital of illegal DVDs, people can watch anything as soon as it airs. Decent-quality knockoffs are available for as little as $1 a movie or $3 for an entire season of a television show.

Technology is also helping people lead healthier lives. Health and wellness apps have become personal trainers, motivating people to push harder and connecting them with others who can inspire their journey to fitness. The balance of power between patients and health professionals is shifting. Patients armed with Internet print-outs now challenge doctors during consultations, their white coats no longer a symbol of sanctity. The Internet is empowering people to make informed decisions about the treatments and medicines they receive and the specialists they see.

But technology is not just about added functionality or connectivity. It is empowering lives in ways no one expected. The Internet is a blank canvas of self-expression, allowing anybody with a unique point of view to become a star. In well-behaved Singapore, Wendy Cheng, a blogger known for her profane writing style and occasional race-tinged rants, gained notoriety overnight. She criticized a disabled man for scolding an able-bodied person who used a toilet designated for the handicapped. In China, Li Yuchun achieved instant fame when she won the nationwide singing contest *Super Girl* in

2005. More than 400 million people tuned in to see her win, and more than eight million voted by text during the finale—an unprecedented exercise in mainland Chinese democracy. What's important is not just that the Chinese voted but for whom they voted. Li Yuchun is not a typical Asian beauty with soft features and a round face: she has attitude and an edgy style. The people, armed with their mobile phones, rose up and said: "We are going to define a new standard of celebrity. We are not going to have the Communist Party apparatchiks dictate to us who we like and who we admire."

Emerging markets are likely to become the biggest beneficiaries of the digital universe as an agent of social change. Technology is already unraveling centuries of top-down patriarchal authority. In Asia social media are giving people a voice; they are able to talk back to traditionally deaf governments and to a certain extent define the agenda. Social media participation counterbalances the large sections of the media that are still state controlled, allowing alternative points of view to proliferate. In Malaysia activist organizations use social networks to spread information about protests against electoral fraud. Images of police trying to shut down the rallies with tear gas and water cannons now quickly fill news feeds, reaching media outlets around the globe.

The Arab Spring shows just how influential social media can be in helping to change the fate of entire regions. As protests against autocratic governments spread throughout the Middle East and North Africa, Twitter and Facebook played an instrumental role in disseminating information to activist groups. In Tunisia the self-immolation of a then-unknown street vendor, Mohamed Bouazizi, sparked an uprising that eventually brought down the government. As Al Jazeera reported, one of Bouazizi's relatives said that people protested with "a rock in one hand, a cell phone in the other."[14] Social media helped spread information nationally and internationally, creating a domino effect across the region.

In Egypt social media were considered so instrumental in the uprising against President Hosni Mubarak that the government scrambled to shut down Internet and cell phone services. Rafat Ali, a social media expert and founder of online media hub PaidContent, told *Wired* that this power caught the Egyptian government unaware. "These despots are five generations older than the youth," he observed. "None of these people in their 60s, 70s, and 80s have ever used Facebook or Twitter."[15]

The stage has been set. The Internet will increasingly intersect with culture and government, pulsing through society and disrupting and reshaping the relationship between rulers and ruled that has existed for millennia. Ultimately we are still humans with the same timeless desires, but technology is opening new worlds of possibility. It is empowering societies and creating new definitions of community. This has major implications for brands.

Bottom-Up Communications

Technology has altered the balance of power between brands and consumers. People will no longer be told what to think or do. The advertising industry is in the midst of a paradigm shift, with consumers actively wresting control. The success or failure of an advertising message is no longer controlled by how many people it reaches but by how well it engages people to reinforce loyalty to a brand. The fate of companies now rests squarely in the hands of consumers.

No one wants to be a passive receiver of information; no one wants to be interrupted by one-way advertising or talked down to by advertisers. Rather, consumers demand commercials that are as involving as any other entertainment option. Consumers want to participate, but this must never become an obligation; a brand that makes its audience work too hard for entertainment is not sustainable. The key is in evoking a desired behavioral response by creating material so engaging that consumers can't help but want to become part of it.

Bottom-up advertising is colliding head-on with its top-down predecessor—and the end goal is not exposure or chasing eyeballs but developing relationships with empowered consumers to engender loyalty and brand advocacy. At its core this approach is multidirectional and interactive. It can be a one-on-one dialog between brand and consumer; it can be intense expressions of dissatisfaction; it can be intimate whispers of delight. This approach begins organically, is rooted in passion, and relies on word of mouth: people are the medium. They can spread the message in unexpected ways.

As a result consumers can, and will, hijack brands. They are prepared to co-create messages and push them to evolve over time so advertising becomes of the people, for the people. This is a scary thought for many brands, which have been pulling the levers for decades. But Cadbury's experience is testament to the awesome power that a brand can release if it is willing to loosen its grip and allow consumers to take a degree of control over creative messages.

The company's "eyebrows campaign" in the United Kingdom started in 2009 with a simple one-minute TV commercial that showed two kids breaking into a wiggling "eyebrow dance" that was perfectly in time with a funky backtrack blasting from a digital watch. The spot was an exuberant expression of Cadbury's longtime "producers of joy" position, but it had no conventional product shot or other branding device. The only way consumers knew it was a Cadbury's commercial was through a closing end line, "a glass and a half full of joy," a spin on the product's well-known story of having a "glass and a half of milk" among its ingredients. The film went viral, racking up four million views within the first three weeks. As Lee Rolston, Cadbury Dairy Milk's marketing director, explained in an interview with the *Observer,* the UK newspaper, at this point the brand stopped trying to control the message and allowed it to evolve at the whim of the public. "TV and online are morphing almost

Cadbury's viral video is a manifestation of the chocolate's "producers of joy" brand idea. It sparked a participatory phenomenon, including the co-creation of the world's longest communal eyebrow dance, and is a simple example of how content can spread spontaneously in the digital era. (Permission of Mondelez International)

daily," Rolston said. "We tend to put our first ads in big things such as the *Big Brother* final or the *X Factor,* then it's immediately online, which becomes a very fluid, organic process. People tend to interact with the films and make their own versions and their own music. We just let it go and see what people think of it."[16]

The response was resounding. The British public embarked on the world's largest communal eyebrow dance, a 24-hour national event during which people created their own dances and shared them by webcam, with the results streamed directly onto the MSN home page. People submitted about 6,000 remixes in eight hours, and the site attracted six million unique users—10 percent of the entire UK population. The American rapper Kanye West promoted the video on his blog; the celebrity gossip blogger Perez Hilton, known for his cattiness, described it as supercool; the multitalented English comedian, actor, writer, journalist, film director, and serial tweeter Stephen Fry described it as "Wrong. Wrong. Yet oddly right."[17] While Cadbury was responsible for the initial framing of the message, the

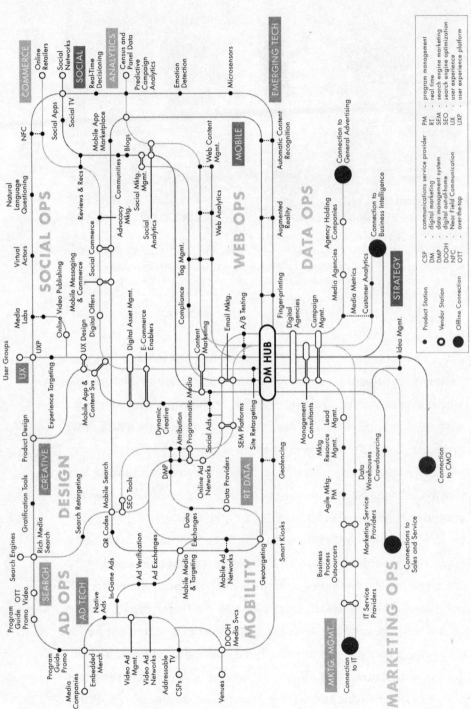

The digital universe is growing ever-more complex, leading many professionals to question whether anyone can navigate its many realms.

rest of the world ran with it. Consumers interacted with the message, made it their own, and deepened their connection to the brand.

Brave New Marketing World

Digital technology and omnipresent data sourcing has also transformed the commercial landscape and reconfigured how brands are able to connect with consumers. "Real-time marketing" companies with new age names such as siSense, Outbrain, Datura, AppsFlyer, and Ubimo optimize engagement with pre-identified consumers at distinct times and places. Ultra-precise targeting could enable, for example, real time delivery of discounts to consumers as they pass through specific points on their shopper journey. By "pushing" the most appropriate offer for a given sales opportunity, marketers overthrow conventional marketing—that is, attracting customers by using a predefined offer.

And then there is the ominous sounding "Internet of Things." "Machine-to-machine" connectivity has the potential to turn any product into a service. The first Internet appliance was a Coke vending machine at Carnegie Mellon University in the early 1980s. Programmers could connect to the machine to see whether it was empty or full. Kevin Ashton, cofounder and executive director of the Auto-ID Center at the Massachusetts Institute of Technology, explains the potential of the Internet of Things:

> Today most computers—and, therefore, the Internet—are almost wholly dependent on human beings for information. Nearly all of the data available on the Internet are first captured and created by human beings by typing, pressing a record button, taking a digital picture or scanning a bar code. The problem is people have limited time, attention and accuracy— all of which means they are not very good at capturing data about things in the real world. If we had computers that knew

everything there was to know about things—using data they gathered without any help from us—we would be able to track and count everything and greatly reduce waste, loss and cost. We would know when things needed replacing, repairing or recalling and whether they were fresh or past their best."[18]

Up until now, clothes were simply worn. Today, they track physical exertion and manage caloric intake. Washing machines do much more than clean clothes. Equipped with intelligent technology, they help repair themselves by sending and receiving information to and from parts suppliers.

"Big data," the algorithmic aggregation of multiple data points from different platforms into predictive behavioral modeling, has enhanced our ability to target with great precision—for example, to identify runners who also like heavy metal music or theater aficionados who love European travel. This new power has, in turn, made media buying and planning sexy again, while unhelpfully de-emphasizing creativity. In fact, the eclipse of the creative department began several years ago. Many communications professionals rue the day media buying and planning functions were taken out of creative advertising agencies and aggregated into powerful media holding companies that control where and when ad dollars are invested. Then came the emergence of a new industry—the high-tech, low-charm "marketing as a service." These vendors help companies manage marketing-intensive activities such landing page creation, campaign design, lead scoring, lead generation, and marketing analytics—capabilities often given short shrift in traditional sales management systems that focus on sales force automation and customer service. Providers of marketing as a service, sporting names such as Eloqua, Primo, and Silverpop, operate in the cloud, hosting applications that ensure integration with existing customer relationship management (CRM) systems.

Thus quantitative rationalism might appear to compete with ideation and inspiration as drivers of behavior change. In truth, both are

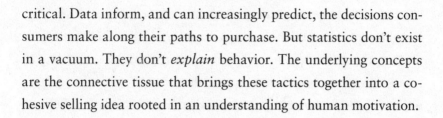

critical. Data inform, and can increasingly predict, the decisions consumers make along their paths to purchase. But statistics don't exist in a vacuum. They don't *explain* behavior. The underlying concepts are the connective tissue that brings these tactics together into a cohesive selling idea rooted in an understanding of human motivation.

DIGITAL DAZE

The communications industry is at an exciting crossroad, with two concurrent models: the timeless top-down approach and the morphing, shape-shifting bottom-up model. Advertisers and marketers need not only be fluent in both but also to find new ways to reconcile the two. This divide is often exacerbated by intellectual and culture gaps. For example, digital agencies tend to celebrate entrepreneurialism and technology-led invention. Experimentation and design are obsessions, traits of a workforce with honed analytic and technical skills. On the other hand, advertising agencies tend to nurture conceptual precision and communication of abstract ideas.

Clive Sirkin, Kimberly-Clark's global Chief Marketing Officer, neatly expresses the reality of needing to reconcile two paradigms: "We don't believe in digital marketing. We believe in marketing in a digital world, and there's a huge difference."[19] In other words, we must permit consumers to participate with brands without surrendering the ability to manage the message and what people say about their products.

Engagement that changes behavior is now the imperative—so let's agree on a proper definition. Most north Asian languages have no equivalent for the word *engage*. Whenever I have to explain it in China, I use the context of an engagement to be married. As Jim Stengel, Procter & Gamble's former chief marketing officer, said back in 2007 at the 4As Media Conference and Trade Show: "It's not about telling and selling. It's about bringing a relationship mind-set to everything we do."[20] Engagement must be a long-term connection that blossoms over time. It is a behavioral commitment between two parties—the brand and consumer—to remain together and withstand challenges over time. It must be dynamic, capable of responding to change and a variety of different needs but also consistent. *Engaging* consumers is not achieved by discrete messages aimed at holding their attention. It is a lifelong relationship.

New technology presents a breathtaking, yet overwhelming, array of combinations. Many marketers have become intoxicated by the sheer scope of what's possible, reassuring themselves that doing something is at least better than doing nothing—How many times have we heard, "Let's create an app" without first asking why? While all brand leaders need to experiment, it's not enough. Marketers need to wield technology to build brand equity and strengthen consumer loyalty. Too often technology does neither.

Mercedes Benz, for example, established dominance in the luxury auto segment by owning "engineering perfection," a fusion of mechanical performance and sensuous indulgence. In a typical ad shot in Taiwan in 2005, the dashing owner of a 700 series Benz celebrates his birthday with colleagues. He is unable to blow out the candles on his birthday cake because he has nothing left to wish for. The message is clear: once a driver has a Mercedes, nothing—or no one—else measures up. However, a few recent high-tech initiatives have done little to reinforce the brand's role as a statement of ultimate arrival in society. And it is worth noting that back in 2006 Mercedes lost its leadership in the luxury segment to BMW. Audi now ranks second.

To promote Mercedes' zero-emissions fuel cell technology, Jung von Matt, the Hamburg advertising agency, created an animated light-emitting diode clock that made the car invisible. The technological innovation turned heads but was inconsistent with Mercedes' aspirational image. A year later in the United Kingdom, Mercedes attempted to "move brand perceptions away from 'sedate luxury' as well as drive 50,000 leads" with YouDrive, the world's first "audience-driven commercial." According to Maxus Global, Mercedes' media agency: "Our young audience hates being passengers. They're used to driving content and conversations. So we gave them power over something they'd never had power over before—the world's first real-time audience-driven TV commercials. Using Twitter, viewers drove the action over three commercials in a single show." The ads centered on a musician, played by Kane Robinson, a British rapper better known as Kano, and a professional driver who are on their way to a secret gig when they are chased by authorities. While the series was designed to promote a new A-class vehicle to younger consumers, plot options had little to do with Mercedes' engineering craftsmanship. Even if this effort managed to boost short-term sales among young car buyers, it probably did little to strengthen long-term equity.

Dan Ingall, the managing director of JWT Shanghai, manages to be both commercially aggressive and conceptually ambitious. He conveyed to me: "In our role as strategically led idea pioneers, we must be better at navigating between what *can* be done and what *should* be done to achieve set objectives, from brand engagement to sales, in order to build the brand and business. We achieve this by knowing—through superior analytic capabilities made possible by the era of 'big data' and technology—and fusing it with the idea. By bridging what can and should be done, we arrive at CASH, a nifty acronym for the ultimate desired outcome of competitive advantage and business growth."

Brand stewards should avoid the temptation to deploy technology in a manner that dilutes long-term equity in exchange for a short-term sales fix. In 2013 several McDonald's franchises in Spain took advantage of their powerful wi-fi network signal to hijack customers who were eating in nearby establishments. By changing their signal name into a message—for example, "Free drink with your McMenu," or "Come eat with us and have a sundae on the house"—the McDonald's franchises lured people into their restaurants. The local stunt was clever and generated a burst of incremental sales. But the fast-food chain missed an opportunity to combine hard-hitting discounts with reminders of why people love McDonald's—that is, its reputation for quality food and family friendliness.

Sometimes even the best brands succumb to high-tech expedience. As I will discuss in Chapter 5, Uniqlo is one of the world's most inspired digital marketers. The Japanese apparel retailer sells stylish mix-and-match clothing so even fashion-challenged individuals can create their own style. Ahead of the 2010 reopening of its UK e-commerce site, Uniqlo ran a "Lucky Counter" Twitter promotion in which more tweets yielded deeper discounts. A temporary web "micro-site" displayed ten items. When users clicked on an article, a tweet appeared with the hashtag #luckycounter that users could personalize and send. Prices dropped in relation to the number of tweets elicited by each article. This exercise in unabashed discounting lacked even the faintest brand message and as such did nothing to enhance brand equity or strengthen loyalty.

Even more pernicious than random digital discounting is the rise of an e-commerce business model based on "deals-of-the-day" or "flash sales" in which online retailers offer a single product for sale for a period of 24 to 36 hours. Potential customers register as members of the deal-of-the-day websites and receive online offers and invitations by e-mail or social network. Gilt.com was at the forefront of flash-sale sites, which sell excess inventory at deep discounts for a limited period. As the *New York Times* reported, "Most of the sites took off in 2009 when even wealthy people cut spending. They solved a range of e-commerce business problems, particularly the risk of buying inventory upfront, because flash-sale sites generally buy on consignment."[21] In the process virtual bargain basements have degraded even luxury brands such as Rolex, Valentino, and Vera Wang.

Compare the debasement of flash sales with the inspiration of "Project Re: Brief," rolled out jointly in 2013 by Google and

Coca-Cola. The breakthrough initiative captures the spirit of the famous "Hilltop" advertisement from the early '70s in which all colors of humanity bonded on a mountain with a Coke. Internet users can record a message and send it with a Coca-Cola to someone on the other side of the world at a specially designed vending machine. And the receivers can then send a thank-you message back to the sender. Technology, properly deployed, can deepen engagement between people and between consumers and brands.

two

the value of
strong brands

*Strong brands provide more than just superior function-
ality. They forge emotional connections with consumers,
project exclusivity, and help the user achieve a certain identity in society. Winning new customers is much more expensive than retaining existing ones, so a marketer's primary
objective is to develop consumers who not only commit to
the brand but also recommend it to others. A strong brand
therefore adds tangible value to a company's bottom line,
enabling it to charge higher prices and make expenditures
for media more efficient.*

Noah Green is an ordinary British teenager with an extraordinary
predilection for Apple products. On September 16, 2013, the then-
17-year-old college student lined up outside the company's flagship
London store. Four days later photographers and camera crews jos-
tled to get Noah's picture as he became the first person in the country to buy the iPhone 5S. "It's the best feeling in the world; I'm the
first in the whole of the United Kingdom," he jubilantly exclaimed,

holding up a limited edition gold device, as the crowd applauded. "And I have the best phone!"[1]

This wasn't the first time Noah had camped out for the introduction of an Apple product—he had lined up days in advance of every one since the iPhone4 in 2010. His devotion is extraordinary but not, it seems, entirely unusual: Noah is one of thousands of "Apple fanboys" from New York to Shanghai to Sydney who do this on a yearly basis.

More than six years after it introduced the first iPhone, Apple continues to enjoy unrivaled buzz, as customers scramble to be the first to buy the latest iteration of the handset, test its operability, and share their verdict on the product through social media and sites that post consumer reviews. Apple is without doubt the leading brand when it comes to instilling such fanaticism among consumers around the globe.

Why are some brands so deeply loved, while others draw indifference at best and cynicism at worst? The key to Apple's success lies in the provision of multidimensional benefits to consumers. Its products have both functional and emotional qualities (often superior to competitors in both areas), providing a platform for consumers to shine. In this new era all marketers must strive to satisfy these needs, not least because of the financial benefits they can accrue. Creating deep affinity with consumers can substantially boost company profits. Strong brands are consistently found to outperform the stock market, in good times and bad.[2] Generally speaking, strong brands weather economic crises better than their weaker counterparts and grow faster during boom periods.

This strength derives from an ability to amass supremely loyal consumers, which in turn enables companies to charge higher prices for their products. By forging deep connections with consumers, strong brands can focus on reinforcing, rather than establishing, their messages. Sustaining an existing campaign often costs about

40 percent less than establishing a new one. Simply put, consumer engagement pays off.

THE VALUE OF STRONG BRANDS TO CONSUMERS

The fundamental quality of a successful brand is its ability to provide superior functional benefits to consumers. Google changed the way people find information; Apple elevated computers from hardware to objects of beauty; Nike no longer just sells sportswear, it helps people train harder, and it has turned a smartphone into a personal trainer with its Nike+ apps, thereby bringing the user one step closer to achieving performance goals.

But it bears repeating: strong brands provide much more than functional benefits; they also forge emotional connections with consumers. The best-performing brands are those consumers feel add value to their lives through a deep understanding of their needs and desires. A 2009 study in the *Journal of Marketing* asked respondents to name brands that provide a "strong experience." Apple, Nike, Google, the Body Shop, BMW, Starbucks, and HBO all made the cut. When asked to describe them, respondents said, "This brand intrigues me"; "I am part of a smarter community"; "I really feel Apple products go with my way of life"; "A BMW is the symbol of my success"; "I want to be with the people that share the values that brand promotes"; "With Google, I change the way I organize and interact with information."[3]

Clearly just as people spend more time with friends who add value to their lives, who are fun to be around, and who share their values, so they will gravitate toward brands with which they have an emotional connection. The *Journal of Marketing* study also shows that the world's strongest brands often provide social value to consumers. They are more than a companion—they help consumers project a certain identity in society and connect with like-minded individuals.

Apple's "Think Different" campaign in 1997 was not just a catchy slogan. It was a line in the sand, a statement of intent, a rallying call to those who shared the brand's values. The opening lines of the commercial introduced this proposition, saying: "Here's to the crazy ones. The misfits. The rebels. The troublemakers. The round pegs in the square holes. The ones who see things differently." This was as much about Apple consumers as it was about the company. There was no sales push or presentation of product functionality. It was simply about the values and beliefs held by the company and therefore the people who buy its products. It cemented Apple as a religion that would amass thousands of followers who wanted to be part of this great alternative ideology.

Mastering these rules has paid huge dividends for Apple, with analysts predicting it could become the world's first trillion-dollar company by 2015. In part Apple has enjoyed such extraordinary success because it has accrued a fan base like no other. The website Mac|Life recently ran a list, the "50 Reasons We Love Apple." The iPod ranked eighth, the iPhone fourth; even Steve Jobs, an icon of the twenty-first century, came in at only number three. The number one reason why Mac|Life loves Apple is its community of loyal devotees. "Apple may be a company, but it's the community that's gathered around that company that makes it special," the website noted.

> We've sold more Macs for Apple than any commercial because we believe in the products. We stick together when times are tough, and we share a sense of pride when the company releases something spectacular. . . . That community is why we are here. Look around—do you see a Dell magazine? Even the Windows-centric magazines talk about the Mac. Mac|Life, like Apple, is here because of that community and its desire to make the most of Apple's products. Wherever you live, that community's reach is a magazine or a few mouse clicks away. Because we are everywhere, and we are Apple.[4]

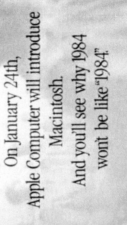

On January 24th,
Apple Computer will introduce
Macintosh.
And you'll see why 1984
won't be like "1984."

Apple's "Think Different" position was first explicitly articulated in 1998, but the belief in technology as liberating humanity and inspiring each of us to challenge convention was powerfully conveyed in the company's classic "1984" television commercial, aired in 1984.

Harley-Davidson achieves a similar standing among its loyal following. Its logo was once the most popular tattoo in America. Harley fanatics continue to gather in packs to race along America's highways and thereby prove their dedication to the exclusive club. On a Yahoo! message forum, a user innocent to the depth of love for Harley-Davidson among its loyal fans wrote simply: "The way I see it, they are overpriced, under-engineered, slow, heavy, and loud. I don't understand it. Why pay more money for something that lacks quality, performance, and reliability?"[5] It was a straightforward question, but it elicited angry responses from Harley-Davidson devotees, culminating with this comment: "I wish I knew where you lived so I could take one of my overpriced, under-engineered, slow, heavy, loud, lacking quality, performance, reliability motor-cycle's [sic] AND BLOW YOUR DOORS OFF. By the way your [sic] obviously an idiot!!!" For its fans Harley-Davidson is more than the nuts and bolts of the machine. It is a physical manifestation of the American ideology of freedom. It is an overt rebellion against the constraints of society.

I should stress that Apple and Harley-Davidson did not collect some of the world's most loyal fans through one commercial. Forging a deep-rooted connection with consumers requires meticulous construction—the company must embed brand values in all communications and product development. A consistent brand idea is the bedrock of all marketing activity that establishes and reinforces relations with consumers. By defining the role they want to play in life, strong brands are able to rally employees as well. A company that is oriented to the future, expresses a clear goal, and is able to articulate its objectives will be more likely to recruit and retain staff who live and breathe the brand principles. Suitably motivated, they have the confidence to reinforce the brand spirit in innovative ways. It is no coincidence that people regard as the best places to work the companies that make some of the world's strongest brands. Google tops the list of a LinkedIn study of companies most people would like to work for. It is followed by Apple, Microsoft, Facebook, and Unilever.[6]

BRAND CYNICISM

Though all brands may aspire to this level of affinity, few achieve it. Some products are inherently unable to create such a connection with consumers. Not many people would write on message forums about their love for toilet paper brands, for example. And there is a definite movement away from branded products in certain corners of the world, particularly in Western countries such as Australia, a market notable for its cynicism about advertising. This trend has several causes, not least the global economic crash. Yes, spending power is constrained, but it is also true that brands in all categories are finding it more difficult to reach the hearts and minds of consumers.

While brands still hold a sway in developing markets, brand indifference is becoming quite real in developed markets. According to Deloitte's 2013 "American Pantry Study," brand loyalty across multiple grocery and household goods categories had been in decline for three consecutive years.[7] An Ernst & Young survey showed only 28 percent of consumers globally believe that a product's brand influences their purchasing decisions. Brand indifference was highest in South Africa, Western Europe, and the United States. Emerging markets, however, are relatively more loyal. In China 40 percent of people claim that brands play a role in their purchasing decision, followed by 34 percent in Brazil and 32 percent in India.[8]

There is no denying that consumers worldwide are increasingly willing to purchase products that do not bear a company's logo, as societies shift away from conspicuous consumption. Fewer than one-third of Australian respondents to Nielsen's Global Consumer Survey said they liked to buy products that carry famous brands, compared to a global average of 47 percent. In the United Kingdom many shoppers see little difference between branded goods and private labels when purchasing grocery staples. A study by Canadean, a consumer market research company, showed 44 percent of UK shoppers believe private label and store brands originate in the same factories. Furthermore 70 percent believe private label canned foods are just as good as or better than branded items in terms of quality.

Does this mean that the consumerism that has pervaded society for more than 100 years in the United States, Australia, and Europe is about to crash? No. While there is certainly *active* cynicism about brands in the Western world, which means marketers face greater challenges in forging bonds with consumers, the consumerist society is unlikely to disappear anytime soon. In a world filled with new choices and opportunities, brands simplify the consumer landscape and reflect the aspirations of people who use them. Maybe the relationship is a little tarnished, but if marketers get the formula right, they still will be able to create an affinity between brands and consumers, just like the one between Apple and Noah Green.

STRONG BRANDS PROVIDE TANGIBLE FINANCIAL BENEFITS TO PARENT COMPANIES

Forging a deep relationship with consumers must become the holy grail of marketing, not least because the financial benefits of doing so are too huge to ignore. The world's strongest brands are consistently found to have enormous economic value: they outperform the stock market, collect loyal consumers, are able to charge higher prices, and can benefit from reduced media costs.

Strong Brands and Stock Market Value

During the mergers and acquisitions frenzy of the 1980s the idea of the financial worth of brands began to emerge, changing how companies are valued. For decades organizations were priced according to their tangible assets—financial balance sheets, land, manufacturing plants, and so on. In 1981 such assets accounted for 82 percent of the total bid for any given company, yet only six years later that figure had dropped to just 30 percent. The key shift resulted from the recognition of intangible assets like brands, trademarks, and patents. Soon companies were being snapped up at prices significantly higher than their stock market value. When Grand Metropolitan opened its initial bid for Pillsbury in 1988, it offered $60 per share—$21 more than Pillsbury's trading price at the time[9]—while Rowntree had a prebid market capitalization of about £1 billion when Nestlé bought it for £2.5 billion that same year.[10] Financial capitals around the world had awakened to the idea that brands, not bricks-and-mortar assets, were companies' most valuable property.

Today the economic value of brands is indisputable, and their creation and nurturing has become a major preoccupation of CEOs. According to a 2002 study conducted by Interbrand and J. P. Morgan, brands contribute, on average, more than one-third of the shareholder value of a company, and some of the world's strongest brands contribute much more.[11] Coca-Cola contributed 51 percent of the market capitalization of the Coca-Cola Company. The McDonald's brand meanwhile accounted for a massive 71 percent of its parent company's market capitalization, and it was 68 percent across all parts of the Disney-branded empire. The strength of these brands has been fundamental to these companies' ability to consolidate their positions in existing markets and expand into new ones.

The corporate owners of strong brands have been found to outperform the stock market, growing faster during boom times, and seem to be protected from the full adverse effects of downturns. Marketing communications holding company WPP's annual study, "BrandZ Top 100 Most Valuable Global Brands," carried out by Millward Brown Optimor, one of its marketing consulting arms, provides strong evidence of the impact of brand building on stock market performance. WPP's BrandZ Top 100 Strong Brands portfolio, comprising a diverse set of leading companies, appreciated 58 percent between 2006 and 2013. The S&P 500 gained only 23 percent during the same period. Furthermore, during the global financial crisis that began in 2008, the BrandZ's Top 100 Strong Brands suffered significantly less and recovered faster than the S&P 500. This suggests that, particularly during periods of financial volatility, buying the stock of companies that have strong brands can offer investors more risk protection than they can find elsewhere.

In many cases the stronger a brand, the higher its parent company's stock price-to-earnings ratio, a measure of growth potential. Of course brands are not the only mitigating factor; a company with strong brands is likely to be equally robust in product development, supply chain management, operational efficiency, and corporate governance and have staff adept in each of these areas. However, an

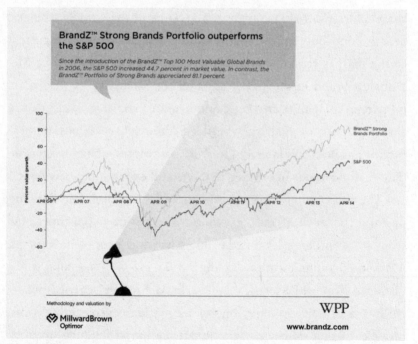

The link between strong brand equity, as measured by WPP's proprietary BrandZ methodology that focuses on loyalty and return on shareholder investment is clear. Strong brands boast high price/earnings (P/E) ratios.

association with strong brands provides greater confidence in the delivery of financial returns. Such companies have built the foundations for sustainable success.

Strong Brands and Customer Loyalty

One key reason strong brands generate value for their parent companies is they are able to foster customer loyalty. McKinsey & Company suggests there are two types of loyal consumers. The first are "passive loyalists," who continue to buy a brand but are not fundamentally committed to it, perhaps because of laziness or confusion resulting from the array of choice. The passive loyalists follow certain brands and will make repeat purchases, but they remain open to messages from competitors that present them with a reason to switch. The "active loyalists" not only commit to a brand but also recommend it—and clearly these are the consumers on whom marketing strategies should primarily focus. Ultimately marketers must forge connections so deep that consumers become advocates of a brand, spreading its message to friends, relatives, and strangers the world over.

Loyalty may be harder to achieve these days, but it still pays off financially and therefore must remain a major corporate goal. It is no coincidence that Apple—a brand with some of the most loyal consumers in the world—is also one of the world's largest listed companies by market capitalization. Loyalty is an economic force. Many leading brands today began life more than 150 years ago during the industrial revolution; they were able to grow and prosper because customers kept buying their products.

The impact of loyalty on profitability is multifaceted. First, a protected customer base helps a company maintain its market share, acting as a shield against aggressive pricing strategies from competitors and, more acutely, public relations disasters. In the 1980s Johnson & Johnson came under enormous pressure after a consignment of the painkiller brand Tylenol was contaminated with cyanide, killing seven people. The company's market share plummeted from 37 percent to 7 percent, but one year later the brand had clawed back its lost ground. Its reputation intact, Tylenol controlled 30 percent of the market, and the drug continues to be a leading brand around the world. The transparency of crisis management efforts were consistent with J&J's image as "tender" and "caring." More recently Nike and Apple have repeatedly overcome accusations of producing their goods with sweatshop labor in developing countries yet remain among the strongest brands globally.

Second, consumers who are loyal to a brand are more likely to devote a much higher proportion of their category spending to that brand than consumers with lower levels of affinity. Millward Brown's research shows 14 percent of consumers who are bonded to a certain brand of packaged goods devote about 66 percent of their category spending on that brand. If they are only aware of a brand, it is likely to receive only 28 percent of category spending. Loyal consumers give brands a greater share of their wallet, but they have also been found to spend more over time as they become aware of other product lines, and the loyalists show greater willingness to experiment with brand extensions. A loyal long-term consumer is not easily replaced by a new customer, who will incur acquisition costs and whose initial spending will likely be considerably lower. This is true in "low involvement" packaged goods—for example, food and beverages, inexpensive clothing, and household items—in which buying habits are often entrenched and need to be altered. The cost of conversion in "high involvement" categories such as cars and computers is even higher. For these goods, consumers have already dedicated significant amount of time and energy to determine brand preferences. Companies have a clear imperative to ensure their brand devotees remain devoted.

When these two factors of market dominance and strong loyalty converge, a self-perpetuating benefit cycle is created, helping companies maintain market share and enabling them to repeatedly generate superior profits. Indeed businesses with strong commercial positions (a market share greater than 50 percent) have benefited from rates of return more than three times greater than companies with a market share of less than 10 percent.[12]

Strong Brands Can Charge a Price Premium

If customers feel a brand offers strong functional or emotional benefits, or adds value to their lives, they are willing to pay more for it. Companies with strong brands are therefore able to charge price premiums higher than the category average without experiencing a drop-off in demand. This phenomenon is most visible in the luxury goods market. People will pay huge sums for better-quality goods, not least because of the perceived social value that the latest Mulberry handbag or Prada wallet will add to their lives. Millward Brown analyzed 209 brands of consumer packaged goods in the United States that people had a "higher opinion of than others" and found they enjoyed median prices 11 percent higher than the category norm.[13]

Millward Brown's Value-D study looks at the price premium concept from a slightly different angle, examining the impact of "desire" on perceived value, or price. The study, based on data for about 7,000 brands worldwide, shows that growing desire for a brand enables greater price flexibility. A product with a high price can be considered as either too expensive or having a "justified premium." If a product or brand generates a sufficiently high level of desire, consumers would be prepared to pay more for it. Likewise consumers may see a brand with a low price as good value or poor value, again depending on the level of desire it creates. Brands with justified premiums included Pampers, Coca-Cola, Apple, and Microsoft.[14]

Premium value varies in relation to sociocultural context. Asians today are conspicuous consumers. They exhibit a greater willingness to pay a premium for goods consumed outside the home because brands allow people to project a certain identity in society. In China visiting Starbucks or a Häagen-Dazs store ensures the individual is seen as part of a new middle-class elite. Chinese so revere labels that a Mont Blanc pen or Cartier watch can be the passport to upward advancement almost all by itself.

Of course not all strong brands will be able to charge a huge price premium. But consumer perceptions of where and how a higher price is justifiable can make an enormous impact on company profits. For example, it means companies can avoid the murky depths of price promotions. They have no need to resort to short-term discounts to attract and retain customers, which ultimately constrain margins and reduce the amount of money available for brand building and other investment.

Even a marginal price increase marketwide can radically boost profits. McKinsey & Company suggests that a price rise of 1 percent for a product sold by an S&P 1500 company would, if volumes remained stable, result in an 8 percent increase in operating profits.[15] The impact on the bottom line would be more than three times greater than that of a 1 percent increase in volume. A price premium of a few cents can therefore lead to huge changes in profitability.

Benefits run in the other direction, too. In some cases consumers themselves actually feel reassured by higher prices; they see them as a mark of superior quality.[16] Clearly this assumption must be delivered upon, or the reassurance will not hold, prompting consumers to look elsewhere for value. But if a branded product warrants a higher price, and consumers are willing to pay that premium, companies can achieve the dual advantages of boosting their bottom line and delivering consumer satisfaction.

Strong Brands Enjoy Smaller Media Budgets

Finally, strong consistent branding allows companies to significantly reduce their media spending. It is useful to think about this in the context of other relationships—after all, I am talking about the connection between brands and their consumers. A young man prepares for his first date with a young woman by investing in some nice clothes and then takes her to an expensive restaurant and then a movie. However, familiarity breeds economic prudence. As the months go by, their dates become trips to KFC and then a subway ride home to watch an illegal DVD from the couch.

It is the same with media costs. Whenever marketers introduce a new message or brand, they have to invest more to buy enough media space required to establish the message in consumers' minds. Once that relationship with the consumer has been built, the imperative shifts from *introducing* a message to *sustaining* it, and the media costs come down. By creating a consistent message that unifies each new campaign required for different sales objectives, media planning becomes more efficient. The company does not have to repeatedly spend higher sums to define what a brand stands for—consumers already know. In my experience with media planning, sustaining a campaign can cost about 40 percent less than seeding a message.

Although Samsung is the world's largest smartphone maker, it has a much smaller share of the market in America, where home-grown Apple remains the dominant player. ComScore figures show that in July 2013 Apple owned 40 percent of the market, compared to Samsung's 24 percent. To try to close the gap the Korean manufacturer has been forced to aggressively increase its spending to flood billboards, TV spots, and print in a bid to win over American consumers. According to data from Kantar Media, Samsung increased its media spending by 414 percent between 2011 and 2012 to total $401 million through efforts to promote its mobile phone products in the United States.[17] It is clearly working much harder to build awareness on Apple-dominated turf than it has to elsewhere. Conversely Apple is still able to sell thousands of iPhones because it has such a strongly embedded proposition and deep-rooted relationship with American consumers. The company also increased its media spending between 2011 and 2012 but only by 32 percent, to $333 million.[18]

In years past companies spread their media dollars across TV and print. The explosion in advertising channels prompted by the advance of digital media means budgets must stretch further than ever. Forging a relationship with consumers, reinforced by consistent messaging, is a sure way to ease pressure and write savings into media planning.

three

insight into consumer behavior

Insight into consumer behavior, not technological adventurism, is the starting point for all branding, communications, and product development, explaining the fundamental motivations of behavior and preference. Marketing budgets are worthless if the marketers they support fail to embrace psychology and cultural anthropology in order to penetrate the souls of the consumers with whom they are trying to connect. The most effective insights are about conflicts within the heart of the individual—between needs and wants, pleasure and guilt. Consumers will spend more time with brands that resolve these conflicts, and this loyalty translates into price premiums.

The first character of the word *insight* in Chinese is *dong,* which means hole. It is a fitting parallel; insights into consumer behavior are deep. They go far beyond simple observations of what people say or do. They use cultural and human truths to explain fundamental consumer behavior, seeking to answer the question "Why?"

I'm Jewish. I have been living and working in Asia for more than 20 years, and whenever I want to make mainland Chinese both like me and fear me, I say, "*Tian bu pa, di bu pa, jiu pa youtairen jiang Putonghua.*" It translates into English as "There is nothing to fear in heaven or on earth except for a Jew who can negotiate in Chinese." The Chinese have countless books about the secrets of Jewish people because the Chinese think we are clever. And they think that because we ask "Why?" until it can be asked no more. This is exactly what marketers need to do when trying to understand the fundamental motivations of human behavior and find the insights that will help create products, branding, and communications that truly resonate with consumers.

Insight into consumer behavior has always been the secret sauce of advertising—the starting point for all branding, communications, and product development. As forming relationships with consumers becomes a greater imperative than ever before, logic demands that marketers first need to understand them better. So I believe that being fluent in explaining the raw drivers of consumer actions has also never been more important.

The first point to make is that insights into consumer behavior have to explain the fundamental motivators for behavior and preference and answer the question "Why?" Until we understand why consumers behave in the way they do, we are rudderless. We must aspire to become psychologists and cultural anthropologists. The millions of dollars spent on marketing and communications are for nothing without an ability to penetrate the souls of those with whom marketers are trying to connect.

Consumption goes to the core of human desire, but a conflict within the individual is usually what prompts it. These tensions can be between almost anything: needs and wants; pleasure and guilt; family and career; a gourmet dinner and the time it takes to make one.

Brands aim to help resolve conflicts. And by reconciling two diametrically opposed needs, a brand is able to increase its value in a consumer's life. Doing so endows the brand with a purpose that it might not have had before; the brand's other product lines and communications may suddenly resonate because consumers, consciously or subconsciously, perceive that it understands the dilemmas they face. By basing insights on a dilemma, rather than on a one-dimensional desire, such as "I want to indulge," the marketer can establish a much more powerful position. For example, an individual might want to indulge but also worries about putting on weight. This insight into consumer behavior has been the basis of the appeal of diet soda for decades. Similarly, since its debut in 1957, Dove soap has been solving the conflict between consumers' desire to stay clean and concerns that soap will dry out their skin. Its formula, with one-quarter moisturizing cream, addresses both problems.

Consumers are likely to spend more time with brands that can resolve the conflicts in their lives, and this loyalty means the manufacturer can adjust product pricing accordingly. Insight into consumer behavior is therefore the font of robust profit margins—a truth often overlooked because of a preoccupation with the latest technological innovations.

UNEARTHING INSIGHTS INTO CONSUMER BEHAVIOR: HUMAN TRUTHS THAT UNITE US

When mining insights into consumer behavior, a useful first step is to think about human truths that hold true across societies. These are the fundamental motivators of behavior, the things that unify all of us. Whether we were born in Australia or China, America or Indonesia, we share certain goals. They can be physical—a need for food, water, and shelter—or driven by emotion—a desire for freedom, love, nurturing, respect, and admiration.

The hierarchy of needs—the psychological theory of motivation developed by Abraham Maslow in the 1940s—goes some way toward explaining the shared drivers of human behavior. He suggests that there are five broad categories of human motivations, including both physiological needs and emotional imperatives. Although Maslow formulated his ideas more than 70 years ago, they remain a cornerstone of management school curricula and corporate training presentations.

Maslow's theory is often presented as a pyramid, with the five categories stacked atop one another. The idea is that we humans start at the bottom of the pyramid and ascend each tier gradually throughout our lives, reaching one tier before we can go on to the next. At the bottom of the pyramid are the physiological motivators—the essential physical needs driven by the imperative to survive (including needs for food, water, and shelter). Nobody can exist without first satisfying these physiological requirements.

Maslow's hierarchy of needs remains a powerful framework for describing universal human truths. Our desires begin with safety, progress to establishing productive engagement with society, and, for the lucky few, culminate with self-actualization or transcending convention.

Once these essential needs are met, an individual develops a desire for safety. This is about the need to feel protected, to avoid danger and illness. In emerging markets the desire for safety is acute and often is a fundamental motivator of consumer behavior. In China, for example, the best-selling soap is Procter & Gamble's Safeguard. For years P&G has built this brand on a germ-killing proposition, which is directly about safety and restoring order to an unpredictable and dangerous world. In fact in all emerging markets the leading soap is almost exclusively about physical and safety benefits, not the brands that tout sensuousness or indulgence that often dominate more developed markets, where safety fears often already are addressed. (Later in this chapter I will discuss the strategic benefits of differentiating consumers in emerging markets from those in developed markets.)

The next stage is the need for love, affection, and positive relationships, whether with family, friends, peers, partners, or society at large. Once humans reach this level of the pyramid, they are no longer motivated by physical needs, according to Maslow. What they crave is a sense of belonging. It may be stronger in some countries than others, but it is universal. Next come the "esteem needs"—self-confidence, independence, and freedom. (As humans approach the zenith of the pyramid, their needs become purely emotional, firmly rooted in societal acknowledgment.) At this stage all humans crave respect—from themselves and others—status, recognition, and appreciation. If we can satisfy all these needs, Maslow argues, we are firmly on the road to feelings of adequacy, of being necessary in the world. A failure to satisfy these needs leads to feelings of helplessness and inferiority.

The apex of the pyramid is self-actualization, when we are able to transcend the restrictions of society and define for ourselves the meaning of morality. At this point people are motivated purely by what they are interested in; they are able to escape the limitations of structure, hierarchy, bureaucracy, and social mandate. Achieving self-actualization means different things for different people. It could mean becoming the ideal mother or an artist or an Olympic athlete. According to Maslow, few people make it to the summit of the pyramid—he estimated that, during his era, just 2 percent of the population were self-actualizers. Among those he considered to have reached this plane of self-possession were Albert Einstein and Abraham Lincoln.

There are, of course, caveats to this model, notably the sequential nature of the pyramid. Many argue that life doesn't follow such discrete patterns—it is far more complex, and different things motivate us at different times. Regardless, it serves as a useful starting point, reminding us that despite hugely varied geographies, cultures, and beliefs, humans share some universal truths.

Human Truth Versus Human Truth

A number of brands have built up consumer loyalty and market share by resolving tensions that arise between two competing human truths. The Belgian condom brand Zazoo used a hugely successful yet controversial ad that goes to the heart of an insight that holds true for virtually all adults. The 45-second commercial shows an exasperated father trying to deal with a kid who is having a tantrum in a supermarket, ending with the beautifully simple tagline: "Use condoms." It won multiple awards, including a Silver Lion at the International Festival of Creativity at Cannes. The ad is effective—and remains memorable—because it is based on a simple recognizable conflict: I want to have sex, but I don't want to worry about the consequences.

These tensions exist in all categories. Another example is Unilever's detergent brand OMO, which is marketed on the basis of a behavioral insight about parents around the world: they want their kids to be kids, but cleaning clothes is a hassle. A 30-second commercial for the China market shows a kid covering himself in dirt

Singapore artist Jooheng Tan was commissioned by Unilever's OMO detergent to depict the career ambitions of children, an emotional territory that would not be possible without OMO's evocative brand idea "Dirt is good."

as he tries to learn how to tie his shoelace. The ad positions OMO as the savior, in that it allows kids to continue to play and explore but also reduces the burden on parents of washing clothes. Through OMO's stain removal power, dirt is transformed from bad to good. Once a brand taps a strong insight like this, it becomes free to create other ideas that engage consumers. OMO went on to physically project the idea that "Dirt is good" with its campaign in Singapore that brought in Jooheng Tan, a world champion sand artist, to create unique sculptures that depict children's dreams for their future. The 18-ton "dirt sculptures" are a physical manifestation of an insight that goes beyond functional benefits and creates a proposition that resonates with parents all over the world.

HBO has for many years also successfully tapped two opposing human truths. The brand has revolutionized American television because the writing for its shows is extremely incisive, with character-driven shows like *Six Feet Under, Sex and the City,* and *Game of Thrones.* For many years HBO's tagline was "It's not TV. It's HBO." The idea is that the writing for HBO's shows is so sharp viewers feel like voyeurs—they are no longer passively watching a fictitious plot unravel on screen, they are peeking into other people's lives. Through HBO, viewers are able to resolve this dilemma: they want to know the gossip but know they should mind their own business. This insight not only underpinned HBO's programming strategy but also became the basis for its marketing communications. In 2007 the company ran its "Voyeur" multimedia campaign, designed to showcase HBO's storytelling capabilities. The campaign began with a team that distributed invitations on the street to a "week-long summer evening New York event" and directed people to Manhattan's Lower East Side. There they found a short film projected on the side of a building; the crowds of onlookers felt as though they were watching a drama unfold in eight different apartments. The spectators became voyeurs, witnessing scenes depicting life, birth, and redemption. The campaign then moved online, with updates,

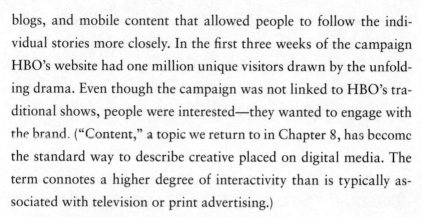

blogs, and mobile content that allowed people to follow the individual stories more closely. In the first three weeks of the campaign HBO's website had one million unique visitors drawn by the unfolding drama. Even though the campaign was not linked to HBO's traditional shows, people were interested—they wanted to engage with the brand. ("Content," a topic we return to in Chapter 8, has become the standard way to describe creative placed on digital media. The term connotes a higher degree of interactivity than is typically associated with television or print advertising.)

These communications are based on a basic but surprisingly powerful insight. And once that insight is harnessed, engaging people and infiltrating their lives in unexpected ways becomes easier.

CULTURAL TRUTHS THAT SET US APART

Insights that are rooted in cultural truths are not universal—geographic, historical, and environmental factors dictate these needs. Globalization and technology have begun to break down some of these boundaries. News is globalized, reaching smartphones within seconds from Twitter; cities are multicultural; people travel internationally at levels never seen before; and on a Saturday night a London consumer is just as likely to sip sake in the latest Japanese restaurant as head to the pub.

Yet people are still largely defined by where they were born or raised. Economic development does not equate to cultural dilution. The spotlight might be on Indonesia, China, and India as the new powerhouses of global growth, but as these markets emerge on the world stage, they are not becoming Westernized—the global village comprises starkly different neighborhoods.

Peoples' desired engagement with society might vary greatly depending on whether they were born in Confucian China, Buddhist Thailand, or individualistic America or Europe. But defining culture in traditional geographic terms doesn't capture the full picture.

Hippie culture, for example, was united by a belief that the older generation was corrupt. Hippies came of age during the Vietnam War, when dissatisfaction with societal constructs and prevailing politics was widespread, and they and other baby boomers sought to challenge the established order and offer an alternative ideology. While this culture began in America, it spread across geographic boundaries, making its way across the Atlantic to the United Kingdom. Hippies didn't identify with a particular country but a set of shared beliefs. They were to some extent defined by the clothes they wore and the music they listened to, by flowers in their hair, free love, and marijuana. More recently hip-hop culture emerged in the late 1970s and early 1980s, a new art form and means of expression definitively different from its predecessors and initially driven by the black community. The movement swiftly gathered social momentum, transcending ethnic distinctions to become part of mainstream culture today.

A successful marketer must therefore be mindful that cultures are not always dictated by geography, and marketers must identify the nuances in different cultures in order to make communications relevant. In the 1970s the social psychologist Dr. Geert Hofstede began to research the different dimensions that define national cultures around the world, and his work continues to be recognized as one of the first empirical models of its kind. Hofstede's theory, set out in his coauthored book *Cultures and Organizations: Software of the Mind*, created a new way of understanding how cultural elements affect various aspects of life and business. It is based on five dimensions:

1. **Power distance index**—how different cultures view the idea of hierarchy and inequality in society, defined as "the extent to which the less powerful members of institutions and organizations within a country expect and accept that power is distributed unequally."

2. **Individualism**—whether people define their self-image in terms of *I* or *we*. It relates to the notion that some societies are more individualistic; people are driven by what is beneficial for them. Conversely, in nonindividualistic societies people do not exist independently of their obligations to others.

3. **Masculinity**—the degree to which competition and achievement drive a society. In these societies individuals must be the best in their field to be regarded as a success. However, feminine societies tend to define success according to the individual's ability to care for others and the general quality of life.

4. **Uncertainty avoidance index**—the extent to which different cultures feel threatened by ambiguity. A high score would suggest that a society does not accept uncertainty; such societies do not tolerate behavior and beliefs that fall outside the norm. At the opposite end of the spectrum are more easy-going societies whose members are more comfortable with the idea that the future is largely unknown.

5. **Long-term orientation**—how societies view the future. A society oriented to the long term favors investment and perseverance as means of achieving results. Conversely a society oriented to the short term focuses on more immediate gratification.

Individualistic America Versus Confucian Asia

Hofstede's dimensions can be used to identify and understand patterns that emerge between different cultures. America scores 91 for individualism, compared to 20 for China, 17 for Taiwan, 18 for South Korea, and 25 for Hong Kong. America, at the high end of the scale, clearly is a highly individualistic society, with the assumption that the individual, not the clan, is the basic unit of society engrained in the national psyche. In America, and like-minded countries in Europe, individualism is to be cherished, and its productive potential liberated. Parents want to raise independent kids—they consider it a shame if their 19-year-old is still living in the family home. And once parents reach a certain age, children are willing to put them into assisted living or nursing care—in 2011 1.4 million elderly were living in more than 15,000 nursing homes across the United States.[1] There are geographic and economic reasons why American senior citizens are loath to reside with their children. But cultural factors also play a role. Most parents are reluctant to move in with their kids because the parents would see this as sacrificing their independence.[2] This is directly related to the notion that Americans value freedom and independence above all else; it is the bedrock of the American Dream.

American individualism explains why many of the most popular US brands are rooted in uniqueness or originality. Levi Strauss, for example, positions its blue jeans, produced since 1851, as the "genuine article" and has appropriated quintessential American totems such as cowboys and the Wild West for its iconography. The brand is part of the mythology of James Dean and Jack Kerouac, heroes to those striving to find themselves. Between the 1950s and 1980s Levi's became popular among a wide range of youth subcultures, including greasers, mods, rockers, beatniks, hippies, and skinheads. High-fashion European jeans have adopted the rebellious ethos of Levis to gain street cred. Diesel, an Italian youth label, equates anti-intellectualism with unconventional creativity. Diesel's print and digital campaigns encourage young hipsters to "be stupid" with such copy as "Smart listens to the head. Stupid listens to the heart," "Smart says no. Stupid says yes," and "If we didn't have stupid thoughts, we'd have no interesting thoughts at all."

Individualism is also the rallying cry for faded American brands looking for a quick burst of relevance. In the early 1980s Playtex controlled 25 percent of the bra market, but its share has eroded significantly in recent years. The brand introduced a 2013 campaign that encourages women to "be uniquely you." Tricia Bouras, director of marketing for Playtex, explains: "Women love and trust the Playtex brand because we recognize that a woman wants a bra that matches her personality, allows her to show her individuality and provides the fit and support she expects from Playtex." Likewise, Dr Pepper was famed for a 1970s advertising jingle that began, *I drink Dr Pepper and I'm proud. I'm part of an original crowd.* The cola attempted to recapture youth magic with its 2012 "One of a kind" and 2013 "/1" campaigns. The newer spots motivate young adults to be "one of one, not just one in a billion" and feature individuals whose uniqueness is reinforced with graphically presented statistics. Dr Pepper's director of marketing, Leslie Vesper, adds: "Now, in an age of YouTube stars, Tumblr, and Twitter, people more than ever are putting their individuality out into the world. That's why the '/1' campaign features real people with real stories that make them like no one else."[3]

Across Asia, however, individuality—or, worse, rebellion against convention—is verboten. The idea that children would leave home at 19, or that parents would be placed in an old people's home, is less acceptable. Confucian Asian societies like China, Korea, Hong Kong, and Taiwan are based on the notion that the basic unit of society is the clan. In contrast to their counterparts in Western society, individuals in Asia do not exist independently of their obligations and responsibilities to others. The Chinese do not look favorably on stepping outside the norm—rebellion results in a one-way ticket to the land of outcasts. And this clan-driven culture dictates the way businesses as well as families operate. Filial piety—respect for parents and ancestors—binds societies together: workers in China send money home every month to their parents, whether the children can afford to or not; adult children care for their elderly parents, almost regardless of the sacrifice involved. The dynamic is now shifting as increasingly fast-paced lives constrain a family's abilities to observe these traditions. But it also fair to say that per capita nursing home occupancy in Confucian societies across Asia will never match the rate of individualistic societies' like America and the United Kingdom.

Whenever I am asked what makes China really different from the West, it's not just the Confucian lack of individualism—it is the level of ambition. In China everyone is ambitious. Women want their piece of the sky, just as men do. A study by the Center for Work-Life Policy found that just 36 percent of college-educated women in America described themselves as "very ambitious," compared to 65 percent in China. A further 76 percent of women in China aspire to hold a top corporate job, compared to 52 percent in America.[4] The "tiger mom," forcing extracurricular activities upon her child to make sure he gets into Harvard 10 years later, is not a myth. Not all mothers are like this, but ambition remains a palpable force in Confucian societies. They were the first to become socially mobile societies; engrained in the Chinese psyche is people can achieve success by mastering convention and internalizing the rules. The desire to get ahead binds people together. From the bourgeoisie in the bustling metropolises of Seoul, Beijing, and Hong Kong right down to the farmers in the fields, all want to be an emperor of their small corner, no matter how modest their origins.

This Confucian ambition transformed Singapore in 50 years from a small backwater village into one of the world's most innovative and leading economies. In fact the notion of *kiasu*—the fear of losing—is a common driver and cultural thread throughout Singaporean society. The philosophy impacts all behavior, and every day minibattles take place across the country. Drivers nudge their cars forward at a traffic light, seeking to be the first to shoot off when it turns green. Drivers rarely give way, lest they be considered as having lost out. With temerity that would make rough-and-tumble New Yorkers blanch, commuters pile onto the subway without waiting for people to get off the train first. Singapore prides itself on its multiethnicity—a melting pot of Chinese, Indians, and Malaysians— but it is still a profoundly Confucian society. Chinese Singaporeans constitute about 74 percent of the population. The country's lead-ers and political system are also Confucian at the core. Singapore's first prime minister, Lee Kuan Yew, was a quintessential Confucian leader who had a top-down idea of how to orchestrate society, and he facilitated the city's step-by-step transformation into a shining city on a hill. As recently as the 1960s Singapore was considered a third-world jurisdiction; in 2012 it had the third-highest gross domestic product per capita, trailing only Qatar and Luxembourg, according to a *Forbes*' analysis of International Monetary Fund data.[5] Some-what unbelievably, millionaires head one-sixth of all households in Singapore. That is the power of Confucian ambition.

Secular Northern Asia Versus Spiritual Southern Asia

Asia is an incredibly diverse region with unique cultural truths. In this sense a comparison of Western and Confucian ethics goes only so far when examining the influence of geography on consumers' outlook. Within Asia are differences between northern and south-ern Asia, and these can be subdivided again and again. Each coun-try has unique nuances, but a fault line divides societies in northern Asia (China, Japan, Hong Kong, and Taiwan) and southern Asia. The former are largely secular, and the latter are more spiritually driven.

Indeed northern Asia is home to some of the world's most non-religious societies. According to a recent WIN-Gallup survey, just 14 percent of people in China describe themselves as religious, and overt religion does not play a big role in the country.[6] The Cultural Revolution of the 1960s saw religion actively stamped out, lest it become a counterforce to Communist ideology. During this period the Chinese either desecrated or transformed temples and cultural sites into nonreligious buildings, and the legacy lives on. China con-tinues to ban formal religious education not directly overseen by the state, and Communist Party members are not allowed to engage in religious practice.

The WIN-Gallup survey also revealed that in Japan just 16 percent of people claim to be religious. South Korea, Taiwan, and Hong Kong are also largely secular societies. Of course spirituality does exist to some degree in these countries. Multifaith South Korea, where neon crosses illuminate cityscapes and Buddhist thought still holds sway, is religious by northern Asian standards. And although the Japanese describe themselves as nonreligious, Jordan Price, senior planning director at JWT Japan, says many still follow traditions and customs that are rooted in spirituality and religion. He told me, "When visiting a new town in Japan the first thing most people would do is go to a shrine or a temple and drop a bit of money in the box or say a prayer. So Japan is not religious in the sense that people are aligned to one particular religion, but they do follow the customs of Buddhism and Shinto on a regular basis."

But these pockets of activity are nothing compared to southern Asia; a theological core runs through the entire region. From Buddhist Thailand to Islamic Malaysia and Indonesia to Catholicism in the Philippines, spirituality underpins south Asian societies. In the Philippines Catholicism is visible everywhere: rosaries hang from the mirrors of "jeepneys"; office workers stop by parish churches on their way home to light candles and pray for favors; and a modified image of *The Last Supper,* showing Jesus eating with Filipino street kids, adorns the walls of many homes. And people are united in their fervent belief in God—in the face of crises and misfortune it helps them maintain their optimism that things will turn out right. As the local saying goes, when all else fails, "*Diyos ang Bahala*"—Leave it up to God. The same is true across much of Southeast Asia. In Malaysia, Indonesia, and Pakistan the Muslim call to prayer reverberates through towns and rural areas. Kuala Lumpur, Jakarta, and Islamabad are seas of women in headscarves. Indeed the Malaysian government's stated goals include one to actively "infuse Islamic values"

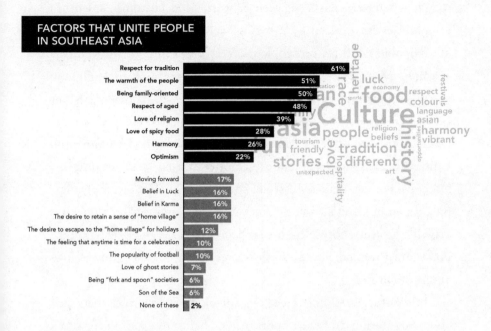

FACTORS THAT UNITE PEOPLE IN SOUTHEAST ASIA

Factor	Percentage
Respect for tradition	61%
The warmth of the people	51%
Being family-oriented	50%
Respect of aged	48%
Love of religion	39%
Love of spicy food	28%
Harmony	26%
Optimism	22%
Moving forward	17%
Belief in Luck	16%
Belief in Karma	16%
The desire to retain a sense of "home village"	16%
The desire to escape to the "home village" for holidays	12%
The feeling that anytime is time for a celebration	10%
The popularity of football	10%
Love of ghost stories	7%
Being "fork and spoon" societies	6%
Son of the Sea	6%
None of these	2%

Cultural "country clusters" exist. Countries across Southeast Asia, for example, are more religious and less future-focused and ambitious than countries, especially Confucian China and Korea, in Northeast Asia.

into society. In Pakistan religion plays a huge role in everyday life, even within the younger generations. A study by JWT Pakistan found that three-quarters of Pakistani youth (younger than 30) expect their friends to be religious. To many young people, their identity as Muslims is much more important than their identity as Pakistanis.[7]

Cultural Truth Versus Cultural Truth

Identifying the unique cultural drivers in societies is critical if marketers are to create meaningful connections between their brands and consumers. While the imperative may be greater for global companies looking to localize their offerings, domestic players must never become complacent about identifying with customers. Every society has its tensions, but they are especially pronounced in Asia today, where the clash between centuries-old customs and other possibilities introduced by growing incomes and the Internet create palpable conflicts in people's hearts and minds. In China, for example, Mont Blanc is held in such high regard that the company recently opened its largest flagship concept store in Beijing. Mont Blanc's trademark has always been its six-pointed star, which appears on the cap of every pen and is a special design element for the Chinese because it is a potent projector of status. The star, graceful but conspicuous, makes a distinct statement. The act of simply clipping a pen in a suit's front pocket or taking notes during a meeting artfully projects both elegance and power. This unexpected combination of refinement and flash is precisely what the Chinese love about the brand.

In Confucian China "face" is a sociological construct that is all about reputation and the importance of being recognized for one's success. It is a social currency to be bought, sold, traded, lost, won, and earned. Wearing the wrong watch at a business meeting can result in loss of face.

When I arrived in Shanghai in 1998 I wore a US$400 Longines watch—the one that now boasts the feminine tagline "Elegance is an attitude." In one of my first meetings agency staffers kept their eyes focused on the table, and I instinctively asked myself, "Have I said something wrong? Did I make a mistake?" Finally, after a meeting with a client, a group of staffers said, "We have something serious to discuss with you. It's your watch. Every time you go into a meeting with a client wearing that Longines, the entire company loses face. You cannot, as managing director of JWT Shanghai, wear a Longines." They escorted me to a department store to buy a US$5,000 midrange Cartier. Several years later I got promoted, and they came into my office again and said, "You cannot wear a midrange Cartier." I was forced to upgrade to a more elite brand. In this way face is the path to upward advancement, and its preservation is absolutely essential to Chinese who must succeed.

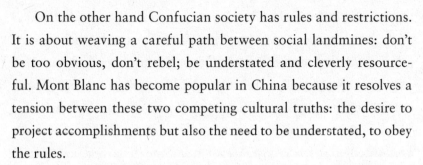

On the other hand Confucian society has rules and restrictions. It is about weaving a careful path between social landmines: don't be too obvious, don't rebel; be understated and cleverly resourceful. Mont Blanc has become popular in China because it resolves a tension between these two competing cultural truths: the desire to project accomplishments but also the need to be understated, to obey the rules.

In Southeast Asia—the location of some of the world's most rapidly developing countries—societal shifts are causing other tensions to surface, especially among younger generations. In Indonesia, for example, society has traditionally been built on notions of conformity and collectivism. Faced with the challenge of unifying the diverse archipelago, Indonesia's first president, Sukarno, declared Pancasila (the five pillars) the philosophical foundation of the nation, a fusion of social justice, nationalism, and monotheism. Sukarno used his call for consensus as a means of social control—a way to forcefully unite a diverse and sprawling group of cultures. But as the country opens up to the world, allowing alternative points of view to proliferate, Indonesians have a different understanding of how they should embrace consensus. They believe that unity should come from within, that people should celebrate differences in culture and opinion and encourage individual achievement. The overriding tension in society is that Indonesians want to fit in yet stand out.

Similar tensions exist in Thailand. Local people are very nationalistic, in part because the country has never been colonized, but the country's long rich cultural identity is also built on the idea of collectivism and the Buddhist ideal to maintain harmony at all times. A common phrase is "mai pen rai"—never mind, you're welcome, or don't worry. People in Thailand say it all the time, even when they are angry, because they find it hard to express their real feelings in case doing so upsets the need for order and balance. On the one hand Indonesians need collectivism and harmony, but, on the other, just as in Indonesia, Thais also want to stand out, to be noticed. This tension has intensified with the emergence of social media, which allow people to show off their achievements and communicate with other cultures. Indonesians want to plug into an exciting modern world but also be true to their heritage. When *Vogue* recently began a Thai edition, its commercial underscored this tension. It shows Thais as fashionistas, able to compete on the world stage yet still acknowledging the importance of tradition. In a nod to cultural nuances models assume "nang pap piap"—the seated position for a traditional Thai woman, which involves bending the legs to one side—with one crawling on her knees to meet her elders and tilting her head and body as a mark of respect.

Elsewhere, in some of the more developed Asian markets like Hong Kong and Singapore, some people are questioning the values that helped to bring about growth. Hong Kong is a city on steroids—the pace of life is phenomenal—but stress levels are soaring. People feel as though they are racing on a treadmill, having lost sight of where they are actually trying to go. Their dilemma is between the embedded Confucian need to succeed and anxiety about what the future holds. In Singapore it is much the same. For decades Confucian ambition was summarized with the idea that residents value the "five C's" above all else: cash, credit cards, cars, country club memberships, and condominiums. Overt material wealth was always the hallmark of success in Singapore, but in recent years people have begun to question these values, and attitudes are changing. A more rounded definition of what winning looks like has replaced material definitions of success.

Singaporeans have the Confucian dragon of power in their hearts and still have the ambition to own their piece of the sky. But the world is changing, creating an anxiety that perhaps the old ways are no longer best. Brands have been tapping these tensions quite successfully. A recent survey by OCBC Bank found that fewer than 4 percent of Singaporeans actually wanted a country club membership, and less than 12 percent desired a luxury car.[8] The resulting ad campaign for the bank coined a new set of five C's: control, confidence, community, can-do spirit, and fulfilling career aspirations. The bank's "Strive for more" work included online videos of taxi drivers chatting about their personal views on wealth, as well as a provocative outdoor campaign that articulated the tension in Singaporean society. One billboard read: "To zig when others zag. To speak up for yourself when no one else does. To quit your job when you've stopped enjoying it. To stand tall where others fall. Strive for more."

HUMAN TRUTH VERSUS CULTURAL TRUTH

The third and final tension revealed by insights into consumer behavior is between competing human and cultural truths. This is when urges that unite people clash with the pressures arising from their cultural, historical, or geographic identities. Nike became an iconic brand in the United States because it resolved a tension between human and cultural truths in American society. People want to succeed on their own terms—to be only who they want to be and not worry about the opinions of others. However, even Americans exist in a rules-based society; they understand that unbridled selfishness is not sustainable. Pure individualism bucks against the need to respect a certain order. Nike's resolution is the "Just do it" philosophy. Goods sold by the brand—running shoes, apparel, the Nike+ apps—liberate individuals to break free of limitations. The basketball court becomes a temple of individual expression and cleverness, the soccer pitch a platform of powerful release during make-or-break moments. And in the process Nike becomes a brand American consumers cherish. (As I will discuss in Chapter 4, Nike's success in non-Western markets has benefited from a nonrebellious interpretation of individualism that suits collectivist cultures.)

"Women hold up half the sky" is one of Chairman Mao Ze-dong's most famous sayings, and more than 60 years later it still rings true—Chinese women are strong. Like men, they want to be acknowledged for their successes; they want to stand up and be counted. China is one of the most equal societies when it comes to employment. Unlike many of its neighbors, the country has an exceptionally female-driven workforce; about 85 percent of women who have children remain employed. But this desire for acknowledgment clashes with the cultural truth that women should be loving and gentle, understated. And therein lies the tension. It is why the Chinese love diamonds. The sparkle is delicate, not like the brash unsubtle glare of gold—the diamond captures attention but does so in an understated way. In Taiwan De Beers harnessed this tension for its "Blame It on the Diamond" commercial, which shows a woman admiring herself and her jewelry in her reflection in a mirrored restaurant window. Little does she know that a couple sitting on the other side of the glass can see her, so the woman is showing off without realizing it. This goes to the heart of the idea that women want to shine but without sacrificing their unassuming femininity.

In Thailand women also face the tension between a longing to express themselves freely and a social requirement to conform to certain standards of behavior and physicality. Thai society is still quite conservative. Thailand's leading brand of cosmetics, Oriental Princess, crafted a hugely provocative campaign that encouraged woman to question society's expectations, asking them: "Why put on makeup? Why shop mindlessly? Why be beautiful? Why change? Why lose weight? Why don't you think first? Why is whiter skin better? Why do you need to be jealous? Why get so emotional? Why do you need to be like others? Why do you need to be slim? Why can't you have a new start? Why believe in others? Why not trust yourself? Why stay quiet? Why tolerate so much? Why be afraid? Women's value, it's for you to create." This campaign resolves the tension head-on. The brand is offering an alternative for Thai women to rally behind, encouraging them to embrace natural beauty and, in the process, define their own self-worth, to break free from societal expectations and express themselves, to be who they are.

In Latin American cultures the universal desire for upward momentum in life often runs up against a lack of faith in institutions to represent, let alone advance, the interests of ordinary people and results in a *que sera sera* passivity. Puerto Rico's largest Bank, Banco Popular, playfully challenged this laid-back approach to life, which is celebrated in a hugely popular salsa song, "No Hago Más Ná" (I Do Nothing), by the band El Gran Combo. The lyrics include lines that extol the pleasures of living life lazily, "just eating, sleeping and not working." Banco Popular worked with El Gran Combo on a new version of the song with new lyrics that subvert the song's original spirit into a celebration of productivity and "moving forward, never backwards." The bank then started a successful campaign to make the new song the most popular track in Puerto Rico, generating about $2.3 million in free publicity in the process.

TECHNIQUES TO UNCOVER HUMAN AND CULTURAL TRUTHS

Research is the method marketing organizations use to understand what motivates consumers. Since the early twentieth century, research has been instrumental in efforts to determine attitudes toward particular brands and their competitors. In 1924 Procter & Gamble was among the first companies to set up a market research department, which studied the preferences of consumers and their buying habits. Although techniques have evolved since then, exploration remains a top priority for marketers—even though almost everything else in the advertising industry has changed. Marketers and advertising agencies now have a range of qualitative and quantitative techniques at their fingertips. Quantitative methods like usage and attitude surveys are a good starting point when analyzing what people say about a brand or category. They help marketers understand various metrics, including how often people use or buy a product, how they feel about that product, and the standing of the brand compared to its competitors. Likewise, mapping studies address the different consumer segments for a category, uncovering the different factors motivating each one. This is all valuable information, but used in isolation it is unlikely to generate powerful insights into consumer behavior or contribute to an understanding of the tensions within the hearts of consumers.

Focus groups also have their place. Asking a cross section of a target group of consumers how they view a product, its benefits, and drawbacks, and how they would respond to certain communication plans or product developments, has clear advantages. Most important, using a focus group introduces individual voices that might cut through the reams of data and make simple yet prescient and actionable observations. However, a big bias is baked into any findings that come out of focus groups because their members are expressing opinions about brands and products in front of other people. People in a group have been known to hide their emotions and fail to provide feedback that is completely truthful. And the more sensitive the category, the greater that bias is likely to be. While a man might have no problem sharing his deepest thoughts about his shampoo preferences, he may find it more difficult to talk about how different condom brands affect his sexual performance. Likewise, women may find it harder to talk openly about feminine hygiene products. Ethnographic techniques that focus on observing people in their natural environment hold slightly more promise. The idea is to enter people's lives to understand exactly how they interact with brands or products. It can be done on a narrow basis, such as looking in people's kitchens and seeing what is in their cupboards, and watching how people prepare food.

In some situations simply being an observer of humanity and different cultures is enough to make an informed marketing decision. When I think of how I develop my insights about China, I realize that they often come from my cultural immersion. I get a lot out of research that is descriptive and observational, but nothing can replace walking around and talking to people.

Giant manufacturers of fast-moving consumer goods—Unilever and Procter & Gamble, for example—spend huge amounts of money on research, particularly in emerging markets. Although research alone cannot describe the tensions within the hearts and minds of target audiences, it must be the starting point. Then the information should be analyzed with proper perspective. Analysts should use qualitative and quantitative techniques with a curious mind to uncover the fundamental motivations for consumers' behavior and preferences. As such, marketers and advertising agencies must be willing and able to enter the realms of psychology and cultural anthropology. There is no substitute for curiosity and persistence when asking "Why?" until it can be asked no more.

INSIGHTS ABOUT EMERGING MARKETS
AND BUSINESS STRATEGY

Generally speaking, the psychology of consumers in emerging markets is distinct from their counterparts in developed nations. This does not discount the importance of cultural factors in shaping buying behavior—Confucian values will always be less individualistic than Western values, no matter the per capita value of a country's gross domestic product. But a country's level of economic development is an important factor, and marketers should adjust their strategy accordingly.

Institutions designed to protect the political and economic interests of consumers—for example, independent judiciaries and reliable social welfare schemes—are relatively immature in emerging markets. People are less vested in having a civil society, and they seldom take safety—physical, emotional, and societal—for granted. Consumers in these markets focus more on the scale and reassurance of big brands; projection of status and adherence to tradition that characterize hierarchical societies; and benefits that "do good" rather than "feel good." In the developing world, the watchwords are *protection* and *pragmatism*. That is why Safeguard, Procter & Gamble's germ-killing soap, is especially popular in places like China and the Philippines; in economically developed countries consumers are drawn to hedonistic benefits. These consumer commonalities lead to a number of crucial strategic imperatives. Marketers should

1. Introduce megabrands (brands with offerings across several related categories) rather than stand-alone brands
2. Adjust their products to maximize perceived value
3. Capitalize on trends driven by the country's stage of economic development
4. Compete across, not within, categories
5. Develop communications that are rational and linked to social context

Megabrands. Well-known brands are reassuring. According to the 2013 edition of *Roper Reports,* 79 percent of consumers in developing Asian markets and 61 percent of Latin American consumers "only buy products and services from a trusted brand." In Western Europe 46 percent of consumers agree with that statement, while in developed Asia—that is, Japan and South Korea—the level slips to 42 percent. In developing countries 53 percent believe "it's better to buy well-known brands because you can rely on their quality" compared to only 28 percent in developed countries. Familiarity also tends to reassure consumers in emerging markets. A survey by McKinsey & Company, the management consulting firm, found that 28 percent of Chinese consumers prefer to "stick to brands I have used in the past rather than try new ones" versus only 16 percent in the United Kingdom and an exceptionally low 4 percent in Japan.[9]

Lack of confidence in the integrity of the manufacturing process, as well as the weak link between category and brand common across emerging markets, explains the reassurance consumers derive from mass-marketed products. In the Philippines one brand, Magnolia, sells a broad array of categories—from water to cheddar cheese to chicken cutlets. This does not happen in the United States, where Kraft equals cheese and Aquafina equals water. In China, Chunlan, a state-owned enterprise, produces everything from motorcycles to water heaters, while Yunnan Baiyao, originally known for an ointment that stanches bleeding, now has a portfolio that spans medicated bandages and toothpaste.

"Conglomerate brands" are comforting. South Korean *chaebols* are corporate behemoths that arose during a period of postwar economic deprivation. Today they control, directly or indirectly, approximately 70 percent of economic activity. Samsung Corporation, the largest of these companies, still wields its eponymous brand to promote an extensive array of categories, including mobile phones, consumer electronics, insurance, and medical equipment. In the West, Procter & Gamble is a corporation, not a brand. Consumers know Pringles potato chips and Downy fabric softener; P&G is only a corporate stamp of reassurance.

Manufacturers in developing countries also benefit from the inherent efficiency of corporate brands. Media costs are rising faster than per capita spending in any category, so forging brand awareness is an expensive proposition. In Australia and the United States, where annual per-child spending on toys is approximately $500, Mattel has been able to establish discrete consumer franchises under the Thomas & Friends, Barbie, Hot Wheels, and Monster High brands. In developing countries establishing four stand-alone brands is less feasible.

Multinational brands operating in developing markets are learning quickly. Many have either expanded their footprints into contiguous categories or rebalanced their focus in favor of the master brand. Nestlé's Maggi is a brand of bouillon cube in developed markets, but in India it is used to sell instant noodles, milk, sauces, and soup. L'Oréal began as primarily a skin care and cosmetics brand in Europe and North America, yet in China it entered the market fully diversified into shampoo, hair coloring, and styling products. In China, Southeast Asia, Mexico, and Southeast Asia, Kellogg is evolving from corporate to master brand with advertising and activation events that reinforce a campaign for the entire cereal portfolio that promises "breakfast for better days."

Value justification. Consumers in emerging markets are nervously optimistic. A kaleidoscope of change heralds new, albeit uncertain, opportunity. In this context manufacturers often deploy international brands as weapons on the battlefield of life. They are expensive compared to local competitors but achieve success because new consumers are more sensitive to value for money than low price. Lack of confidence in local products and services can result in what could be called a "penalty of poverty"—that is, higher prices than in developed markets. This phenomenon occurs in categories in which contamination fears are rife, such as infant formula or bottled water, as well as in highly regulated sectors like financial services, where interest rates for microfinancing are higher than those charged by mainstream banks.[10]

Marketers should concentrate on increasing customers' perceptions of value as much as lowering their out-of-pocket expense. Ways to achieve this include value engineering, introducing composite products, and adding purpose to pleasure.

Value engineering. The Nokia 1100 mobile phone, introduced in 2003, created a new value equation in developing markets by redefining standards of durability, an area of concern among lower-income consumers. The model, now discontinued, became the world's

Nokia's seminal 1100 mobile phone, introduced in 2003, redefined the value equation for developing markets. The model's durability was particularly relevant to lower-income consumers.

best-selling mobile phone. Improving sensory satisfaction also can enhance perceived value. Nestlé originally tailored its RMB1 wafer for the China market, where chocolate still suffers from being perceived as too yang—causing excessive heat that requires yin, or cooling, foods to maintain internal balance. By increasing the wafer-to-cocoa ratio while lowering the cost of goods, Nestlé was able to sell a chocolate bar for the first time as an everyday snack, not an occasional indulgence. Nestlé's three-in-one coffee has been a hit because the product is designed with sweetness to balance bitterness. Minute Maid enhanced the value perceptions of its Pulpy by ensuring that it imitates the mouthfeel of pure juice, and in the process it became a power brand.

Composite products. "Frugal innovation" is the creation of mass-market products that offer more for less. These items often take the form of composite products that boast multipurpose, multibenefit design. Procter & Gamble's Olay Total Effects is an affordable moisturizer with a "seven-in-one" antiaging formulation. Pfizer's Centrum, a multivitamin supplement, has achieved success in China and India, driven by its "complete from A to Zinc" composition.

Preference for composite products in emerging markets has shaped the strategic vision of leading electronics manufacturers. Western consumers prefer special devices for specialty applications— Microsoft's Xbox is specifically for games, while Apple's iPad largely helps consumers access digital media and provides entertainment. Consumers in emerging markets, on the other hand, expect a single device to cover a wide range of functions. Nokia's lack of success in eroding the dominance of high-end smartphone manufacturers in Western markets masks impressive gains in feature phone sales throughout developing Asian, African, and Latin American markets. It designed the Nokia 105, for example, to appeal to first-time phone buyers and build value perceptions with a variety of preloaded functions such as an FM radio, multiple alarm clocks, a "speaking" clock, dust and water resistance, and a flashlight. The phone also has a color screen and an impressive 35-day battery life.

Purpose over pleasure. Brands should focus on external payoffs rather than internal satisfaction or release. In an insecure and competitive environment, celebrating indulgence is risky. Starbucks has established its stores as gathering sites for the professional elite eager to display new-generation cool rather than the "third space" between work and home that Howard Schultz, CEO of Starbucks, intended. Premium yogurt should focus on "digestion that gets you going" rather than taste satisfaction, while Wrigley's Extra chewing gum fuses great taste with oral care. Danone established its premium Evian brand, popular in the West, on a platform of purity. The company's Mizone, distributed largely in Asia and South America, is a nutrient-enhanced "energy water." Mattel is repositioning its toy brands to more explicitly align fun with learning or discovery.

Trend Arbitrage. Other factors being equal, economies—and consumer motivations—evolve in predictable ways. As markets progress from emerging to developed, marketers can stay a step ahead by introducing products in niche categories destined to achieve broad scale. In food, for example:

- Emerging markets are at a basic stage in which protective benefits dominate. Products are often unbranded or locally produced, and familiarity establishes trust—"a brand I grew up with." Natural ingredients with traditional "do good" properties do well, as do those that reinforce claims of purity or being free of chemicals. Health benefits are rooted in immunity or "more is better" nutritional propositions. For example, claiming "4 times [the essential fatty acid] DHA" helped Mead Johnson's Enfagrow, an infant formula, build a leadership position in several markets. In China, Kellogg introduced breakfast cereal by claiming it provides "well-rounded and complete nutrition."

- Middle-income countries are at a modernist stage. As taste indulgence comes to the fore, chocolate and salty snacks appear on store shelves, and high-calorie products proliferate. Increasingly stressful lifestyles also give rise to convenience products. Nutritional benefits flip from protective to transformative—that is, taller, bigger, smarter. Nontraditional foods, from fast food to red wine, become more popular, especially if consumed outside the home as a signal of middle-class modernity. "Detox" food and beverages offset unhealthy diets. Suntory introduced its black oolong tea in Southeast Asia as a postmeal drink—an antidote to greasy foods—with ingredients that slow fat absorption.

- Postmodernist marketing is a reaction against overindulgence and can be summed up as less is more. Developed economies, including those of Japan, America, and Western Europe, are at this stage, where nutritional benefits, such as balanced or light, are more nuanced. "Back to nature," illustrated by Evian's "live young" purity claim or the proliferation of the Body Shop's green cosmetic counters, emerges as a powerful motivator. Consumer awareness of the goodness of organic food grows, with "feels good" trumping "tastes good." Kellogg's Special K, a low-calorie grain-based cereal and snack that also promotes female confidence, is poised to become a more diversified brand that plays a broader role in women's lives.

Companies can exploit the knowledge of how markets evolve. To establish the vanguard positions in the competitive mainland China market, the Tingyi Holding Corporation and Uni-President Corporation, Taiwanese snack food manufacturers, anticipated the emergence of convenience benefits and introduced instant noodles and then cups of noodles. Shaklee Corporation, an American manufacturer and distributor of natural nutritional supplements, was equally prescient. The company's weight-loss protein powder already generates annual sales of more than $100 million in mainland China.

Food categories are not the only ones that evolve in predictable ways. In emerging markets newcomers to luxury products are drawn to such goods as conspicuous badges of status. The shiny "double G" Gucci belt buckle or diamond-studded gold Rolex are marks of sophistication. As their incomes rise, luxury buyers want to demonstrate their connoisseurship and refinement, so branding cues become more understated. Louis Vuitton's highest-priced bags, for example, do not carry the famous "LV" logo. Of course economic development does not eliminate cultural differences. In Western countries private luxury—products or services only a few know about—is coming of age. But in China and other Asian markets the most advanced buyers demand personalized luxury—noticeable product flourishes tailored to the specifications of individual buyers. Andrew Wu, who heads the China division of the luxury group LVMH, said to me, "The Chinese believe there's no point in paying a lot of money for a brand if no one knows what you own."

Cross-category competition. Consumers in emerging markets are, by definition, new consumers. Advertising should work hard to convey a compelling reason for them to switch from one category to another. The competitive landscape is primordial and the frame of reference—the range of categories that compete with one another to fulfill a specific need —is in flux. In markets with low coffee consumption, for example, Nescafé competes with tea and other beverages. In markets with high coffee consumption, it competes with other instant coffees. Advertising in developed markets targets category users who are already familiar with existing brand alternatives so enhancing the salience of yours is key. Elsewhere, advertising should trigger more fundamental changes in behavior.

What constitutes an effective reason to change one's behavior depends on the nature of the category. Across Southeast Asia, for example, Mattel's Fisher-Price Play IQ is a winning proposition because the brand resolves the tension between childhood advancement and fun. In other categories, from cake mix to frozen dinners, convenience needs become more acute as daily life becomes more hectic. B&Q, a UK home improvement retailer, provides free decorating advice at an on-premises design center, a service traditional mom-and-pop shops are unable to offer. For goods consumed in public, status sells. Chinese first-time car buyers purchase the majority of automobiles, many of which cost more than 100 percent of the buyer's annual income. Auto brands must therefore announce entry into the middle class, with benefits externalized to facilitate progress up the social or professional hierarchy.

Contextual rationalism. Consumers in emerging non-Western, nonindividualistic markets have not yet attained confidence in their material stability and are disoriented by a surfeit of new brand alternatives. Advertising can point them toward the rational benefits of the product and demonstrate product value within a social context.

The importance of developing market rationalism is apparent in many ways: effectiveness of in-store activation in providing information that can change buying decisions near the point of purchase; reliance on authoritative online opinion leaders and information portals in shaping preference; acute price sensitivity, especially for goods consumed in private; the importance of "reasons to believe" in increasing persuasion. Consumers in emerging markets are not robots, but they can differentiate products emotionally only after their left brain—that is, logic-based—imperatives have been satisfied.

Once marketers have addressed the pragmatism of consumers in emerging markets, they can emphasize the emotional relevance of their products by highlighting how they enhance buyers' social standing. The context of external acknowledgment broadens as incomes rise. Men of modest means want the admiration of friends and immediate family. New-generation Yuppies aim higher, for accolades from the business community and beyond. A related note: most advertising in emerging markets benefits from the use of celebrities or authority figures because they reduce the risk of buyers fearing losing face.

CONCLUSION

The starting point for powerful communications is insight into the fundamental motivations for consumers' behavior and their preferences. In my experience the best insights spring from tension between or within human and cultural truths. If a brand resolves a conflict of the heart, that brand's role in life is greater. Prices can therefore be adjusted accordingly. Insight remains the font of robust profit margins, and it is rooted in an appreciation of sociocultural forces that drive consumers' behavior—whether common the world over or geographically nuanced—in different markets. In a commercial universe pulsating with high-tech possibility, it behooves brand owners not to ignore this timeless marketing truth.

four

the brand idea

Insights into consumer behavior can often be articulated as a conflict in the heart, between or within cultural and human truths. If a brand can resolve that tension, its role in the consumer's life becomes greater, as does the potential for deeper engagement and the cultivation of loyalty. Marketers root this resolution in the brand idea, a fusion of insight and unique benefits offered by the brand that articulates the long-term relationship between consumer and brand. It is an abstract but ubiquitous presence in all communications, ensuring a consistency that ideally endures for years, regardless of the changing media landscape.

In 2009 JWT was about to lose a major account in China. In the midst of the global financial crisis, Unicharm, the Japanese manufacturer of Asia's largest feminine hygiene brand, Sofy, put us on notice. JWT had handled the account for twelve years, and losing it would have had a major impact on the business. We faced a significant profit hit, layoffs, and plummeting morale.

Over the years we had based Sofy's advertising on the brand's functional benefits. The tone and manner across commercials were disjointed; the only consistent elements were meticulously engineered demonstration sequences of the product's "leakage protection." In terms of emotional benefits the brand skipped from "liberation of your adventurous spirit" to "security at night." Sofy was not as vibrant or consistent as it needed to be and did not connect with young women. For a variety of reasons we had never managed to imbue Sofy with a brand idea—the nucleus of any vibrant marketing effort—and this was frustrating. No one, within the agency or at Unicharm, was satisfied.

As a gesture of respect for twelve years of partnership, Unicharm's board of directors invited JWT to Japan to present a brand idea that could ensure strategic and creative consistency across all current and future product variants (daytime, active slim, nighttime, a "fashion" range); be effective throughout Asia; demonstrate our insight into the motivation of Asian young women; and unify creative executions across mass media, promotional, and digital communications. A friend at Unicharm whispered to me that our trip to Tokyo, while well intentioned, was mission impossible.

JWT retained the business, and four years later Sofy is the market leader in Japan, Thailand, Indonesia, and Taiwan and is coming on strong in other countries. In China, where the brand has dozens of local competitors, its share increased 7 percentage points between 2010 and 2012. On a national level the brand has eclipsed Procter & Gamble's Whisper, Sofy's major multinational competitor, and achieved leadership in several first-tier cities such as Shanghai and Beijing. Prices and margins have increased, whereas those of rivals have dropped. JWT continues to handle the account throughout the region and, for the first time, in Japan as well.

None of this would have been possible if we had not pushed a compelling brand idea. To differentiate the product from the market leader, Procter & Gamble's Whisper, we reduced the age of our target segment from professional to younger women. We sharpened and articulated the insight into consumers as this inner tension: "I want to lead a more colorful, active life but 'those days' make it difficult." The product differentiator remains leakage protection, but we fused it with sharper insight into the brand's younger consumers, which led to the tagline "Shine without a pause." We have now unified Sofy's communications and marketing efforts across product, time, and geography by dint of conceptual cohesion, not high-tech

Sales took off when Sofy, Unicharm's feminine hygiene brand, targeted younger Asian women who crave lifestyle liberation. Communications were unified with the brand idea "Shine without a pause." Sofy is now the leading feminine care brand in several Asian countries.

wizardry. Sofy became a lifestyle liberator. Social media activities such as the online Miss Sofy Club provide a platform for consumers to share new "special sparkles." Even premiums breathed the brand idea, including a series of plush *kawai*—Japan-style cute—toys that are popular among young Asian women.

Unicharm, a rare but happy exception in a land of corporate conservatism, is now a believer in the beauty of brand ideas.

Insight into consumer behavior is the starting point when constructing a brand idea. It involves fusing insight and a "unique brand offer," or UBO—in other words, the most important differentiating characteristic of the brand or product in question. The brand idea is more than a positioning statement. It transcends ordinary what's-in-it-for-me benefit statements—such as "makes your skin soft" or "provides shiny hair"—and individual creative executions

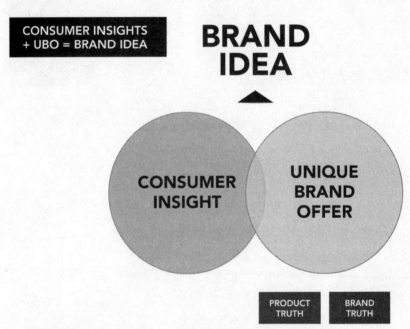

The brand idea is a long-term, two-way relationship between consumer and brand that remains consistent yet capable of dynamic evolution. It is a fusion of consumer insight and Unique Brand Offer, the latter born of either a product or brand truth.

and campaigns. The brand idea is strategic, a work of both conceptual precision and forward-thinking inspiration. Indeed it defines the very soul of the brand and, barring dramatic change in the operating environment, should endure for decades.

The brand idea may assume the form of a tagline, but it is more fundamental than this. Meticulously articulated, it represents the long-term *relationship* between consumer and brand. Inherently bilateral, the brand idea provides the raison d'etre for subsequent engagement across both digital and analog media. Like a good marriage, it represents a commitment between two parties, something that remains consistent but evolves over time and place. The brand idea is abstract, but its presence should be felt in every television commercial, consumer promotion, microsite, in-store activation program, and social media campaign. It is nothing less than a brand's life force, forging conceptual order from chaos. In an era of exploding communication channels, both digital and traditional, a clear brand idea is more important than ever. It ensures coherence across a brandscape overflowing with new media outlets and vehicles for engaging consumers.

The irony is that, despite the value derived from a strong brand idea, most consumers do not believe brands stand for much of anything at all. This may be at least partially because our industry is increasingly—yet naively—seduced by technological razzle-dazzle at the expense of clear brand messaging.

HISTORY RECAP

Consistency has always been the core of successful branding. During the industrial revolution, it made modern marketing possible. A product was branded with an attractive-sounding name and supported by advertising that conveyed its unique qualities. Ivory soap introduced its claim of "Ninety-nine and forty-four one-hundredths pure. It floats!" in 1881. Such message uniformity made it possible for consumers to trust a product regardless of whether they purchased it in Bangor, Maine, or San Diego, California. As efficiencies in manufacturing and distribution networks increased, the national, and then multinational, brand was born. Concurrent breakthroughs in mass media, starting with national print and culminating in coast-to-coast television broadcasts, greatly enhanced the ability of manufacturers to control their content and placement of advertising. Communications were largely one way and, for the most part, remained unadulterated by word of mouth.

Of course shoppers have always been savvy, holding strong opinions about the Brand A versus Brand B. But the digital revolution has upended the balance of power between consumers and manufacturers. Through blogs, Facebook, Snapchat, Instagram, Pinterest, Medium, and countless other channels, communication between buyer and seller is instantaneous. And, in an era of social networks, advertising has evolved from wisdom imparted by marketers and received by grateful buyers to a shape-shifting dialog involving three parties: the manufacturer, the consumer, and online friends. Communication channels—which in the mid-1990s were limited to television, radio, print magazines, and newspapers, with a smattering of direct marketing thrown in for good measure—have multiplied.

Seduced by these new forms of technology-enabled engagement, many marketers and their advertising agencies have foundered, leading to a disintegration of craftsmanship and consistency in messaging, as well as a parallel rise in disjointed creative executions. This fractionation has occurred for a variety of reasons, but the most important are erroneous assumptions: (1) that new forms of technological engagement imply a fundamentally different relationship between consumers and brands, and (2) that each technological application requires different creative ideas. A few years ago, at the Cannes advertising festival, the chair of the judging panel for cyber creative began his opening remarks by declaring, "We are no longer creative people. We are inventors!" Many found this disconcerting and rightly so. Communications professionals should embrace the noble goal of reconciling clear top-down messaging with the dynamism of consumer-led engagement fueled by digital platforms. We should harness the power of technology in the service of great creative ideas that unify media, not mistake the medium for the idea itself.

BRAND "EXPERIENCE" VERSUS BRAND "IDEA"

So-called traditional advertising (radio, print, television) verbally and visually communicates the brand and product benefits. In an era of consumer empowerment, we should immerse consumers in the brand by stimulating as many senses as possible. "Experiential marketing" involves anything from in-store sampling to pop-up stores to the sound emitted when a can of cola is opened. The goal of experiential marketing is to form a multidimensional emotional connection between consumer and brand that reinforces loyalty.

Some communications experts prefer the modish expression "brand experience" to "brand idea," deeming the latter too uni-dimensional and "advertising-y" relative to the interactivity and holism of the former. I beg to differ. A brand idea, the long-term *relationship* between consumer and brand, is dynamic and multifaceted. It must breathe life into every interaction—or "touchpoint"—that connects consumer and brand. Each experience, hi- or low-tech, must reinforce a clearly defined proposition—an idea born of conceptual craftsmanship.

LEGO, a brand that has celebrated creativity since 1932, gets it. The name LEGO is derived from Danish phrase "Leg godt," which also means "I put together" in Latin. Every manifestation of LEGO's brand idea, "inspiring the builders of tomorrow," strengthens brand equity. The company's award-winning retail outlets are designed with innovative displays and spaces for family "building" events and kid-friendly exploration areas. At several locations worldwide,

LEGOland encourages kids to open their imaginations at construction sites that dot the theme parks. To the tune of almost $500 million in global ticket sales, the 2014 film *The LEGO Movie* is perhaps the most successful branded entertainment in recent years. It tells the tale of an ordinary construction worker, Emmet, battling nefarious Lord Business whose ambition is to glue everything in the adaptable LEGO world into place. In the words of Kjeld Kirk Kristiansen, the grandson of LEGO's Danish founder Ole Kirk Kristiansen: "I seek to take the LEGO idea [beyond building things] and encourage children to explore, express and experience their own world. A world without limits."[1]

Google, the ultimate twenty-first-century power brand, does not really sell many of its own services. From French patisseries in New York to study abroad programs in Japan, it brands the services others sell, largely through its search engine. The brand is unified by experiences that add dimension to Google's brand idea, "bringing the world together through technology." This mission transcends advertising. Every piece of information generated by an online search is associated with the warm glow of Google. In the process, the company's proprietary tools—airline status, mapping, street view, auto correct, and so on—are demonstrated. Every technology does this, including Google Glass, a wearable product designed for "those on the move." The experience of using the product makes the world a smaller place. Google's vivid relationship with consumers stands in marked contrast to erstwhile Japanese titans such as Sony, Panasonic and Hitachi. It is probably no coincidence that these brands, now tech also-rans, never had clear brand ideas.

GREAT BRAND IDEAS: FROM CONCEPTUAL UNITY, STRENGTH

As the digital revolution turns the advertising industry on its head, consistency and conceptual craftsmanship have become forgotten imperatives. Bob Jeffrey, JWT's global CEO, presaged the problem at the Next Big Idea Conference in California back in 2007: "In our zeal to crack the next big thing, we're simply latching on to the latest thing without thinking about how it links up to a big brand idea. Today, the 'bits'—the executions, the tactical side of things—overshadow brands. Despite the changes that our business and our clients' businesses are undergoing, some universal truths remain, most crucially the idea that creative work needs to be rooted in building a client's brand."[2]

If brands are to weather today's challenges of globalization and media fractionation, consistency should be the bedrock of everything they do. If not, things fall apart. Brand ideas that define what a brand stands for and the role it plays in consumers' lives ensure consistency. The brand idea must crystallize a long-term relationship between consumer and brand that endures over time. Brand ideas should evolve but not stray from their conceptual underpinning.

Nike lives and breathes the "Just do it" spirit across all media. This spirit is not simply a call to participate in sports, it is a rallying cry to push against convention and define oneself independent of society. Through Nike, through a relationship with a brand that has forged a meaningful role in life, a paraplegic can ignore preconceptions and compete in a long-distance marathon. A short woman can defeat trash talkers on the basketball court. Nike's spirit didn't appear out of thin air or drip from a Twitter feed. It is the exquisitely refined vision of Phil Knight, the company's cofounder and CEO, and Nike has reinforced it at every level and in every corner of the organization for forty years.

Apple's brand idea is equally inspired. When Steve Jobs exhorted the masses to "Think different," he was not simply encouraging them to buy a product but establishing Apple as a quasi-religion, a belief in the humanizing power of technology. The company's most famous products are *sublimely* elegant. They provide balm in a frenetic depersonalized world—hence, the fanatic loyalty of users.

Great brand ideas are precise, the fruit of meticulous thinking. They possess four characteristics:

- They are seamless fusions of insights into consumer behavior and a unique brand offer. The UBO must directly address the need revealed by the insight. Through "strong stain removal," OMO detergent's "Dirt is good" brand idea resolves the tension between a mother's wish for her kids to explore the world and the hassle of getting tough spots out of clothes.

- Great brand ideas should be surprising, which ensures they have a long life. Until HSBC shifted its strategy from a focus on retail banking to money management, its brand idea was "The world's local bank." The combination of global heft and local savvy, of towering scale and cultural empathy, was unexpected. For more than two decades the unifying power of HSBC's brand idea kept an expanding network from falling apart.

- Brand ideas must be evocatively written. Whether they double as taglines or not, they articulate the brand's soul and role in life, serving as a manifesto that calls an organization to arms. *Lian ziji,* the brand idea of the Chinese sportswear producer Anta, is more electrifying than its English translation, "Forge yourself." The character for *lian* has a fire radical that connotes a transformation of blood, sweat, and tears into shining glory. (Brand ideas also should convey their drama with a range of stimuli, including brand identity manuals and videos that use powerful visuals and music.)

- The brand idea must be written in a way that feels "of" a specific category. Rolex's "Timeless champion" uses watch language, aligns that language with success, and alludes to the brand's heritage of craftsmanship. "Live for Greatness" or "Tell History, Not Time," two of Rolex's recent campaigns, would never have materialized without an enduring brand idea that springs from category-specific cues.

In some parts of the world age is a barrier, in others an advantage. You can be written off or revered.

At HSBC we work for 125 million customers, all over the world, on a daily basis. And what we've learned in our travels hasn't just broadened our mind but opened it too.

One thing is certain, people will always have different points of view on life. And that's good no matter what your age.

yourpointofview.com

The world's local bank

This ad is an example of HSBC's "points of view" campaign. It is an expression of HSBC's retired brand idea "The world's local bank": powerful positions often achieve differentiation via an unexpected juxtaposition of ideas. (Photography by Henrik Knudsen)

Brevity is also critical because it simplifies strategic imperatives and competitive differentiation, but sometimes you can be too terse. In 2006 the advertising icon Maurice Saatchi introduced the concept of "one-word equity"—a single word that embodies a product or service. Arguing that Google owns *search*, while America's one-word equity is *freedom*, Saatchi writes in the *Financial Times*:

> Take great care before you pick your word. It is going to be the god of your brand. Try this simple test on your own company's products or services. Pick a brand. Any brand. Now, think of what you are trying to say. Can you precisely describe, in one word, the particular value, the characteristic, the emotion, you are trying to make your own? If it runs to a sentence, you have a problem. A paragraph? Sell your shares. Why? Because, nowadays, only brutally simple ideas get through. They travel lighter, they travel faster. One-word equity is the most priceless asset in the new world of the new technologies. Discover it and you have the route to salvation and eternal life.[3]

Sweat comes from the ruthless paring down of the paragraph to the sentence and the sentence down to the word. Brand ideas must be ruthlessly simple, but reducing them to a single word carries the brevity imperative too far and risks losing people completely. Such brief foundations can rarely support full relationships. Simple does not mean simplistic—brand ideas should comprise one *idea* but not necessarily one *word*. A diet food's position as "tastes great, lose weight" contains two thoughts that the marketer must dramatize, always a tough challenge. "Guilt-free indulgence" is one idea. A breakfast cereal that "kids love, moms like" has two ideas, but "delicious nutrition" or "sugar-coated pill" has one. Single words—most of the time, anyway—lack sufficient nuance to describe a brand's soul and how it fits into the lives of consumers.

THE UNIQUE BRAND OFFER:
RESOLVING THE INSIGHT

Either a product truth or a brand truth can serve as the basis of the unique brand offer. I call them truths because they are fundamental elements of a brand's DNA rather than mere characteristics or product claims. The product truth is physical, a functional characteristic that exists within—that is, *inside*—the product itself. It can be tasted, tested, quantified, counted, supported, and demonstrated. The brand truth is abstract but does not appear out of thin air. It is something associated with a brand by dint of relentlessly consistent communication. It can be tangible—for example, Coca-Cola's red hues or the "no tears" formulation of Johnson & Johnson's baby shampoo. Or it can be intangible—for example, perceptions of Tsingtao Brewery as China's first beer or Vivienne Westwood as modern punk.

The UBO is the most compelling way to describe what sets the brand apart from competitors. Unlike the brand idea, it does not articulate a mutual relationship between consumer and brand. While relevant to consumers, the UBO is something a bit less than the relationship; rather, it is the most powerful way to describe why people should choose a product. The insight is the recognition of a conflict between or within human and cultural truths for a specific group of consumers; the UBO resolves that tension. Owning a UBO is a prerequisite for achieving competitive differentiation and hence loyalty. Differentiation usually relies, at least partially, on emotional cues, but unless these are underpinned by function, benefits ultimately dissipate. In any case without a compelling UBO, margin enhancement is impossible. There is no scientific way to select the best UBO: research can quantify the relevance of various propositions, but the language must be crafted as meticulously as the brand idea. And, like brand ideas, UBOs are inherently subjective.

The Product Truth: Goodness Inside

Articulating the product truth is necessary to reinforce relevance and uniqueness. For example, a toothpaste claim of "calcium and fluoride protection" is a lousy product truth, because it neither differentiates nor clarifies why we should care. Does the formulation create "strong teeth" (a mass-market benefit)? Does it "eliminate germs that cause bad breath" (a middle-class benefit in an emerging market)? Or does it provide "total oral care" (a therapeutic claim in developed markets)? If a breakfast cereal highlights "fortification with 12 vitamins and minerals," it won't sell. The description may be accurate, but no one will care unless the benefit is obvious—"total nutrition" works in lower-middle-income China, whereas "balanced nutrition" is right for Korea and Japan. Here are a few products and their product truths that have stood the test of time:

- *Sunsilk*. Unilever's shampoo brand, popular in Asia, claims "black sesame for black and shiny hair." Note repetition of "black . . . black." Even more important, a natural ingredient believed to bring out shine seals the deal. This element resolves a tension in many Asian women between desire for beauty (a human truth) and an acute fear of chemicals (a cultural truth).
- *Cadbury*. The candy manufacturer doesn't advertise that its chocolate provides the minimum daily requirement of vitamin D. Its product truth is "a glass-and-a-half of milk," reinforced by an image of milk pouring from two glasses. Cadbury's truth is a memorable way of resolving a mother's conflict between not wanting to give her kids junk food and their demand for tasty treats. Chocolate becomes "creamy goodness."
- *Sofy*. The product truth for Unicharm's feminine hygiene item is "'side gatherers' for leakage prevention." Procter & Gamble's Whisper had dominated global markets for decades with an absorption benefit. Absorption of liquid is horizontal, so Sofy went

Cadbury's product truth is "A glass and a half of milk," a powerful descriptor that resolves a tension between junk food avoidance and delicious taste. The claim is reinforced by a cut-through visual mnemonic device. (Permission of Mondelez International)

vertical and staked out a point of difference relative to the market leader. "Leakage prevention" and "side gatherers" convey images of dams. The UBO also aligns product performance with the removal of lifestyle barriers implicit in the "Shine without a pause" brand idea.

- *JetBlue Airways.* For years the discount airline's product truth was a series of vivid contrasts between high and low, an offering that could be expressed as "luxury, even in cattle class." (Cattle class is the epithet Americans use to describe economy-class service.) Advertising compared JetBlue's unexpected delights—individual TV screens, drinks, baggage checking, smiles—with the spartan offerings of other airlines. It is no coincidence that, despite a disconcerting spate of flights canceled by bad weather, 2013 was the ninth consecutive year JetBlue earned the highest score in the J. D. Power & Associates North American Airline Satisfaction Study.

- *Dove.* Unilever's soap has focused on "¼ moisturizing cream" since the brand's debut more than 50 years ago. Disarmingly simple, this claim highlights important points. First, product truths can be functional rather than emotional; this one resolves a tension between skin that is both clean and dry. Second, the language of differentiation should be precise. "One-quarter" implies enough lotion for soft skin but not so much that Dove is no longer a soap. Furthermore, moisturizing is a benefit, not technobabble.

- *Philadelphia.* Kraft's cream cheese, one of the most profitable items in American supermarkets, has used the product truth "half the calories of butter," allowing weight watchers to have their cake and eat it, too. Philadelphia doesn't say "reduced fat" or "50 calories per two-tablespoon serving." Instead, it uses butter as a frame of reference to address the tension between taste and staying slim.

- *Double A.* The Thailand-based leading premium brand of printing paper in Asia has a powerful product truth: "No jam" (which links to the brand idea of "Run smoother"). Just one word aligns a feature of paper superiority with the actual experience of using it. Double A could have highlighted any number of characteristics, including weight, thickness, smudge resistance, or image sharpness. But office workers' moment of truth occurs at the photocopier. When sheets glide through the machine effortlessly, product quality and lack of hassle become mutually reinforcing.

Dove soap's long-standing product truth of "¼ moisturizing cream" resolves a basic "functional" tension between a desire for clean skin and avoidance of dry skin. (Reproduced with kind permission of Unilever PLC and group companies)

The Brand Truth: Equity That Surrounds

Brand truths are associations with a brand that have been built over time. Unlike product truths, they already resonate with consumers—they are "core equities" that communications have dramatized for many years. Tangible or intangible brand assets can be the basis for brand truths, which are not brand ideas. Again, brand ideas define relationships between consumers and brands.

Tangible brand assets. Brand truths often include specific brand assets that can be touched, seen, or heard.

- *Packaging.* For nearly one hundred years Coca-Cola's advertising has featured the cola's contoured bottle design as the source of small moments of happiness. Wieden + Kennedy's recent "Happiness Factory" campaign depicts bottle interiors as delightful wonderlands. Separately, the curves dominate the design of ubiquitous vending machines. In college cafeterias around America, posters asked students, "Do you know where happiness will strike next?" and then special vending machines spit out everything from free cans of Coke to animal balloons to pepperoni pizzas. Meanwhile the squat transparent bottle used by Absolut vodka has been a defining asset of that brand since 1979. Its unique shape stands out in a sea of taller, sleeker bottles and reinforces perceptions of the purity of the vodka. The outline is iconic as a result of long-running ads that featured an Absolut bottle-shaped object and the headline "Absolut _____."

- *Colors. National Geographic* magazines and other media properties of the National Geographic Society would not be instantly recognizable without the yellow rectangular border, a property used since the beginning of the twentieth century. Tiffany & Company's jewelry would not captivate women without its pale blue box and bag. The ability of "Tiffany blue" to intoxicate is so great that the girlfriend of one of my Chinese colleagues broke up with him after she learned that the Tiffany box he gave her was genuine but the gift inside was not.

- *Symbols and logos.* Nike's "Just do it" requires no verbalization; the logo says it all. The swoosh was originally designed to embody the spirit of a winged goddess who inspired Greek warriors. Today it is one of the most recognizable brand symbols in the world. McDonald's golden arches also are iconic, particularly among children. When squabbling kids on a family trip catch a glimpse of those twin peaks in the distance, peace reigns. The golden arches become a heavenly gateway to family harmony.

- *Taglines.* Catchy slogans, regardless of whether they state the brand idea or are an encapsulation of it, are powerful. Nestlé KIT KAT's "Have a break, have a KIT KAT" is an invitation to let off steam in new ways. (Nestlé produces the candy everywhere except the United States, where it is made and distributed by Hershey.) In 2012, when weather delayed Austrian Felix Baumgartner's record-breaking sky dive from the edge of space, KIT KAT stepped in to offer some light relief. It sent a KIT KAT bar strapped to a weather balloon aloft with a recorded greeting. A video of the flight went viral across social media, accumulating ten million Twitter impressions, 6.5 million Facebook views, and more than $15 million worth of free media coverage. In Singapore JWT created the world's first "social media break" app, a widget from KIT KAT that offers users respite from the demands

KIT KAT *created history with the 2013 launch of Android KitKat 4.4, the first co-branding activity between Google's operating system and any brand. The browser is now a natural platform for cyber breaks.*

of blogging, tweeting, and commenting. Tailored responses were automatically sent to Facebook postings or Twitter feeds. And the brand made history with the 2013 introduction of Android KITKAT 4.4, the first-ever cobranding activity involving Google's Chrome operating system.

- *Jingles and sonic devices.* The best advertising jingles trigger feelings of nostalgia, and people remember them for decades. Kraft Food's Oscar Mayer, a leading meat brand, has consistently refreshed two jingles beloved by Americans young and old. The hot dog song—*Oh, I'd love to be an Oscar Mayer wiener. That is what I'd truly like to be. 'Cuz if I were an Oscar Mayer wiener, everyone would be in love with me!*—first aired in 1964. The bologna jingle—*My bologna has a first name. It's O-S-C-A-R*—was originally sung in 1973 by a seven-year-old boy. Both jingles continue to be valuable assets. They transform Oscar Mayer's brand idea, "Through the eyes of a child," from a strategy statement into a playful escape from adult reality. Meanwhile Microsoft Window's cheerful four-note sonic device, "Jingle Bells," reminds professionals that Monday's tidings are upon them.

Intangible assets. Brand truths can also spring from intangible assets, associations similar to Maurice Saatchi's concept of one-word equity. They are embedded in consumers' perceptions of brands and can evolve, with skilled marketing. Volvo means safety. A decision to position the brand as a sports car would end in tears, but it could become "exciting safety." Johnson & Johnson's current equity of "mother love" is incompatible with the introduction of condoms, but it could be used to introduce infant formula. Rugged Harley Davidson can never be urban, but it can become more stylish. BMW's "driving machine" can incorporate sleekness but not "sensorial indulgence," which is the territory of Mercedes. "Demure" Victoria's

Secret can blossom into "tasteful liberation," but it should not go so far as to sell items sporting leather or chains, the domain of Frederick's of Hollywood.

LESSONS FROM THE BRAND IDEA FRONT

Not all brand ideas are created equal. First, internationalization is a frequent stumbling block, with companies treating it as a direct goal for their brands rather than the inevitable by-product of work in other areas. Second, success is impossible without a strong consumer insight that, when used properly, can help an underdog upset the established order. Third, for global success a brand idea must tap into emotions that transcend borders but at the same time are expressed differently within different cultures. Fourth, cause marketing, which emphasizes a brand's commitment to corporate social responsibility, works only when the message is linked to tangible product benefits. Finally, the best brand ideas liberate, rather than constrict, creativity.

Internationalism: Necessary but Not Sufficient

Marketers, more often in developing economies, dream of following in the footsteps of Honda, Samsung, and Kia Motors, local brands that have morphed into global powerhouses. But they forget globalism is the result, not the cause, of success and should be treated as such in communications. Western brands should also keep international street cred in perspective. If a brand has not cultivated a distinct position in its domestic market, it will never succeed abroad. Japanese automakers traditionally have won abroad because of superior reliability and attention to design detail. Kia has taken off because of its unique combination of value for money and stylishness. Samsung boasts a uniquely broad range of innovative mobile phones with "open architecture." This reality might seem basic, but many brands in emerging markets make the mistake of trying to convert international credentials into a sustainable competitive advantage. This never works.

The Chinese sportswear manufacturer Li Ning provides one of the most vivid cases of international image fixation, the only consistent element of its long-term strategy. The brand, until recently a point of pride on China's primordial brandscape, could have been a contender. Viewers of the 2008 Beijing Olympics broadcast probably recall that Li Ning, the iconic gymnastics champion who founded the company, lit the Olympic flame while suspended in midair. This bold move announced China's, and by extension Li Ning's, arrival on the world stage. Starting in 2006, Li Ning lifted its sights to compete directly with Nike and Adidas. To reinforce an image of international quality, the company invested millions of dollars in global sports stars, including such NBA celebrities as Shaquille O'Neal, Chuck Hayes, Damon Jones, and Baron Davis; the Russian pole vaulting star Yelena Isinbayeva; and the tennis player Ivan Ljubičić, as well as a smattering of international team sponsorships ranging from a team in the Spanish soccer league to the American Olympic table tennis team. Li Ning also opened showcase stores in Singapore and the United States, despite the lack of a consumer franchise in those locations.

In the meantime Li Ning altered its positioning several times in just a few years. It certainly never had a robust brand idea. Starting in 2005, the company celebrated a "Chinese style of play," rooted in understated, clever resourcefulness. Next, its advertising investment shifted to support casual apparel with an appeal to the post-1990s generation to "make the change." Since 2011 the brand has returned to its domestic roots and now sponsors the China Basketball Association. Furthermore Li Ning never decided on a category development strategy—it flip-flopped between basketball and running and flirted with other sports, such as badminton and women's aerobics.

The result of this strategic incoherence and monomaniacal focus on "international credibility" was consumer confusion and plummeting profit. By 2012 Anta, another local sportswear brand, had surpassed Li Ning to become the second-largest domestic player by units sold. Li Ning dropped to fourth place, down from second in 2009. In the first half of 2011 the company's revenues declined, in stark contrast to an average annual growth of more than 30 percent during the previous ten years. In the next eighteen months Li Ning's stock price dropped by 55 percent, compared with a 20 percent gain for Anta and 36 percent and 45 percent gains for Nike and Adidas, respectively. By 2012 TPG Capital, a private equity investor, had installed one of its partners, Kim Jin-goon, at the helm of Li Ning. According to Kim, "TPG's investment in Li Ning is a long-term one as the turnaround will be a multiyear effort."[4] His first priority was to clear out the inventory built up by third-party distributors. Simply put, Li Ning tried to fake an international pedigree, and it didn't work. Consumers sensed the pretense and abandoned the brand.

Even when global heft is genuine, it is rarely differentiating. The scale of Microsoft is reassuring. But in the case of Nokia, global dominance in mobile phones failed to protect it from massive erosion once Apple and Samsung developed superior products and marketing strategies. It is worth nothing that national heritage is rarely differentiating, even for countries associated with category excellence. Zegna embodies Italian sartorial craftsmanship, but, then, so does Armani. Mercedes' German engineering trumps General Motors's but not BMW's. Country of origin is often an invaluable element of a brand's personality and appeal, yet the provenance of few, if any, brands seals the deal. Even Levi Strauss, maker of the quintessential American blue jeans, celebrates universal dreams of individuality, not the American Dream.

Great Brand Ideas: Impossible Without Insight

In 2011 Anta reported a profit of $250 million, four times greater than Li Ning's earnings. Although neither local brand boasts the credibility of Nike or Adidas, Anta's financial performance has been relatively steady, particularly given the standards of wildly gyrating domestic brands. Young people in small and medium-sized cities nationwide have embraced the company's brand idea, "Forge yourself," as a rallying cry. Anta's target has not been ambiguous: mass-market youth who do not reside in tier-one cities such as Shanghai, Beijing, Guangzhou, and Shenzhen. The company's market position springs from the deep insight of cultural truth: the unresolved tension between ambition for externally acknowledged success and a regimented social structure in which opportunities are not evenly distributed. "I want to be the greatest! But life isn't fair."

In 1992 Deng Xiaoping, who succeeded Mao Zedong as China's paramount leader, embarked on his historic Southern Tour, an endorsement of private enterprise that fostered the emergence of the country's first generation of entrepreneurs. "To get rich is glorious," Deng proclaimed, thereby establishing the acquisition of wealth as a human's newest and most worthy pursuit. The definition of success, divorced from self-driven Western individualism, has always been government-mandated, in both dynastic and Communist China. Deng also tipped his hat to the inevitability of capitalistic income disparity when he said, "Let some prosper first." This acknowledgment had nothing to do with economic rights. Indeed Deng proclaimed the generation of capital to be the individual's most sacred *obligation* to the nation as China sought to assume its rightful position on the world stage. Since then the country's economic transformation has been nothing short of dazzling. Since the mid-1990s real per capita income has more than quadrupled. But, according to the Gini coefficient, a standardized measure of income inequality, the gulf between haves and have-nots is one of the widest in the world. Given the keen longing for externally acknowledged success in Confucian societies, the perception of blocked opportunity among the lower tiers of China's new generation has led to great frustration and suppression of "the dragon in my heart."

Anta shoe's "Forge yourself" brand idea has remained consistent since the company achieved critical mass in China during the mid-2000s. Its competitor, Li Ning, has suffered from scattered communications.

Since its inception Anta's brand idea, "Forge yourself," has addressed this frustration. A 2006 thematic television commercial encourages young Chinese to "let your scars become badges of honor." Through sports, "an elevated heartbeat is your declaration of intent." The brand tagline, *Yong bu zhi bu,* roughly translated as "Never stop moving," implicitly promises glory as the manifestation of sweat and hard knocks, both literal and figurative. As Anta expanded into such categories as tennis and basketball, the "Forge yourself" brand idea was interpreted to reflect the dynamics of each sport. For example, Kevin Garnett, an NBA star who, because of his own struggle to overcome adversity had become a hero to young Chinese, encouraged basketball enthusiasts to "reach higher." The campaign urged tennis players to "let courage perfect every stroke." Product advertising aligned the brand's functional and emotional benefits by enabling runners to "defeat heat" with sweat-resistant shirts and "conquer rough terrain" with shock-absorbent shoes. As Anta became the official sponsor of the Chinese Olympic Committee, a collective declaration to "rock the world," scored to the beat of Queen's "We Will Rock You," spread across the nation. And then, as the rising tide of China's economic growth marginally lifted the fortunes of lower-income consumers, the tone of Anta's communications evolved while remaining true to the brand's spirit of perseverance. A video that went viral, "Basketball Is Life," incorporated this sense of budding optimism: "Life is a gift from heaven. It's the sun that rises every day. You can feel its power, for it unleashes your ambition and desires. It makes you want to live on the edge, even though pain and hurt are facts of life."

Anta's rise has not been unblemished. Its product line is not particularly innovative, and its investment in international and local sports properties has been insufficient. And, like most local companies, Anta is overly dependent on television advertising relative to newer digital platforms. Most analysts agree, however, that Anta's insight into the motivations of mass-market youth has been a critical factor in taming Li Ning.

International brands can also leverage cultural relevance to make their mark. Because of concerns about product quality and safety, in China the dairy sector is one of a few dominated by multinational brands despite their high prices relative to domestic competitors'. When the Netherlands-based Friesland Dairy introduced baby formula in 2011, largely focusing on developing countries outside the West, it was entering an arena in which the likes of Nestlé, Wyeth, Mead Johnson, Meiji, and Dumex were already well established, particularly in premium segments. Through effective use of consumer insight, Friso defied those who predicted its failure.

Without exception, premium infant formula is sold in Asia as a way of enhancing intelligence and brain development. Not unsurprisingly, mental agility is regarded as essential to winning the game of life, particularly in northern Asia. However, brand differentiation exists only on the "reason to believe" level—for example, nutrition that is "balanced" for infants versus nutrition that is "easily absorbed" by newborns. Dumex focuses on "memory as a weapon." Enfantbon strengthens information retention *and* creativity, while Wyeth claims its balanced formula produces "multidimensional intelligence." Most advertising features babies performing cerebral tasks, with proud parents and doctors in lab coats hovering in the background.

Friso took a different approach. First, the brand overcame its late-to-market disadvantage by focusing on direct-to-consumer marketing (or CRM, customer relationship management) and e-commerce strategies that deepened engagement with new moms. Second, Friso tapped into the emerging unease of so-called progressive middle-class parents, who want their children to achieve but also feel guilty about putting so much pressure on them. This tension is exacerbated by the adults' lack of confidence in their parenting skills, particularly in countries where modernity arrived fast and furious, leaving the citizenry disoriented. Friso crafted a

Friso's "Growing up together" brand idea achieves differentiation versus other infant formulas that usually have a monomaniacal focus on intellectual achievement. Friso stakes a middle ground between encouraging academic performance, which it acknowledges as fundamental to development, and promoting childhood joy. This journey of shared discovery has inspired all elements of the marketing mix, including packaging design.

brand idea, "Growing up together," that elegantly fuses achievement with joy by recognizing that experience is the best teacher. The brand became a bridge between mother and child, transforming a rigid guardian-dependent relationship into a more intimate bond strengthened by shared discoveries and endless exploration. Learning morphed into wonder, both natural by-products of a loving fun-filled relationship. Copy on packaging, websites, video, and print aligned function and a unique emotional payoff: "We can freely experience more together. Friso nutrition keeps him [her] strong from the inside. More freedom. More childhood." One popular ad shows a mother and daughter camping out in their backyard and exploring the delights of nature. Friso built this journey around a multistage product line.

Throughout its communications and downloads of its theme music, Friso popularized the song "Incredible Journey," which celebrates a new relationship between mother and child:

We've only just met
But I feel sure
We will be best friends
Sharing the joy
Of every step
We take together.
This journey that we're on
Where both of us grow strong.
This journey that
We'll make it together.
Love the wonder in your eyes,
The thrill of each and every first time.
The whole world is new.
Baby, hear it call for me and you.
Stumbles and falls they may come.
But I know that they'll make you stronger.
Through the rain and shine,
We learn about life
And grow together.

By 2013 Friso had become a billion-dollar brand.

Global Ideas, Human Truth, and Cultural Relativism

Global brands are inherently efficient. When a brand idea is consistent around the world, savings on everything from media buys and creative development to research and packaging design are evident. Global brand ideas must be rooted in insights or motivations common to all human beings. De Beers roots a diamond ring's appeal in the expression of love, a universal emotion. Even Kimberly-Clark's Kleenex tissue maintains consistent positioning by fusing functional "soft, strong, and absorbent" with emotional release, a desire that transcends borders.

However, as I have shown, most categories are susceptible to cultural differences. Rigid centralization usually fails. Global brand ideas must be aligned with local imperatives. Many luxury brands, ruled with an iron fist by creative directors in Milan or Paris, are aspirational but emotionally inaccessible to the new middle class in Asia and other emerging markets. The segment, despite explosive growth as a whole, remains a glob of glitter. BMW's Asian sales, on the other hand, took off when its global "driving machine" proposition evolved into a projection of masculine power, a key imperative in non-Western societies that value pride.

Marketers' principal error when stretching global brand ideas across geographic clusters is assuming that cultures converge. As economies evolve, people become more modern, more internationalized, but not more American. Western individualism, or a belief in the right to pursue one's own definition of happiness, springs from a combination of monotheistic spiritual empowerment and Greek rationalism. Deeply ingrained in European and American thought, individualism is reinforced through institutional structures that consider the individual the basic productive unit of society. In most non-Western countries this unit is the clan, and the individual does not exist independent of obligations to others. In order for global brand ideas to resonate far from home, marketers must embrace cultural relativism. Their communications must reflect the importance of social context in dramatizing benefits and must acknowledge, at least implicitly, the low appeal of internalized benefits relative to externalized ones. Outside Europe and the Western hemisphere, "how it makes me look" always trumps "how it makes me feel."

Nike did not adapt "Just do it" to reflect Asian cultural sensibilities until just before the 2008 Beijing Olympics. Previously American individualism—or rebellious challenge to convention—was central to the concept, with creative executions largely imported from the United States. In a 2005 ad Nike flirted with disaster when Kobe Bryant, depicted as an animé cartoon character, slayed a Chinese dragon, the ultimate symbol of Chinese potency. The classic late 1990s commercial in which Pete Sampras and Andre Agassi play a tennis match in the middle of a New York City intersection, flouting authority throughout, remains off-putting to many Asians, even those of the pierced and tattooed younger generation.

Now Nike's communications are more culturally attuned yet remain rooted in the universal appeal of self-actualization. In Asia "Just do it" has become a means to an end. In a 2012 campaign Nike encouraged Chinese youth to *yong yundong*, or use sports. Self-possession became the path to achievement and ultimately acknowledgment by society for being special. The destination was as important as the journey. The brand achieved a harmony of opposing forces, a resolution of yin and yang. Juxtaposed against quintessentially Nike images, including an armless relay swimmer and a young girl outperforming the boys on the basketball court, a voiceover proclaimed this manifesto:

Use sports.

Use sports to get everything you want.

Use sports to go with the flow.

Use sports to have fun.

Use sports,

Even if they all say that you can't.

You still make it, little by little, then move on.

Use sports to meet your idols.

Use sports to live a splendid life . . .

To make friends . . .

So you can go home late.

We are all brothers and sisters

You can fail once, twice, even three times.

But you will win eventually,

No matter who you are or where you're from.

Because sports will never say, "You can't."

Likewise, the failure (because of a hamstring injury) of the hurdler Liu Xiang at the Beijing Olympics was alchemized into "heroic courage" during a comeback bid at the 2012 London Games. Nike's advertising put Liu's "inner strength" on display, resulting in one of the most buzzed-about social media campaigns of the year.

De Beers has also succeeded in adapting its global brand idea, "A diamond is forever," across cultures. The company's skill at establishing diamonds as "love jewelry" is an outstanding example of elegantly blending human aspiration and a non-Western worldview to drive purchasing decisions. The engagement ring is now a cultural imperative across Asia. In these societies marriage is considered a union between families as much as between individuals, the universal desire for "romantic love" coexisting uncomfortably with a non-Western requirement to tangibly demonstrate commitment. Also important is that as material security has increased, the optimal balance between passion and pragmatism has shifted. In the 1990s, when few recently engaged couples were buying diamonds, all advertising and promotional efforts stressed a woman's need for security. Diamonds as a representation of passionate love—the meat of all American and European copy in which the presentation of the diamond occurs in tandem with a musical climax—has become more prominent over time in Asian promotions. The safety message has become less obvious, skillfully integrated into the diamond offering. De Beers's first Chinese ad, "Moongate," was spectacularly nononsense. It depicts the wedding of a young couple who have grown up together; although they are clearly in love, the "don't worry: he won't leave you" message is explicit. In 2004 "Swimming" opened with an attractive couple walking toward a pool at a luxurious resort. She says, "Ah, the moon is so romantic." Proving his allegiance, he volunteers, "I'll go grab it for you." Valiantly he dives into the moon's reflection on the water's surface. Before he emerges, his hand appears with a huge rock glistening in the moonlight. She takes the ring and pushes him away, ever so playfully.

Now more than 80 percent of couples in Shanghai, Beijing, and Guangzhou seal their engagement with a diamond; in tier-two cities such as Chengdu, more than 50 percent of newly engaged women sport diamond rings. Sales in India are strong but not as head turning as in China. Nonetheless engagement rings are de rigueur for young middle-class couples in Mumbai and New Delhi, despite lower incomes than in China.

Kimberly-Clark, a long-time client of JWT, expertly manages the balance of global consistency and local relevance. The Kleenex brand of tissues, for example, is rooted in an insight into human behavior—"I have feelings I want to release, but I shouldn't wear them on my sleeve"—and a powerfully simple unique brand offer, "soft, strong, and absorbent." Emotional liberation and functional performance are beautifully aligned. However, the company is equally committed to local relevance, exemplified by the cultural astuteness of the "Let It Out" campaign, which debuted in 2007. It recognizes that Western, particularly American, expression of emotion can be celebratory, even over the top. In individualistic societies seeing a psychologist is nothing to be ashamed of and, for an apparently broad swathe of the population, neither is watching *The Jerry Springer Show* or *The View*. In the United States activities centered on a blue couch in open public squares and the revelation of poignant personal stories. Television ads were unabashedly sentimental, accompanied by music that tugged heartstrings. Viewers were then led to a website, www.letitout.com, where they were encouraged to "Let it out. It's time to laugh until you cry, scream until you spit. Show your heart and show some tears. Sing at the top of your lungs. Jump for joy. And when tons of stuff stuffs up your nose, blow it loud and blow it proud." Kleenex promoted its UK "Let It Out" campaign with a YouTube video in which an actor also sat on a blue couch, inviting passers-by to join him for a chat. A box of tissues was always on hand to mop up any tears. The video includes the line "Are people ready to let it out? Turns out all it takes is a good

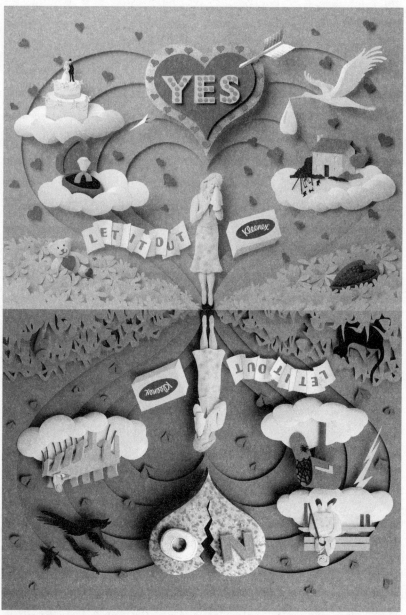

Kimberly-Clark's Kleenex tissue has long associated emotional release with soft absorbency. These print executions, designed in the United Kingdom, are quintessentially Western, a bold celebration of emotional expression. Driven by cultural imperatives, the Asian "Let it out" work is understated, but equally powerful. (Illustration by Gail Armstrong)

listener and Kleenex tissues." A series of British print ads were bright and bold, displaying contrasting color palettes based on whether the girlfriend says "yes or no," the soccer team has "glory or failure," and the entrepreneur is "king or fool."

Asian audiences, particularly those in northern Asia, tend to giggle in embarrassment when they see this work. People in nonindividualistic societies dislike expressing their emotions openly—cues to what they are feeling are subtle; feelings must be understated. Kimberly-Clark's creative work reflected this imperative. Videos that went viral showed *families* resolving long-standing differences, encouraged by an empathetic yet persistent counselor. Family members' eyes were misty, but the tears did not flow; a husband's hand grazed his wife's arm, but no one hugged. Clever posters and packaging designed for in-store sampling were equally subtle. A faceless widow in black lies on one side of a bed with tissues pulled from a slit that marks "his side." In another, identical twins sit silently on a bench, apparently separated by a lifetime of unspoken resentment— and a Kleenex tissue is released into this gap.

Even Mattel's Barbie doll, the epitome of Malibu sunshine, is becoming a worldly girl. The full-on liberation of its global brand idea, "Anything is possible," has been subtly softened by Asian restraint to "Let dreams blossom."

Cause Marketing: Not Enough

Corporate social responsibility (CSR) is a term that became popular in the 1960s. CSR functions as a built-in self-regulating mechanism whereby a business monitors and ensures its active compliance with the spirit of law, ethical standards, and international norms. It often goes beyond pure legal compliance and encourages actions that promote social good. In recent years CSR has given rise to "cause marketing"—a brand's positioning with consumers incorporates "do-good" initiatives. According to a 2013 study by Nielsen, 50 percent of global consumers surveyed are willing to pay more for goods and services from companies that have implemented programs to give back to society, up from 45 percent in 2011.[5]

However, evidence is scant that advertising exclusively rooted in an appeal to our better angels actually works. As the business strategist Saj-Nicole Joni, author of the 2010 book *The Right Fight,* notes, "This particular road is richly paved with good intentions, but it can to lead to hell if not approached deftly. The fundamental problem is that too many idealistic managers suffer from cause-marketing myopia. They forget that in reality their company's first commitment is to performance and results."[6]

Cause marketing can fail because of perceived hypocrisy. BP's "Beyond Petroleum" ads, meant to position BP as an environmentally conscious corporation, were compromised by the 2010 oil spill in the Gulf of Mexico.

Cause marketing also ends with a whimper when lofty messages are not linked to concrete benefits of the product. Consumers everywhere want to know, "What's in it for me?" The "Real woman" brand idea for Unilever's Dove soap is probably the best-known example of advocacy that, while widely applauded, did not improve loyalty and sales. Dove advertising featured full-figure models who were not conventionally beautiful. "The Campaign for Real Beauty" was conceived as a social movement, a celebration of women with the confidence to define their own standards of attractiveness. Two spectacularly successful videos, separated by more than seven years, set the online world ablaze and won countless awards at creative award shows. The first, "Evolution," produced in 2006, featured time-lapse photography in which a plain Jane was transformed into a billboard-ready stunner through image manipulation. The message was a none-too-subtle call to do away with artificial beauty ideals and generated more than 16 million YouTube views. The second, "Real Beauty Sketches," debuted in 2013 and has already racked up almost 70 million hits. Following years of stagnant sales for Dove, "Real Beauty" initially made a splash, with revenues jumping 20 percent year-on-year in 2006. However, Dove did not sustain the momentum as competitors with harder-hitting functional messages mounted counterattacks, particularly in emerging markets where the "Real Beauty" ideal never resonated with consumers to begin with. (Defining one's own standards of attractiveness remains a distinctly Western phenomenon. According to the International Society of Aesthetic Plastic Surgeons, 20 percent of all South Korean women have undergone cosmetic surgery in a quest for the finer features society demands.)[7] The clear lesson: product benefits must be aligned with brand values.

The cause-marketing efforts of Procter & Gamble's Safeguard soap, a rival of Dove, are more likely to deepen consumer loyalty. They flow quite naturally from a brand idea—"Freedom from germs"—that has remained consistent for decades, claiming market leader positions in China and the Philippines. Safeguard partners with leading health organizations around the world, including the Pakistan Medical Association, Philippines Association of Medical Technologists, Mexican Red Cross, and Africa Medical Association. Together they promote life-saving hygiene habits among children with hand-washing education programs in the schools. So far Safeguard's efforts have touched the lives of more than 40 million children.[8] At the same time the brand's germ-killing abilities bring tangible value to consumers.

Examples of cause-marketing efforts that drive sales are rare—partly because the public relations department, not the marketing team, usually controls CSR. Furthermore, in order to weave do-good activities into the fabric of marketing activities, a brand idea must be crystal clear, and this is often not the case.

Sharp Brand Ideas Liberate Creativity

I have worked with a few creative-side executives who believe brand ideas limit the potential for creative expression. Some do. When prescriptive, brand ideas dull the senses, but when they are evoca-tively conceived, they stir the soul. They inspire and liberate because how a life force expresses itself has no limits. It evolves, hums with vitality, and adapts to challenges. A brand idea's essence, unique in a sea of competitors, is eternal.

Honda's work in Europe is a stand-out example. Beginning in 2002, the company developed, in partnership with the ad agency Wieden + Kennedy, a series of award-winning ads that rescued Honda from revenue stagnation and consumer indifference and woke up the entire communications industry. One ad, 2005's "Grrr," took home the Grand Prix at the Cannes advertising festival. Others include 2002's "Cog," 2006's "Impossible Dream," 2007's "Choir," and more recently 2013's "Hands." Each expresses a different dimension of Honda's spirit.

The brand idea, one that could be defined as "Driven aspiration," elevates Honda to a near-spiritual plane and infuses the brand's global tagline, "The power of dreams," with emotional depth. The consumer insight is a human truth—the tension between yearning for a better world and the intrusion of reality. The unique brand offer is the company's "never settle" ethos, a samurai spirit familiar to consumers around the world that is fueled by constant innova-tion. "The power of dreams" is, of course, more than words. It has manifested itself in countless ways, from a web documentary series, *Dream the Impossible*, to the 2005 debut of ASIMO, a walking and dancing robot. Its rhythm remains distinctly Honda, regardless of the creative vehicle, irrespective of marketing objective. All ads for Honda have a sense of pushing forward and nonstop acceleration—and making the impossible possible inspires awe. Honda's life force, so distinctive, is now inimitable.

"Cog" communicated the brand's mechanical precision and at-tention to detail. A single-shot masterpiece, the commercial was revolutionary in terms of redefining the creative canvas for automo-bile advertising. It starts with a simple ball bearing rolling into a

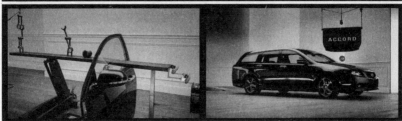

A well-crafted brand idea liberates creative expression. Honda of Europe has produced one of the greatest series of distinct and award-winning work in the history of advertising. Every execution reinforces its "power of dreams" brand idea.

transmission hub. The camera tracks slowly from left to right, following a near-miraculous series of chain reactions across an otherwise empty gallery space. The complexity of the interactions increases as the commercial progresses, growing from simple collisions to zip lines made from a hood-release cable, scales and seesaws constructed from multiple carefully balanced parts, and a swinging mobile of suspended glass windows. At the end of the spot, the ignition button is pushed on, the hatch closes, and an Accord gently rolls off a trailer. The popular storyteller and humorist Garrison Keillor wraps it up with a voiceover: "Isn't it nice when things just . . . work?" An endline appears on the screen: "Honda. The power of dreams."

The "Grrr" campaign marked the debut of a new diesel engine and elevated perceptions of Honda as a responsible corporate citizen. The spot is a trippy cartoon bursting with color, and it portrays an unlikely animated mix of cute animals frolicking in a computer-generated Eden, flying diesel engines, Rockettes-inspired kick lines, and the gravel-on-velvet voice of Keillor. He conveys a simple message: When a corporation cares about the community, miracles can happen. When you hate something, you can change it—in this case the convention that diesel engines must contribute to noise pollution. The lyrics are inspired:

> *Can hate be good? Can hate be great?*
> *Can hate be good? Can hate be great?*
> *Can hate be something we don't hate?*
> *We'd like to know . . . why it is so*
> *That certain diesels must be slow*
> *and thwack and thrum . . . and pong and hum . . . and clatter*
>   *clat.*
> *Hate something. Change something.*
> *Hate something, change something, make something*
>   *better-r-r-r.*
> *Oh, isn't it just bliss when a diesel goes just like this?*

(Purring . . .)
Sing it like you hate it.
Hate something. Change something.
Hate something, change something, make something
     better-r-r-r.

"Impossible Dream" was thematic work—there was no product message—that anchored "The power of dreams" as an expression of Honda's heritage. Re-aired in 2010, it opens on a vintage record player playing a single, "The Impossible Dream," interpreted by Andy Williams. A man reaches for a jacket and helmet, then sets forth from a trailer on a barren landscape. He drives a series of vintage Honda vehicles, starting with a modest minibike and ending with a powerboat that leaps off the edge of a waterfall. He emerges, phoenix-like, from the mist in a hot-air balloon emblazoned with Honda's logo. The original 2006 campaign included a website about a series of vintage Honda vehicles to illustrate the vision of the company's founder, Soichiro Honda.

"Choir," a two-minute chorale rendition of the Honda driving experience, reinvented the relationship between human and car. A week before its release, a teaser microsite asked, "When was the last time you felt a connection with your car? At Honda, we want driving to be fun . . . and involving. So we built Civic. [It's] a car that might change the way you feel about driving." A sixty-member choir, filmed in a stark multistory garage, depicted the sensation of driving. A voiceover intones: "This is what a Honda feels like." Then a finger pushes the red "engine start" button, the choir begins to sing, growing louder throughout, as the camera cuts between the singers and dramatic car-on-road sequences. The sound of driving on a chip-sealed (asphalt) parking garage floor comes from fingers tapped against teeth, while the choir's vocalization approximates the fall of rain. As the car races through fog, the choir reproduces the quickly dropping high pitch of the Doppler effect. The film concludes with the Civic speeding on the highway toward sunset.

In 2013, ten years after "Cog" was produced, Honda introduced "Hands," which captures sixty-five years of "warm engineering" in two minutes. The execution focuses on the "curious hands" of an engineer who seamlessly transforms one Honda product into another, showcasing a commitment to pushing the boundaries of technology. According to Wieden + Kennedy, Honda purchased no broadcast media airtime to support the ad, yet targeted Internet seeding attracted 3.5 million views in one week.

Each of these campaigns communicated different messages and was stylistically distinct. But it bears repeating: The brand idea remained consistent. From the relentless push for progress to the embrace of an impossible mission, Honda's DNA revealed itself in every frame. And this work moved metal. By 2008, just before the financial crisis, Honda Europe had registered record-breaking sales, up 20 percent, the fourth consecutive record-breaking annual performance and the sixth consecutive 12-month period of year-on-year sales gains. Sales of Honda's primary volume driver, the Civic, grew by more than 60 percent from the previous year, another record. Today, in the midst of economic stagnation, Honda Europe faces challenges, as do all car manufacturers, in contrast to robust sales in North America. But, given its uniqueness on the automotive landscape, the company is well positioned to recapture momentum once consumer confidence returns.

In contrast to the crystal clarity of Honda's brand idea, Adidas's appears to be losing creative focus. Until 2011 the brand had a powerful proposition, "Impossible is nothing." Eschewing Nike's ultraindividualism, the German company linked its impressive range of high-tech, high-performance products to the universal aspiration of surpassing human limits. In Japan an award-winning outdoor "live ad" dubbed "Vertical Football" wowed crowds in 2004 with a gravity-defying actual soccer match played on a billboard backdrop twelve stories high.

The mantra of "Impossible is nothing" often took on a collective sheen. The "+10 Dream Team" campaign, a fan favorite, imagined history's ten best soccer players united in common cause during the 2006 FIFA World Cup. At the 2008 Beijing Olympics Adidas depicted the accomplishments of each Chinese athlete as the fruit of national unity, the nation's ultimate competitive weapon.

Since 2011, however, Adidas seems to have gone astray. The company is confusing a brand idea with portfolio management strategy. The new slogan, "All in," refers as much to its fashion items as to athletic shoes and apparel. A two-minute introductory film suggested, "No matter what your goals or challenges, you have to go all in for the ultimate success." The execution was raucous and fun, but the singer Katy Perry's appearance alongside the soccer stars David Beckham and Lionel Messi raised eyebrows. Will Adidas's message disintegrate? In the words of Erich Stamminger, a member of the executive board responsible for global brands at Adidas, "'All in' shows the breadth and depth of the Adidas brand. [This] is the biggest campaign we have ever produced. Its creative concept brings together the diversity of the brand under one strong roof." The "All in" platform resulted in some eye-catching creative executions at the 2012 London Olympics. According to *Campaign,* the United Kingdom's largest marketing-focused trade publication, "The brand, a tier-one sponsor that paid £100 million for the privilege, was the most-talked-about during the Games. And it achieved this with the broadest, most-hard-working marketing." For example, Adidas enlisted the British fashion designer Stella McCartney to design the British team's uniforms, while "take the stage" performances featured collaborations between personalities ranging from the comedian Keith Lemon to the diver Tom Daley and their fans.

However, fuzzy brands confuse creative execution rather than liberate it, and the omens for Adidas are not good. In 2012 Adidas sales were up 15 percent[9] but slowed markedly the following year. In the first nine months of 2013, sales were down 3.8 percent compared to the same period in 2012.[10] A November 2013 *Wall Street Journal* headline proclaimed, "Adidas Loses Traction Against Nike." *Forbes*'s 2013 list of the world's leading brands placed Nike twenty-fourth with a brand value (as opposed to sales revenue) of $18.2 billion, well ahead of Adidas, which was in sixty-first place with $8.4 billion. Apple, not surprisingly, came in first, worth $104.3 billion.

ORGANIZATIONAL BARRIERS TO POWERFUL BRAND IDEAS

Brand ideas are never right or wrong, only good or less good. They are inherently subjective, nurtured by corporations that encourage conceptual ideas and innovation and brought to life by a few evocative words. Within an advertising agency, or between agency and client, debate is necessary. To generate forceful brand ideas, management must forge environments that encourage self-expression, lest they squelch bold ideas or the thinking that can lead to them. Robust brand ideas continue to elude many organizations because creation requires dedicated focus, the courage to articulate the abstract, and a willingness to persuade in the absence of bullet proof evidence.

Brands founder because of cultural and structural issues. The problem is particularly urgent in emerging markets, which have seen a recent explosion of brands that are all chasing relatively small but fast-growing middle-class populations. In the face of this plethora of offers, consumers become confused—and brand switching is rife. Many brands are unable to articulate, even to themselves, exactly what they stand for, resulting in fragmented messages that disorient consumers, who then tune out.

It is important to note that a brand idea is more than an ethereal vision. It is an operational imperative for modern corporations that have invested in a marketing department fully empowered to make long-term budgeting and investment decisions and is not subordinate to sales units. This is not the case in hierarchical Asian companies. For example, in China and other Confucian societies, autocratic CEOs typically run organizations, and their management structures are not built to encourage brand ideas, or any new idea, for that matter. They are driven by sales and dominated by emperor-kings who rule defensively. Quite often these leaders promulgate ambiguous instructions, creating an undercurrent of permanent anxiety at lower levels. Furthermore many managers create rival power centers so competition is horizontal rather than vertical. Ultimately this is a failing of corporate governance—no local management team reports to an independent board of directors charged with ensuring long-term shareholder growth. As a result organizational structures are too centralized, and their planning too short term. Both handicaps are inconsistent with the conceptually adventurous modus operandi required to develop successful brand ideas.

Again, successful brand ideas are produced by organizations that are driven by marketing. These brand ideas are deeply rooted in the history of the company and have the potential to influence the organization's strategy for decades. In companies that are driven by sales, an emphasis on quick wins through discounts and other financial levers overshadows long-term planning. The intangibility of brand ideas is uncomfortable terrain for uncertain managers chasing concrete wins. Formulating brand ideas is both science and art, and it requires a respect for gut instinct. Unless corporate chiefs are committed to the discipline of developing, and then living by, the brand idea, even the most enlightened brand steward will fail.

The benefits of a meticulously crafted brand idea, of course, go far beyond the marketing department. The organization gains purpose, enabling it to attract enthusiastic and passionate employees who become excited about the prospect of joining a mission.

THE BENEFITS OF STRONG BRAND IDEAS

Beyond rallying staff from senior to junior ranks, brand ideas encourage breakthroughs in both communications and product innovation.

Innovative Communications

A brand idea is the basis of a relationship with consumers and therefore the foundation of innovative communications that resonate. Through its "moments of happiness" Coca-Cola has liberated creative executions to inspire consumers with a broad array of groundbreaking communications. Coke inspired the creation of "Small World" vending machines featuring streaming live video feeds that enabled citizens of India and Pakistan, countries divided by decades of hostility, to share happiness. The brand idea also led to the memorable "Overseas Foreign Workers" video that went viral in the Philippines. Coca-Cola orchestrated the surprise reunion of three families for Christmas—a small fraction of the 11 million Filipinos who work overseas and send money back to their loved ones and are unable to save enough to also make the trip home. One man had not seen his family for 11 years. The emotional four-minute video documenting their homecoming has been viewed on YouTube 1.4 million times.

Procter & Gamble's Old Spice recently gained a new lease on life after moving away from dated positioning centered on "nautical freshness." Amid flagging body wash sales, and increasing competition, Old Spice fought back with a much bolder brand idea, "The scent of real men," which equates the brand with sophisticated masculinity. The contemporized brand idea gave rise to the fully integrated 2010 campaign, "Smell Like a Man, Man," one of the most talked-about series of executions in recent years. They feature Isaiah Mustafa, now an international sex symbol, with his call to women: "Hello, ladies. Look at your man, now back to me, now back at

your man, now back to me. Sadly, he isn't me. But if he stopped using ladies' scented body wash and switched to Old Spice, he could
smell like he's me." Old Spice did not abandon its nautical legacy
completely. Mustafa starts out in the bathroom, moves on to a boat,
and ends up on a horse on the beach. But the proposition was new.
Throughout a series of commercials, broadcast on both television
networks and digital platforms, he slyly breaks the fourth wall by
speaking directly to the audience, offering tongue-in-cheek tips on
how to become a paragon of masculinity. In the process Mustafa
invited dialog between the brand and viewers. Almost overnight,
ads from a low-involvement category suddenly became massive talking points on social media, blogs, and media outlets. The 33-second
video was viewed more than 47 million times on YouTube. Old Spice
now has a soul with which consumers can form a bond, and it has
since created a series of successful commercials and other engagement platforms. "Smell Like a Man, Man" won a Grand Prix at the
Cannes Lions International Festival of Creativity, P&G's first in 50
years. In the words of Mark Tutssel, jury president and global chief
creative officer at Leo Burnett, "[P&G] took an old, sleepy brand
and woke it up, and overnight wove its way into popular culture."

Innovative Products

A meticulously defined brand idea also inspires new product extensions, because it provides a focus for innovation. Consumers require
much less of a hard sell because new products are simply another
manifestation of the brand's preexisting role in their lives. NikeFuel,
introduced in February 2012, is an example of diversifying the company's revenue stream beyond shoes and apparel with an elegant re-
inforcement of Nike's brand idea, which is rooted in pushing the
limits of any individual's athletic capacity. The wristband, used in
tandem with Nike+ devices, is a way to measure all kinds of activities, from "your morning workout to your big night out." Designed

to measure whole-body movement regardless of age, weight, or gender, NikeFuel tracks "your entire active life." Global positioning system technology also allows users to calculate their progress and "compare and compete" within Nike's online community. (The profitability of NikeFuel is in question. The FuelBand helped lead the company's equipment division to an 18 percent increase in bottom line earnings in 2011. But in 2014, Nike withdrew from the "wearable technology" market, suggesting that fitness software—that is, Nike+ apps—is more financially bankable.)

It almost goes without saying that Apple's series of rapid-fire home runs would not have been possible if the entire organization were not committed to "Think Different." Business analysts have noted that many of Apple's new products were not technological breakthroughs when they were introduced. The iPad was not the first tablet device; the iPod was not the first MP3 music player. But each item's elegant design and seamless integration with the iTunes store resulted in an exquisite user-friendly digital ecosystem. Apple's website puts it nicely: "You've never been so easily entertained. iTunes is the easiest way to organize and enjoy the music, movies, TV shows, apps, and books you've already got—and shop for the ones you want to get." Since the mid-2000s each Apple innovation has epitomized the spirit of "Think Different," a celebration of technology's power to humanize, to unify rather than divide, communities of the like-minded.

As I have already discussed, De Beers's brand idea, developed in 1947, has been instrumental in making the diamond engagement ring a tradition in cultures both Eastern and Western. More than a slogan, "A diamond is forever" embodies eternal love that deepens over decades. The gift of a diamond keeps flames burning. But the evocative brand idea has also inspired an array of products that extends De Beers's role in life, such as the eternity ring—a symbol of continuing affection and appreciation—and the three-stone trilogy ring, which represents the past, present, and future of a relationship.

De Beers' Trilogy ring is a beautiful example of how product innovation can be inspired by a brand idea. The three diamonds represent a relationship's past, present, and future and are a tangible manifestation of De Beers' long-standing brand idea, "A diamond is forever." (Three-stone ring image provided by Forevermark. Forevermark is part of the De Beers group of companies.)

"A diamond is forever" was also deployed to elevate the "Forevermark," an inscription on the facet of a diamond. Through the brand idea a stamp of product quality has morphed into an eternal mark of love.

Sometimes the fruits of brand ideas show up in unexpected ways. Vodafone's brand idea, "Empowering you," inspired out-of-the-box thinking to help customers in Cairo do more with their hard-earned cash. Because of their limited purchasing power, Egyptian consumers usually buy the smallest-sized package of any product. Merchants commonly hand over small products such as gum, screws, and other random items in lieu of change. To address users' low purchasing power, Vodafone developed prepaid cards worth small amounts of money: 0.5 Egyptian pounds ($.07), one pound ($.14), and 1.5

pounds ($.21). Shifting the balance of power between shoppers and merchants, the company positioned the new cards, dubbed Fakka (Egyptian for "small change"), as a new currency that retailers could give shoppers. Fakka are distributed through Vodafone retail outlets across the nation. The availability of low-denomination cards also enabled cash-strapped customers to talk more without worrying about exceeding daily limits.

Could Old Spice, Apple, or Vodafone have made their breakthroughs without a compelling brand idea? Perhaps. But, more often than not, exceptional brand ideas are the mother of invention.

WHEN TO ABANDON A BRAND IDEA

By definition a brand idea promulgates a long-term relationship between products and consumer that remains consistent over time. It evolves, but the DNA is constant. The world's most respected brands—McDonald's, Nike, Apple—have become more modern, international, and diversified yet still remain true to themselves.

However, nothing lasts forever. When the marketing equivalent of geological cataclysm occurs—our industry calls this disruption, a term coined by Jean-Marie Dru, chair of the advertising agency TBWA—a brand idea will likely have to change. Disruptions can occur within technology, the competitive frame of reference, and a corporation's operating environment. If a brand is to survive these shifts, it must redefine its target market and establish leadership in a new way. It must formulate a new brand idea for a new era.

Disruptive Technological Upheaval

Kodak was an iconic brand because of the role its photographic film products and cameras played in American life. Its major competitor, Japan's Fujifilm, was a perpetual also-ran, with Kodak enjoying an 89 percent market share in the United States in 1976. The company's ubiquity was such that its tagline "Kodak moment" entered the common lexicon to describe a personal event that demanded to be recorded for posterity. The brand idea of "Celebrating the moments of your life," manifested through a wide range of inexpensive and easy-to-use products, shifted consumer behavior from using a camera to record special occasions to taking pictures of everyday delights. Kodak sold a lot of film.

But the company failed to anticipate the convulsion triggered by digital technology. It began to struggle financially in the late 1990s as sales declined. Despite having invented the core technology used in today's digital cameras, it never caught up with the times. In August 2012 Kodak sold its photographic film, commercial scanners, and kiosk operations to stave off bankruptcy. If leadership had had the foresight to align Kodak's emotional equity with opportunities inherent in digital technology—evolving from a passive "capturing moments" to, say, a more participatory "Share a Kodak moment" or "Create a Kodak moment"—it might still be an iconic brand. The company did not evolve its product and positioning fast enough in response to a changing landscape.

Today the company's efforts are largely business to business. It provides packaging, functional printing, graphic communications, and professional services through its Graphic Communications and its Motion Picture Film units. The "Kodak moment" rests in peace.

For years "point-and-shoot" compact digital cameras boomed, pushing analog cameras into ultraniche territory. Like Kodak cameras before them, digital cameras captured the high grounds of portability and preserving everyday memories. The inevitable collapse of the low-end digital camera market has elicited a chorus of "We've seen this movie before." According to Mintel, a London-based quantitative research firm, sales of digital cameras declined by 29 percent in the United Kingdom between 2006 and 2011, results mirrored around the world.

Between Friends—

A KODAK

Of all the gifts that fit the Christmas day, none so timely as the one that provides the means for keeping a picture story of that day— a Kodak.

EASTMAN KODAK CO.

Catalogue free at your dealer's or by mail.

ROCHESTER, N. Y.

The "Kodak moment," one of the most enduring advertising propositions of the twentieth century, never evolved into the digital era.

The "I am Nikon" campaign elevates photography from recording memories to enabling artistic expression. (Photographer, top: Jonathan Tay/Amanacliq; Photographer, bottom: Sven Jacobsen)

In 2013 an Apple ad claimed, "Every day, more photos are taken with the iPhone than any other camera." The rise of smartphones presents gargantuan challenges to manufacturers of digital cameras such as Nikon, Canon, and Fujifilm. The entire competitive frame of reference has inexorably shifted yet again. Mobile devices compete directly with digital cameras, an unimaginable phenomenon only a few years ago, and the market will tilt further in favor of mobile devices as processor manufacturers such as Qualcomm, Nvidia, and Intel ramp up the power. We are on the cusp of a great leap forward in the image quality these devices are capable of capturing. Small wonder Nokia is betting big on camera phone differentiation. The positioning of Lumia handsets as "more than your eye can see" says it all. Models such as the 1020 are supported with a flow of high-tech superlatives: "The only smartphone with a 41 megapixel camera sensor, Full HD video and Nokia Rich recording for incredible audio capture." A recent Nokia ad even ends with a tongue-in-cheek dig at Apple: "Everyday, better photos are taken with Nokia Lumias than with any other mobile." Nikon and Canon don't even merit mention.

The brand ideas of digital cameras require urgent attention. Fujifilm, for example, provides information about its devices on a website called EveryPictureMatters.com, a retread of old-style—that is, passive recording of memories—analog positioning statements. Nikon, on the other hand, is moving in the right direction by concentrating on high-margin digital single-lens reflex cameras that have, thus far, remained unscathed by smartphone competition. Nikon has elevated its target consumer profile, pitching to people who aspire to take more sophisticated photographs, both amateur and professional. Its "I Am Nikon" campaign positions the brand as an enabler of individual self-expression or artistic creation, with television and online advertising depicting real-life scenarios in which people demonstrate their spiritual journeys and broadened worldviews. Still, Rome is burning. To forge a path to the future, all digital camera manufacturers would be well advised to craft sharper brand ideas, ones that confront imminent threats to consumer franchises. This would incorporate digital technology's ability to turn the recording of moments into "image creation" and transform photography from a solitary pursuit into a shared passion among online enthusiasts.

Disruptive Changes to the Competitive Set

China is the world's largest beer market in terms of total consumption, double the size of second-place America. However, China's beer manufacturers face handicaps: the unwillingness of consumers to buy expensive beer except in public on important occasions and fractured distribution networks that preclude the rise of truly national brands. Most international brands remain also-rans because they are so expensive, which explains why global manufacturers have acquired Chinese regional brands to drive future growth. Anheuser-Busch InBev, for example, purchased Harbin, a brand with a strong heritage in northeastern China. All leading brands are domestic, led by China Resources Enterprise's Snow and the independent player Tsingtao.

According to Accenture, a consulting company, about 200 domestic companies and nearly 100 foreign brands are grappling for a share of the Chinese beer market.[11] But even the likes of Snow and Tsingtao dominate only discrete chunks of the country rather than the whole pie. China's sheer size makes it a distribution nightmare, rife with small breweries that benefit from local government protection. That said, in order to survive brands have no choice but to expand their geographic coverage, a trend that will continue until the holy grail of national distribution is achieved.

For this to occur Chinese beers must reconsider their brand ideas to achieve competitive differentiation against both familiar local and new national players. Traditionally their brand ideas rested on themes of trust and familiarity—natural fits for trademarks with deep regional heritage. For example, Qingdao-based Lao Shan has yet to attempt national expansion, and its brand idea of "Good beer for good friends" is typical of a low-priced regional offering. As brands expand, however, they must upgrade their product and, in the process, own a higher order of friendship. According to the research firm Mintel, nearly three-quarters of Chinese consumers say the main reason for drinking beer is to facilitate socializing with friends or family.[12]

When Snow was introduced in 1993, two main breweries produced the beer. Less than a decade later 80 breweries were pumping it out. As Snow's reach expanded, it forged a brand idea of "Adventure beyond boundaries," a proposition that clearly targets a younger market segment and taps into the idea of beer as a social enabler. This confident strategy appeals to ambitious white-collar men who are constrained by the twin yokes of family obligation and professional regimentation. Historically Tsingtao has also been inconsistent in its positioning. But in recent years, through the brand idea "dreams powered by passion," it has moved into more premium aspirational segments. The company's campaign for the London 2012 Olympics revolved around the determination of Liu Xiang, the Chinese 110-meter hurdler, to achieve glory, despite past obstacles, including the embarrassment of withdrawing with an injury from the Games in Beijing. While the advertising efforts of both Tsingtao and Snow are not as sophisticated as creative executions of international leaders, the sharpened brand ideas of these Chinese beers are better suited to a new era of national competition.

China's milk brands have followed a similar trajectory. They recently expanded distribution, confronted new competition, and elevated their brand ideas. According to KPMG, China's raw milk production grew more than 25 percent each year between 2000 and 2006, and it is now the third-largest producer of milk behind the United States and India.[13] But until the mid-2000s dairy products were sold mostly through relatively small-scale distribution networks set up by local dairy companies. As modern trade flourished, chilled storage facilities in supermarkets and convenience stores opened up larger retail markets. Mengniu and Yili, both originally established in northern China, are now distributed nationally. In contrast the state-owned Bright Dairy, based in Shanghai, made halfhearted attempts to expand distribution but faltered because of the incompatible strategic priorities of maximizing shareholder gains and conforming to the political imperatives of the Communist Party.

Before they expanded nationally, Mengniu and Yili were masters of their domains, for decades considered part of the family by local consumers. Brand ideas were rooted in purity and familiarity— "Your mother grew up with us. So, too, will your daughter." Yili, based in Inner Mongolia, focused on "Purity you trust," a position relevant only to people who already knew the brand. Today its brand idea is "Nourishing your life's vitality." The company has successfully forged a deeper connection with Chinese consumers by aligning the functional benefits of its milk—for example, "calcium enriched," "produced from the healthiest cows," or "guaranteed supply chain management expertise"—with a modern lifestyle. Until recently Mengniu, China's leading dairy brand, lacked differentiation, with taglines such as "500 grams every day makes Chinese stronger." Now the brand idea promises "Happiness in every drop," a proposition that, while certainly not worthy of a Harvard Business School case study, reinforces the importance of Mengniu's scale in delivering consistent quality. At the same time it places the brand on appealing, albeit broad, emotional territory.

During the past few years Mengniu's and Yili's product portfolios have expanded dramatically. They now include yogurt drinks, premium yogurt, and infant formula. Such diversification would not have been possible without robust margins afforded by price premiums in their core product lines.

Disruptive Changes to the Business Environment

The Internet has unleashed transformational change in the global aviation industry. Consumer touch points for an airline now stretch

way beyond the airport and the flight itself. In the past carriers re-
lied on travel agents to represent them. Today airlines build direct
relationships with consumers through online booking and multidimensional loyalty programs. In response to major structural challenges, airlines have taken only baby steps in their communications.
In most cases changes have been cosmetic at best, usually focusing
on superior service, supported by undifferentiated product claims. In
2011 Cathay Pacific changed its advertising to declare, "People, they
make an airline," and glamorize the dedication of its pilots and cabin
crews. Qantas now states, "You're the reason we fly," while Virgin
Atlantic introduced its new campaign, "Flying in the Face of Ordinary," to tout its talented workforce. American Airlines also under-
went its first rebranding in 40 years and introduced its "Change Is in
the Air" campaign, an appeal to the put-upon American air passen-
ger. The shifts were driven by pressures that had been building for
some time, given the stiff economic headwinds that have prevailed
since the global financial crisis and the resulting need to cut costs.

Following a protracted period of bankruptcies and consolidation,
investment in stronger communication is a sign that CEOs recognize
the threat to the bottom line when consumers select carriers based
only on price rather than perceptions of superior image and service.
Airlines have not been starved for passengers. According to the World
Bank, the number of domestic and international fliers increased by
more than 50 percent between 2004 and 2012.[14] An extremely price-
sensitive emerging global middle class, however, has fueled these gains.
Airlines have invested hundreds of millions of dollars in business-
class facilities—large video screens, fully lie-flat seats, ice cream sun-
daes—because that's where the money is. Coach fliers are a majority
on almost all trips. But Michael Boyd, chair of the consultancy Boyd
Group International, estimates premium-class passengers account for
75 percent of the revenue on cross-country flights.[15] In economy class,
meanwhile, the masses suffer, with British Airways' newly professed
commitment—"To fly. To serve."—still ringing hollow.

The aforementioned brand ideas will not stand the test of time. They are not differentiated. They are also dated because they focus almost exclusively on upgrading the in-flight experience. But the world has changed. A comfortable seat and friendly smile no longer ensure customer loyalty. Empowered by technology, savvy travelers have begun to shop for the best deals by using such apps as FlightTrack, Gate Guru, WorldMate (a virtual global travel assistant), and SkyScanner (a flight price comparison site). JetBlue's free gift-wrapping service and Delta Airlines's willingness to spend $160 million on a refurbished terminal at LaGuardia airport hint at the amenities consumers now expect from airlines.

Airlines will need to radically rethink how they manage their relationship with customers. They must also harness the power of new business models. An opportunity exists for a visionary leader— a next-generation Richard Branson, Virgin Atlantic's iconoclastic CEO—to redefine corporate engagement with consumers. The future brand ideas of successful airlines must reflect a fundamentally expanded role the category can play in life. From "door-to-door travel companion" (hassle minimization) and "holistic destination orchestration" (combined business and holiday services) to "enjoy more, pay less" (inventory optimization with upgraded services during nonpeak times), the industry awaits its farsighted prophet of profit.

EXTENDING BRANDS ACROSS DIFFERENT PRODUCTS AND CATEGORIES

One of the questions asked most frequently is "How many brand ideas can a brand have?" The answer is simple, albeit deceptively nuanced: one. The brand idea is a long-term relationship between consumer and brand that evolves and deepens over time, like a marriage. That said, the definition of what constitutes a brand is not black and white. Marketers must decide the shape and structure of their brand portfolio. In some companies the corporation is a primary, or master, brand rather than a simple stamp of reassurance. The marketing activities of, say, General Motors and Procter & Gamble are usually limited to corporate public relations and CSR messaging. Royal Dutch Shell, on the other hand, is more ambitious. The energy giant has developed its "Let's go!" campaign to reinforce its commitment to finding multidimensional solutions to the challenges of sustainability. Ford Motor Company's global brand promise is to "Go further," a statement intended to unify three characteristics that underpin the car maker's heritage: people serving people, ingenuity, and attainability. Any large corporation that has a primary brand will also have subbrands. Shell, for example, has many lubricant subbrands, including Helix, Advance, and Rimula, with the Shell icon prominent on each package. Ford's "Blue Oval" logo coexists on vehicles with several of its subbrands, or nameplates, including Mondeo (for business people), Escort (young parents), the Kuga SUV (family), and Focus (young adults).

As a rule, significantly modifying the product offering or market segment requires a new brand idea. Should the spirit of Ford's "Go further" brand idea—a belief in democratizing technology so drivers can live fuller lives or more fully realize their potential—be infused in the positioning of each subbrand? Yes, unless the company is willing to forfeit the halo benefits that a strong master brand usually provides—such as advanced engineering, reliable service, and proven quality standards. At the same time, though, each subbrand requires its own brand idea. Every nameplate requires articulation crafted according to the unique dynamics of each vehicle's product story and target consumers. Great care must be taken to avoid confusion between the positioning of the subbrand and master brand—the child should resemble the parent but maintain a separate identity. A cohesive brand "product family" is efficient, but separation by subbrand is necessary when offering and target differ. For example:

	Ford Escort	Ford Focus	Ford Mondeo	Ford Kuga
Role in life	"Forward-thinking pragmatist"	"Technotalented energizer"	"Refined game changer"	"Family adventure guide"
Vehicle type	Entry-level compact	Midlevel compact	Large sedan	Compact sports utility vehicle (SUV)
Target demographic	Young parents	Single urbanites	Professionals	Middle-income parents
Key product feature	Value for money, fuel economy	Latest technology for dynamic driving	Sophisticated styling	Spacious, easily reconfigured interior

It makes sense to extend brands, and brand ideas, to embrace wider markets and product categories whenever possible. Existing brands should already boast a loyal user base; so long as new products and consumer targets are compatible with the existing franchise, consumers will not resist. Indeed the reassurance of broad scale drives preference, particularly in new markets where manufacturers need to actively earn trust and where shoddily produced goods are the norm rather than the exception. Lipton's tea heritage enabled the brand to extend its product range from teabags to ready-to-drink cans and recycled plastic bottles. At the same time Lipton became a younger, more contemporary, brand. Many producers of luxury items have also elegantly diversified their portfolios, particularly into accessories such as glasses and shoes, without muddying their image.

Maintaining a stable of separate brands is expensive, given that each requires its own investment in media, research and development, on-the-ground activation efforts, and administrative infrastructure. Introducing new brands is more expensive still; the cost of achieving broad awareness is greater for new brands than for ones already on the market. In emerging economies, particularly China, media costs are skyrocketing and competition is intense. Some believe that it is now almost too late for new players to introduce brands unless they are prepared to invest heavily and sustain losses for years.

However, you can't put ten pounds of coffee into a five-pound bag. Brands must not be stretched so far they split their seams— new brands and subbrands must be compatible with existing ones. In China the Alibaba Group owns the leading business-to-business (B2B) e-commerce site. When the company moved into the business-to-consumer (B2C) domain, it introduced a sister brand, Taobao (the name means panning for treasure). B2C is more emotional than B2B, which is driven solely by functional demands such as price, quantity, and delivery. Tata Group is a sprawling Indian conglomerate and has more than 100 independent companies, covering everything from trucks and telecommunications equipment to coffee. Tata has never established coherent brand ideas for any of its subbrands. Chunlan, the self-proclaimed General Electric of China, churns out every-thing from air conditioners to motorcycles. The company is able to stretch itself across multiple categories because scale creates trust among consumers, but it can carry diverse product lines only so far. The strategies of neither Tata nor Chunlan are sustainable if their goal is to have consumers actively prefer brands that maintain price premiums.

Ill-advised brand stretching also occurs in the European and American markets but less frequently. Siemens, the quintessence of German manufacturing prowess, should not launch lifestyle prod-ucts under its brand. The company's mobile phones, designed to ap-peal to "fashion-conscious" segments, flopped. Nestlé's "delicious food" credentials have probably adulterated the advanced nutrition positioning of its struggling infant formula line. Microsoft's cred-ibility is most robust in software for businesses, but it has a strong consumer franchise as well; the appeal of Windows rests on scale-driven reassurance, ubiquity, and—on sunny days—"for the people" accessibility. However, Microsoft has never been, and will never be, hip. Its social network—MSN/Windows Live Spaces—failed because it could not compete with the rise of newer and cooler companies like Facebook, Line, WhatsApp, and WeChat. Conversely Microsoft has succeeded with the gaming subbrand Xbox, a product that appeals to a distinct niche—young men.

Brand extension is also difficult when the target market is *fundamentally* different—for example, either much more premium or more mass-market than the original group. When Honda tried to target wealthier car buyers, it introduced the Acura. HSBC debuted the HSBC Advantage card for subpremium customers and the HSBC Premium card for high-end spenders. In emerging markets extending the brand to lower price tiers is a strategic imperative if multinational corporations hope to achieve both margin and market share. Scale is always contingent on broad distribution of less-expensive variants. Buick, a subbrand of General Motors, introduced its brand with the premium (C-class) Buick Regal and, to avoid brand dilution, competes on a lower price tier (B-class) with the Buick Excel.

It is worth reiterating: subbrands should leverage relevant elements of a master brand, assuming, of course, that it exists. HSBC is known for its cultural sensitivities; its advertising shows a wide range of HSBC products and services in multicultural contexts. Luxury brands like Armani and Ermenegildo Zegna have targeted the younger demographic through their Armani Collezioni and Z Zegna subbrands without forfeiting the cachet of their prestigious flag carriers.

CONCLUSION

The brand idea is a rare asset. It is a life force. It communicates the soul of a brand and its long-term relationship with consumers. That relationship springs from a commitment of mutual loyalty. It is bilateral, rooted in a back-and-forth dialog, and extends over time, perhaps decades, as it evolves to accommodate contemporary circumstances and new business imperatives. The brand idea is a fusion of insight into consumer behavior—understanding the fundamental motivations of a market target—and a unique brand offer, a vivid distillation of what ultimately differentiates a product or brand from its competitors. The conceptual essence of a great brand idea might strike some business leaders as unacceptably abstract or even touchy-feely. But the successes of brands that wield evocative brand ideas suggest otherwise.

five

engagement ideas

The brand idea is the fusion of a consumer insight and unique brand offer, the underpinning for the long-term relationship—that is, engagement—between consumer and brand across digital and other media. While the brand idea remains constant, its creative expression—the engagement idea—does not. Engagement ideas must confront the era of consumer empowerment and digital technology head on. The goal is to do more than just break through the clutter— marketers must convert passive exposure to active participation and trigger consumer reaction by creating ideas people want to spend time with. This can be achieved by connecting to one of the three levels of passion: "me," or helping individuals in their daily life; "we," or creating virtual communities of like-minded souls; and "the world," or broadening horizons for a new global generation.

For years pundits have declared the demise of the advertising industry is imminent. "Never has advertising appeared so pale and lifeless," warned the *Journal of Advertising* back in 1994.[1] "Advertising agencies are dead," said Tony Granger, global chief creative officer at Young & Rubicam, in 2009. "This is the worst time in our business since the Great Depression."[2] A few years later a blog by Bill Lee, president of the Customer Reference Board, helpfully added, "Marketing is dead." He warned, "Many people in traditional marketing roles and organizations may not realize they're operating within a dead paradigm. But they are. The evidence is clear."[3] At about the same time, *Wired* magazine screamed, "Advertising is over!" The authors Stefan Olander and Ajaz Ahmed grumbled, "Planning a start-up and wondering how much of your limited budget to allocate to traditional advertising? We have no doubt the answer is . . . nothing."[4]

Hence the theme for Advertising Week in October 2012: a funeral for the industry. Even JWT got into the act, sponsoring a memorial service. A casket, flying doves, and jingles sung by the Madison Avenue Gospel Choir set the tone. Matt MacDonald, then cochief creative officer, intoned, "We have lost a great industry, a noble profession, a beloved friend." He walked slowly toward the coffin, lifted the lid, and—behold—it was empty. In mock shock the audience gasped. Voice rising, McDonald proclaimed, "The time has come to bury advertising once and for all . . . because then maybe everyone will stop declaring it dead."[5]

In fact advertising is not dead. It's more alive than ever. In 2014 global advertising expenditures were expected to exceed $500 billion for the first time, with the majority invested in so-called traditional media such as television and print. So while advertising, like everything else, must evolve, it doesn't seem useful to pretend there's no link to the old world.

The digital revolution has turned the industry on its head. It has splintered media into a dizzying array of platforms and devices: Twitter, Facebook, WeChat, online video, blogs, and mobile apps. The average person is bombarded by 3,000 advertising messages per day. Half the world's social media users are in Asia; 60 percent are seeking out videos online; 43 percent are using mobile devices to shop. There's simply too little time and too much to see.

The exponential growth of digital channels has prompted a chaotic explosion of disjointed messages, and, in a desperate attempt to engage consumers, brands are scrambling to pump communications through every single one. Never-ending torrents of irrelevant commercials infiltrate online videos, social media feeds, and news outlets. But carpet bombing does not inspire purchase—in fact it makes consumers tune out. Several years ago the ad agency Ogilvy & Mather coined the phrase "360-degree marketing" to reinforce the need to diversify communications channels, but the term has not been helpful. Communications require centrifugal force—unifying ideas—to simplify propositions for consumers.

There are more screens, more channels, and more choice than ever before, and this means a greater number of opportunities for brands to connect with consumers. But that connection has to be truly engaging. When new employees join JWT, we impress on them that we no longer just create advertising; we create ideas people want to spend time with.

The brand idea is the fusion of a consumer insight and unique brand offer, the underpinning for the long-term relationship between consumer and brand. It can evolve, or can be interpreted, to reflect local culture, but at its core the brand idea remains consistent across time and place. The brand idea is conceptual and strategic. Creative execution, however, is not. It can have colors, sounds, music, story lines, images, and graphics vivid enough to affect brand preference and behavior.

Engagement ideas are creative expressions of the brand idea. They can be short term or long term, thematic or promotional. A brand can have one unifying engagement idea or several different ones, so long as all are reflections of the brand idea. I use the term *engagement idea* rather than *creative idea* or *campaign idea* because every campaign provides an opportunity to expand, play with, and build on the engagement idea itself. Through those actions, consumers move closer to purchase. In an era of consumer empowerment accelerated by digital technology, creative execution can transform passive exposure into active engagement. When consumers lean— or, better yet, opt—in to communications, their level of involvement with the brand deepens—and so can their loyalty.

ENGAGEMENT IDEAS THAT
INSPIRE "OPTING IN"

Because the digital revolution has empowered people, creative execution has to be more than interesting. It must do more than break through clutter. Super Bowl Sunday notwithstanding, the days of sitting in front of the television and waiting for cool television ads to air are over. Brands today must create ideas so powerful that they *engage* consumers, becoming part of the conversation and ultimately people's lives. Marketers have to shift their focus from chasing eyeballs to earning a share of consumers' time.

People will welcome brands' messages if they perceive concrete value. According to Guy Murphy, JWT's worldwide planning director, "Our response to these brands will be to want to 'opt-in' to them. Not in the [direct marketing] sense of 'permission' but in the emotional sense of being happy to accept them in our lives." He further predicts people will allow only three to five brands into their inner sanctum. Brand openness will be key. He continues, "In a world dominated by consumer pull, not marketing push, consumers' relationships with a brand will become rather more binary in the future. A brand is either one consumers want to lean in to or one to lean away from. People will either be open to what a brand has to say and do, or they will not."[6]

In a digital era television, radio, print, or outdoor executions are not the only ways to define advertising. Technology inspires brands to push the boundaries of what constitutes an idea. Marketers can create branded services that combine tangible and intangible value and become an integral part of everyday life. "Brands will seem more valuable not just because they *feel* better but because they work better, or serve you better," Guy explains. "This is not a denial of the emotional component of brands, it is just a different way of generating it. It is not only about the power of associations but also the power of reality."[7]

The deep integration of technology into the lives of consumers means some brands are built solely through digital interaction. Users book Uber, a service that offers premium transportation as an alternative to taxis, primarily through a beautifully designed app that handles scheduling and processes payment. Uber does not own the cars or employ the drivers. Online word of mouth and referrals have fueled its growth. Happy customers, given incentives in the form of online coupons to introduce Uber to friends, become advocates—and, as I will discuss shortly, a consumer advocate is the most precious commodity of all. Google has become an iconic brand through its online services—and very little investment in conventional advertising. In the words of Celia Garforth, a Sydney-based strategic planner: "It's now possible to build a brand almost entirely by using [digital interaction] to drive emotional connections. Google's mission to better organize the world's information [and bring the world together through technology] is manifested through a myriad of brand experiences with each one reinforcing the last. This creates countless 'ripples of feel good' that aggregate into a unified brand."[8]

Technology helps marketers make a difference in consumers' lives with innovative products and utilities, new apps, or sleeker and easier-to-use services. But the extent to which most virtual brands will stand the test of time is still very much an open question. By and large real products and meaningful ideas, not by bits and bytes, still motivate consumers. We are people, not computers. Brands must harness technology to engage consumers in the most relevant way while remaining true to the brand idea, thereby expanding the boundaries of the role ideas play in life.

Nike, as discussed earlier, has been in the forefront of this effort for years. By embedding microchips in shoes so that athletes can upload their performance data to smartphones and personal computers, Nike redefined the role of technology in personal training with its the Nike+ series. Thanks to technology, "Just do it" is always on.

Engagement ideas are bouncy, sticky, unstoppable forces. They must go beyond drawing attention to eliciting an active response—participation platforms—not stunts—that inspire consumers to opt in. At the 2014 Grammy awards the fast-food chain Arby's caused a sensation when it poked fun at Pharrell Williams, an American rapper. His hat looked like the one in the Arby's logo, so the company tweeted, "Hey, #Pharrell, can we have our hat back?" It was the most talked-about fashion moment of the show, because it reminded people of pop-culture totems, including Smokey Bear and Harry Potter. The sly move inspired 77,000 re-tweets within 24 hours, and, just like that, Arby's became part of the zeitgeist. But there is little evidence the company sold more roast beef sandwiches.

Our aim is to craft—or *invent*—ideas people want to spend time with. As such engagement ideas must be organic, not only part of the conversation but also part of people's lives. The more time consumers spend playing with and spreading an idea, the deeper their involvement. A strong engagement idea maximizes the individual's involvement with the brand over time.

"BE WATER"

In an era of media fragmentation, engagement ideas must become media neutral—that is, usable on any individual communications channel. Ideas should remain consistent on everything from television to apps to social media networks to in-store shelf talkers to media that defy categorization. (We will return to the topic of unconventional media later in this chapter.) Bruce Lee, the martial arts icon and quintessence of Chinese masculine power, had a philosophy I find useful in discussing media neutrality. During a 1960s television interview, he intoned, "Empty your mind, be formless, shapeless, like water. Now, you put water into a cup, it becomes the cup. Put water in a bottle, it becomes the bottle. Put it in a teapot, it becomes the teapot. Now, water can flow, or it can crash. Be water, my friend. Be water."[9] Water is fluid, adaptable—and this is exactly what an engagement idea must be, assuming the shape of that which it surrounds. It transcends individual media vehicles because the idea has been meticulously defined to adapt to any of them. Marketers no longer create television commercials; they craft an engagement idea that can be broadcast over television. More than semantics, this distinction is a fundamental shift. Creative execution assumes the form *of* various media—it becomes the media—rather than being placed *on* and broadcast *through* media.

Nestlé's KIT KAT engagement ideas are rooted in its long-term brand idea, "Have a break, have a KIT KAT" (Nestlé produces the candy everywhere except the United States, where it is made and distributed by Hershey.) In Japan the candy bar's name is pronounced "Kitto Katto," similar to the Japanese expression "Kitto Katsu," which means "surely win." In 2003 JWT introduced KIT KAT's first *juken* (or entrance exam) campaign, positioning the lucky-sounding chocolate bar as both a lucky charm and stress breaker for students, who face enormous pressure during the university entrance exam season in January and February. The candy's engagement idea was defined as "Your new lucky charm. Take a break from exam stress."

The idea played out in creative executions across all media. Many students travel to Tokyo or Osaka to take the exams. Clerks at hotels handed out a KIT KAT and a postcard of a cherry tree with the expression "May cherries blossom," a Japanese idiom for wishing luck, to students during check-out. The floor of the subway station near Tokyo University, a major exam center, was decorated with prints of colorful *sakura* cherry blossoms and KIT KAT logos. Each step a student took across the subway station toward the exam hall generated more luck. As consumers interacted with the conventionally passive outdoor medium, media and idea became one.

The *juken* campaign has continued during exam season every year since, with new creative executions that leverage the same engagement idea. One television commercial shows a nervous teenager calming herself by praying with a KIT KAT. In other years taxi companies, restaurants, a mobile network operator, and magazines partnered with Nestlé, providing free rides to exam takers, menus offering "lucky sets," and mobile websites where students could post their wishes.

In 2009 JWT Japan turned KIT KAT bars into a whole new medium with "KIT KAT Mail," an award-winning campaign in partnership with Japan Post, the country's postal service. Every spring relatives and friends in Japan send handwritten notes to students to wish them luck with their exams. With KIT KAT Mail people can buy a specially designed box containing a KIT KAT bar at post offices across the country, write a message, and mail it to students anywhere. KIT KAT created a unique distribution channel, selling the boxes at more than 20,000 post offices across the country, where the brand had no competition.

By forging an engagement idea that weaves the brand through the fabric of life, KIT KAT is no longer just a chocolate bar—it has become synonymous with good fortune and success. KIT KAT sales during exam season have doubled since the *juken* campaign first broke, and today one in five students takes a KIT KAT to exams. Furthermore, KIT KAT Mail is still on sale every year during exam season in Japanese post offices. Consumer and brand have a long-term relationship that continues to blossom over time.

KIT KAT's *Juken (or "entrance exam") campaign, positioned the chocolate bar as both a lucky charm and stress breaker for students during the university entrance exam season. The engagement idea inspired invention of new media such as* KIT KAT *Mail, a new way to send good luck. (© 2009 Nestlé Japan Ltd. All Rights Reserved.)*

FROM ENGAGEMENT TO ADVOCACY

What does *engagement* really mean? The answer varies greatly, depending on the specific marketing objective and desired behavioral action. Broadly speaking, however, engagement can take place on several levels.

Engagement can mean ideas that spread or are simply talked about. People will share online content that surprises and delights. In February 2012 Kraft Foods kicked off the hundredth anniversary of OREO with its history print series, a clever campaign that used the image of the cookie to depict milestones in history. In June it followed up with the "daily twist," cute images released across social media of cookies linked to trending world news. There was a Gay Pride OREO, a Psy OREO inspired by the eponymous Korean rap sensation, a Shark Week OREO, even a Mars Land Rover OREO. Across all channels the campaign filtered the world through OREO's distinctively playful imagination and brand idea, "Liberate your childhood spirit." By the time the 100-day initiative ended, OREO had achieved a 280 percent increase in Facebook shares, 433 million Facebook views, and 231 million offline media impressions. It had become part of the conversation.

Burger King's 2007 "Whopper Freakout" was advertising masked as a sociological experiment. Seeking to spur expressions of love for the Whopper, the company took its best-selling burger off the menu in one town, creating a "day of deprivation." Actors posing as Burger King employees explained a new reality to flummoxed customers, offering burgers from Wendy's and McDonald's as alternatives. Emotions flared further. A typical comment: "I hate [expletive] Wendy's! Give me my [expletive] Whopper!" Burger King hired a roving reporter, accompanied by a local news crew, to capture reactions. One perplexed man helpfully suggested, "If Burger King doesn't have the Whopper, they might as well change their name to Burger Queen." After the experiment hundreds of

JUNE 25 | PRIDE

Made with creme colors that do not exist.

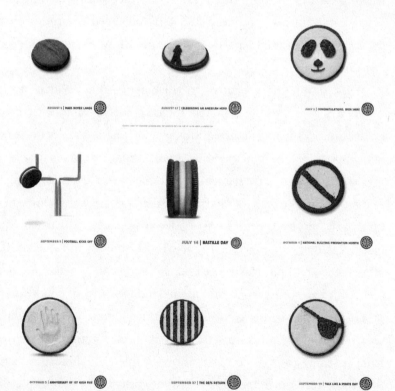

The OREO *"daily twist" leveraged social media to celebrate the cookie's 100th anniversary while integrating the brand into the fabric of American twenty-first-century life. The campaign also made* OREO *the first "gay cookie."* (OREO® *is a registered trademark of Intercontinental Great Brands LLC and is used with permission.)*

hours of footage were cut into 15- and 30-second films broadcast on television and spread virally online. Audio from drive-throughs became radio spots. Ads led consumers to a website, www.whopperfreakout.com, where they could view an eight-minute behind-the-scenes "methodology" video of how "Whopper Freakout" was orchestrated. Consumer recall was the highest ever recorded by IAG Research, which tracks viewer responses to ads. Reaction online was unprecedented, with dozens of homemade parody videos racking up millions of page views.

Involvement can also mean inspiring consumers to actively participate in and shape communications. Old Spice capitalized on the success of its 2010 "Smell Like a Man, Man" campaign by inviting fans to pose questions through social media to the "Old Spice Guy," Isaiah Mustafa. In only three days Old Spice's advertising agency, Wieden + Kennedy, produced 186 tailored video responses on the fly. They were intimate, participatory, and drew 34 million views in just one week.[10]

This level of proactive involvement—that which fosters "advocacy"—is the holy grail of marketing. Weber Shandwick, a public relations company, describes this phenomenon as the act of pledging support for or recommending a brand that translates into brand loyalty. Once they have evidence that consumers are making repeat purchases, marketers can charge a higher price. User endorsements remain the most powerful form of advertising; in a 2010 article McKinsey & Company concluded that word-of-mouth influenced 20 to 50 percent of all purchasing decisions.[11] People now make purchases across all categories based on recommendations from people on the other side of the world. According to Motive Quest, a social media research firm, "The most important, unalterable finding that we draw from listening to and scoring the way people talk about products is that these recommendations—actual advocacy of a brand in online conversations—continue to correlate with offline sales in every category. The type of product doesn't matter; in these conversations, only the level of advocacy influences sales. The best metric of a brand's health in online conversations, we were able to declare, is advocacy—the number of individuals actively engaging with and promoting the brand."[12] In China brand advocates are so influential that nine out of ten online consumers will now buy a product only if opinion leaders or bloggers have posted positive feedback.

Return on Investment Versus Return on Involvement

The mass media benchmarks of recall, persuasiveness, or purchase intent no longer are the only means of measuring success. However, no one has figured out a magic formula to measure advocacy. In the absence of a standardized advocacy index, marketers and agencies have become obsessed with return on investment (ROI). Defined as the causal relationship between incremental spending and sales, ROI is difficult to measure. An obvious—and important—exception is customer relationship management (CRM) programs that comprise one-to-one communications and a series of offers and acceptances that lead to purchases and long-term loyalty. Successful CRM depends on sophisticated management of a database, cross selling, and comparison of test and control offers.

Around the turn of the twentieth century, John Wanamaker, an American merchant considered by some to be the father of modern advertising, famously quipped, "Half the money I spend on advertising is wasted; the trouble is I don't know which half." Things are improving. We can now observe how communication affects behavior, in real time, throughout a shopper's journey, a topic we will discuss in detail in the next chapter. For example, marketers can measure or approximate gains in awareness by number of ad impressions, cost per view, and cost per reach on social networking sites such as Facebook. Meanwhile they also can measure gains in consideration by cost per lead or sign up, cost per trial, and time spent on a site. Assessing advocacy directly is impossible, but marketers can infer it from the number of high response rates, positive reviews, number of re-tweets, fan base size, and spikes in positive social buzz.

It is more useful to think of "return on involvement" than return on investment. Messages that move people to actively participate with brands are by definition involving—and influential. Engagement ideas that are creative expressions of a long-term brand idea should communicate those messages. Digital media are particularly suited for triggering active consumer response, but without a strategic center of gravity, the impact of digital creative ideas will be ephemeral. Josie Brown, JWT's Asia Pacific director of digital, observed to me, "I'm conscious that, these days, great creative content fights with celebrity and stunts that are cheap social currency." Great ideas earn more time; less engaging ones are phased out.

Engaging E-Influencers and Netizens

To foster advocacy, marketers must harness the enthusiasm of two groups of internet users: e-influencers and ordinary netizens. The former are key opinion leaders (KOLs), twenty-first-century disciples capable of shaping the decisions of thousands or millions of consumers. Indonesian fashion circles follow every word from the blogger Ollie Salsabella; Paul Tan, a highly regarded blogger in Malaysia, has more than 70,000 followers on Twitter, and his website is regarded as the number one source for automotive news; the fashion blogger Nicole Warne has 750,000 followers in Australia, which has a population of only 23 million. Every country has both online celebrity voices—the singers Katy Perry and Justin Bieber have almost 50 million Twitter followers each—but also category-specific KOLs with the potential to shape opinions of brands.

Marketers in every category must develop relationships with influencers and communities of influencers by establishing vehicles for them to demonstrate their cutting-edge currency or expertise. Converse, a subsidiary of Nike, extended its brand idea,

"Celebration of originality," to target aspiring fashion designers. A series of shoe design competitions provided a platform for fashionistas to display their creative flair. In 2011 Volkswagen launched the "people's car" project in China, inviting enthusiasts to design the vehicle of the future. Netizens submitted more than 260,000 blueprints online, and a panel of KOL experts selected the finalists. In 2013 the event crossed the offline divide as teams of design students from China's top universities competed to build a winning car. The competition became the basis for a ten-part online documentary series.[13]

Marketers can also harness the power of advocacy among the online population at large. The Internet provides functional benefits like connectivity, access to information, and price comparisons, but it is also emotionally liberating, providing a global platform for release. It is difficult to overstate this emancipation, particularly for

The Volkswagen People's Car Project was a successful digital effort that targeted online key opinion leaders, or KOLs, in China. Engaging the attention of KOLs is an important way of generating brand advocacy, especially in emerging markets where brand alternatives have proliferated. This illustration shows a winning entry, combining the features of a sports utility vehicle (SUV) and a minivan.

Asians, who live in hierarchical societies where daily life is regimented. The Internet allows them to assert their individuality to a degree simply not possible in the offline world. Internet cafes in China are the size of football fields, each populated with legions of *wǎngyǒu*—or net mates—looking to forge identities on a blank canvas of self-expression. The virtual world brings power to people.

It is worth noting that this release has a dark side. Throughout large swathes of Asia, emotional investment in their virtual identities makes people susceptible to Internet addiction. As early as 2007 the China Communist Youth League claimed that more than 17 percent of its 13- to 17-year-old members were addicted to the Internet. The following year China became the first country to declare Internet addiction a clinical disorder and one of the top health threats to its young people. Four hundred institutions have opened nationwide to wean 24 million young people off compulsive Internet use or, as they call it, "electric heroin."[14]

Dangers aside, creating engagement ideas that inspire consumers to "opt in" must be a goal for all marketers. But netizens are unlikely to act unless they gain a reward. Broadly speaking, brands can tap into three levels of motivation to maximize engagement: helping individuals in their daily lives ("me"), creating virtual communities of like-minded souls ("we"), and broadening the horizons of a new global generation ("the world").

Me
Individuals are receptive to ideas that entertain, enrich, or empower them. A brand could do this by providing something useful or simply providing a platform for individuals to show off their talent.

Offer Fun Apps
If brands are to gain a share of consumers' time, they must provide tangible benefits. One tactic is to offer a fun, entertaining app. As

always it must be consistent with the existing brand idea—brands cannot simply adopt the latest technology or gee-whiz app. The ultimate aim should be to reinforce an existing relationship between consumer and brand.

In 2007 the fast-fashion brand Uniqlo created a phenomenon in Japan with its "Uniqlock" blog widget, which told time through dance and music. Throughout the day dancers wearing Uniqlo apparel performed energetic-but-controlled dance routines, moving to the "tick, tick, tock" beat of the Uniqlock. Every hour they performed a different dance. The engagement idea was unconventional, but it worked because it reflected Uniqlo's brand idea of "Style for real people," which has always been underscored by mix-and-match clothing. The company's success in Asia lies in their sleek yet conservative garments that enable consumers to create their own style without crossing into "stylish rebellion." Uniqlo's Asia-friendly brand character infused the steady beat of the Uniqlock—always progressing, always changing. Koichiro Tanaka, creative director for the campaign, explains further: "The challenge was to design the best fusion of dance and sound as a clock. The point was that the clock should be ever-lasting, ever-changing media. We shot as many different dance components as possible, and had [the sound artist] Fantastic Plastic Machine compose time-signal-sound components. We developed the Flash system that shuffles dance and sound elements randomly so the audience felt they hadn't seen repeats. We created catchy and hypnotic experiences that could be shared."[15]

More functionally the widget also served as a screen saver and alarm, as well as a link to Uniqlo's online store. The initiative ran throughout the year but changed with the seasons. During summer dancers wore Uniqlo polo shirts; in the fall they donned cashmere sweaters and scarves. To reinforce the brand's internationalism the widget always displayed the number of worldwide online fans. Dance audition videos ran on YouTube and were viewed more than half a million times. In 2008 Uniqlock won a Grand Prix in the Titanium and Cyber categories at the Cannes Lions International Festival of Creativity.

Unilever's male deodorant brand Axe developed the "sexy wake-up call" alarm clock, an expression of its "Irresistible attractiveness" brand idea. In Japan almost all young men use their mobile phone as an alarm clock but few use deodorant. Axe titillated men to encourage them to change their behavior. It created a branded app that allowed guys to be awakened by different young women. The men could pick their "Axe angels" and would receive a personalized video wake-up call every day during a three-week period, along with a reminder to wear Axe. The app resulted in 3.5 million page views, 27,000 mobile alarm downloads, and an increase in repeat purchases of 27 percentage points.[16]

Schick (Wilkinson/Sword) in France has long adhered to the brand idea "Sharp man, smooth face." In 2007 it leveraged mobile gaming technology to encourage men to "fight for kisses." A teaser that went viral introduced the initiative with the depiction of a grown man and his infant son competing for a woman's tender caresses. As the baby does sit-ups and practices karate, viewers know he means business. A baritone voice intones, "There was a time when babies had a great life. The softness of their skin got them all their mom's attention. Then, one day, fathers discovered a special weapon [the Wilkinson Sword razor]. From now on, father and sons can fight on equal terms. Men can take revenge and win back their wives." The trailer directed people to an online video game that they could download to their mobile phones. Fight for Kisses, reminiscent of the 1980s Street Fighter arcade game, pitted players against their own babies. The platform racked up more than 11 million website visits, 400,000 registered downloads and six million trailer viewings on YouTube and Daily Motion.[17]

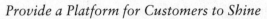

Provide a Platform for Customers to Shine

The Internet is a stage on which the average person stands up to exclaim, "Hello, world! I'm here!" Engagement ideas can provide a platform to shine. The impulse for self-display is powerful and, by the way, probably explains why "selfie" was selected by the *Oxford English Dictionary* as the 2013 word of the year.

In 2007 PepsiCo's "Get on the Can" campaign turned packaging into a talent showcase by offering consumers the chance to get their picture on a special edition can. Harry Hui, then director of Pepsi China's marketing efforts, noted, "We wanted to create YouTube on a can."[18] Participants ranged from monks and pets to macho military men and online gamers. People submitted thirty million photos via mobile phone or microsite, and cast 163 million votes. Pepsi chose 84 winners to run on four regionally distributed cans, and 21 went on to appear on nationally distributed cans. During two waves of six weeks each, the engagement idea, an expression of Pepsi's brand idea, "The choice of a new generation," generated more 750 million unique page views.

In 2011 Vancl, China's leading online fashion retailer, created a platform for netizens to open their own online Vancl store. For Chinese, face is about more than being cool—it is social currency, the fuel for upward advancement. While reinforcing its brand idea, "Create your own style," Vancl made looking good pay. After registering to open stores, netizens uploaded pictures of themselves with tagged Vancl clothing, and a microsite program then transformed photos into stylish posters. If shoppers clicked on the ad to purchase a displayed item, the model earned a commission.

We

Engagement ideas can also offer benefits to individuals who share common interests. Durex's brand idea is "Bringing couples closer," and a recent campaign in Australia—the "Fundawear"

172 twitter is not a strategy

experiment—made sexual intimacy possible for couples separated by distance. Durex equipped underwear with motorized sensors activated by a smartphone app, and partners could "turn on" areas of the garment and control the intensity level. In the words of Durex's technology director, Ben Moir, "It's about transferring touch across vast distances."[19] Within two weeks a demonstration of a couple's "Fundawear" experiment became Australia's most popular YouTube video. Durex saw a 4,000 percent increase in its rate of Facebook fan growth.[20]

Pedigree, a Mars pet food brand, is known for its advocacy of animal welfare. Its brand idea is disarmingly simple: "Dogs rule." Pedigree's Australian affiliate introduced an engagement platform so that a community of animal lovers could promote adoption of stray dogs. This included the 2011 "best mates" pet adoption drive, a rare corporate social responsibility (CSR) campaign that was actually inspired by a brand idea. The effort featured a canine search engine to capitalize on a surprising observation: people choose pets that look like them. Individuals uploaded pictures to the "dog-a-like" smartphone and Facebook app, and then face recognition technology matched the person with the dog that most resembled them. The app drew more than 5.8 million users and became Australia's most successful dog adoption campaign, resulting in a 36 percent increase in adoptions.[21] Through an engagement idea dog lovers rallied in common cause.

Nike has used engagement ideas to resolve a universal tension between self-actualization and affiliation. This conflict is particularly acute in Asian societies, where an individual's ultimate goal remains acknowledgment by society. The NikeFuel band leverages technology so runners can share their achievements or compete within virtual communities. Nike China's 2013 "Summer Nights" campaign encouraged individual athletes to join together to express their "Just do it" spirit. In a country where sports participation is low, a call to play sports after dark is almost a declaration of insanity. Nike's campaign began with a slightly self-confessional online teaser that announced sotto voce: "Come out, come out wherever you are." Nike enlisted celebrities to spread the word, with the American professional basketball player Kevin Durant starring in a call-for-action video. A competition pitted key online opinion leaders against each other using Nike+ and NikeFuel uploads. Activities crossed the offline divide, with numerous nighttime events across the country at which people had an opportunity to practice with their idols. Twelve men joined the basketball star Kobe Bryant in training exercises.

Running is individualistic and fundamentally Western. As Jesse Owens, who won four gold medals at the 1936 Berlin Olympics, said, "I always loved running—it was something you could do by yourself, and under your own power. You could go in any direction, fast or slow as you wanted, fighting the wind if you felt like it, seeking out new sights just on the strength of your feet and the courage of your lungs." In Australia Nike created a platform for solitary runners to form local nighttime running clubs. Nike introduced the initiative after it learned that most women predominantly ran alone but often were afraid of running solo at night. Efforts to forge a new community culminated in a 2012 night race for women, dubbed She Runs the Night. Spurred by social network feeds, more than 3,200 women descended on the iconic grounds of Sydney's Centennial Park for a 13K race. The inaugural event was part of the Nike Women's Race Series taking place in 15 cities around the world and involving more than 50,000 women. A postevent party offered live music, massages, trials of the Nike Free Run+ 3 cushioned shoe, Nike+ demos, and a photo booth they could use to share their success on Facebook. Participants posted their best shots to Instagram and tweeted through the night, helping #NikeSheRunsAU become the highest-trending hashtag in the country. The campaign, in Nike's words, "brought the women of Australia together to share their passion for running and sport."[22]

Starting in 2010, Canon Australia's engagement idea of "EOS photochains" transformed photography from a solitary endeavor into a group passion. Offline advertising invited photographers to contribute to a continually growing chain of photos in which each shot inspired the next. The idea was an interpretation of Canon's *kyosei* philosophy, admittedly not quite a brand idea but a corporate philosophy of "living and working together for the common good." Artistic inspiration spread from person to person, resulting in collective creation. After taking a photo, the photographer uploaded it, then tagged a specific detail to provide stimulus for the next photographer, and the process was repeated until the photographers had created a sequence of thematically interconnected images. Combinations of photos pulled from the chain appeared in outdoor and print advertising. As the initiative gained momentum, photographers explored narrower topics consistent with the *kyosei* philosophy—for example, a "chain of love" or "hero's chain." People could track the journey of their photos and follow other photographers. By connecting photographers online, the brand created a network of enthusiasts who then became the base for direct-marketing activities. Photographers uploaded at least 100 high-quality photos every day, amounting to 20,000 during the campaign's first six months. Engagement with the brand helped Canon EOS increase its market share in Australia to a record 67 percent.[23]

The World

Finally, most netizens want to plug in to something bigger than themselves. The Internet has no boundaries—it beckons us to expand our worldview in ways earlier generations never dreamed possible. Thanks to the digital revolution, we can be part of history.

Help Consumers Be Part of Greatness

In 2008 Adidas New Zealand introduced a high-tech engagement idea, "Adithread," that encouraged the nation to join forces in support of its beloved rugby team, the All Blacks. "Impossible is nothing," the brand idea at the time, was a tribute to the transformative power of the collective. Through a microsite fans put their names on a virtual thread, which was then transferred to actual thread and used to stitch a national symbol, the fern, on the jersey worn by Richie McCaw, the team captain, during a tour of Europe. Thanks to nanotechnology, more than 100,000 fans had their names placed on the chest of a national hero.[24] In a faraway land, propelled by unity, the All Blacks won five straight matches.

Support Dreams

Pepsi's began its Refresh Project in 2010 with the lofty aim of making the world a better place by allowing netizens to vote for projects that support local communities. Winners were awarded grants worth $5,000 to $250,000. Communities submitted more than 1,000 plans within the first week, with celebrities such as Demi Moore and Kevin Bacon spreading the word by promoting their own ideas. More than 87 million votes were cast for projects that funded schools, parks, playgrounds, shelters, and housing for low-income people. Majora Carter, an advisory board member for the Pepsi Refresh Project, expressed her pride in the initiative: "All across America, people from every walk of life are producing powerful, creative and fun ideas that can create positive change. Pepsi's Refresh Project is going to help move ideas from wishful thinking to reality—and that's an incredibly exciting effort to support."[25]

Pepsi elevated refreshment from a physical to a spiritual plane and added new significance to the old tagline "The choice of a new generation." Did the campaign's idealism buck the urgency of hedonistic young adults? Perhaps. Just as Dove's "Real Beauty" campaign failed to increase its market share, Pepsi Refresh Project did not drive sales. The tidal wave of participation, however, suggests the emotional power of iconic brands *can* be harnessed through technology if tightly linked to a clear brand idea.

Start a Movement

In 2008 India celebrated its fiftieth anniversary as an independent nation. The country's leading newspaper, the *Times of India,* orchestrated "Lead India," a three-act social movement to forge a more empowered, less bureaucratic society. Amitabh Bachchan, arguably the country's most famous film actor, appeared in a two-minute broadcast appeal that was consistent with the newspaper's mantra and de facto brand idea, "Let truth prevail." He began, "There are two Indias in this country. One India is straining at the leash, eager to spring forth and live up to all the adjectives that the world has recently been showering on us. The other India *is* the leash. One India says, 'Give me a chance and I'll prove myself.' The other India says, 'Prove yourself first and then maybe I'll give you a chance.' One India lives in the optimism in our hearts. The other India lurks in the skepticism of our minds. One India leads. The other India follows." Bachchan urged the nation to allow a dynamic new India to emerge, "for history is turning a page." During the next few months the film became a topic of burning debate. The *Times of India*'s website became an arena for passionate Indians around the world to express their hopes for the nation. One typical comment: "Our politicians are not the only agents of change. All citizens should become active participants in a thriving democracy."

On Indian Independence Day the Bollywood heartthrob Shahruhk Khan introduced the second phase of the movement with a film broadcast on television and online. A full-page ad also appeared on the cover of the *Times of India.* The headline was one word: *Do.* Provocative body copy asked, "The last time we decided to do or die, it changed the map of the world . . . Today, the eyes of the world are upon us again. So what are we going to . . . do?" Millions of Indians seized the moment. A new generation of professionals, industrialists, members of parliament, lyricists, poets, social workers—even Miss World—came out in support of the campaign. A series of advertorials, "If I Ruled the Country," ran in national and local newspapers.

Grassroots initiatives sprang up across the land: fire drills for slum dwellers, funding for orphanages, microfinancing for farmers, placement in top-ranked universities for the underprivileged.

During the final stage of "Lead India," eight change agents were selected by viewers of a highly rated reality television series. Evocative advertising encouraged viewer participation and ended with "Seeking tomorrow's leaders, today. The search is on." The newspaper awarded the winner, R. K. Mishra, a scholarship to Harvard University's Kennedy School of Government and gave him a $100,000 grant to fund his initiative to educate members of the middle class on matters of public policy. All eight finalists joined public life at the national level.[26]

In 2008 less than 5 percent of the population regularly accessed the Internet, so it is not surprising that "Lead India" was low tech. But it doesn't matter. The initiative was a creative expression of the *Times of India*'s long-held mission to "Let truth prevail," which marketers call a brand idea. The movement's spirit was modern, and the paper treated its readers as active agents, not passive receivers of information. Millions returned that respect by lifting their voices and opening their hearts.

NEW ENGAGEMENT WITH
TECHNOLOGY VERSUS IDEAS

The digital revolution has liberated people's imaginations. However, too many brands scramble to deploy the latest app. New forms of technological engagement are not, in and of themselves, creative ideas. Technology is useful for making ideas more powerful—but advertising professionals have been and always will be the crafters of ideas.

Tesco's experiment with mobile commerce is an example of a technological breakthrough that failed to enhance the brand's stature. Known in Korea as Homeplus, the hypermarket (a big-box

The Times of India engagement idea, "Lead India," is a powerful example of how a creative engagement idea can become a social movement that inspires change. (Times of India)

store that includes a supermarket) opened a virtual grocery store in a Seoul subway station as a convenience for busy workers. Home-plus installed an electronic screen that pictured actual supermarket shelves and refrigeration cases. Commuters could use their smart-phones to scan quick response (QR) codes and create a virtual shop-ping basket. Home delivery was also possible.[27] The initiative won the Media Grand Prix at Cannes, but the concept had two prob-lems. First, many ad industry professionals believed the effort was a scam—that it was nothing more than a mock-up created only to impress judges at awards competitions but never adopted on a wide scale. Second, Homeplus's virtual store had neither a brand idea nor an engagement idea; nothing associated it with the retailer other than the brand's name. There was no strategy, no creative execution, nothing the brand could own. It was just technocool. Any positive impression would have evaporated shortly after the virtual store was taken down.

Technology must be used in conjunction with a coherent brand proposition. A few months later Homeplus's major competitor in Korea, E-Mart, put Homeplus to shame by introducing a real e-commerce service wrapped in a simple and effective creative con-cept, "the flying store." E-Mart's truck-shaped balloons, equipped with wi-fi, floated across the city, including locations far from bricks-and-mortar stores. A downloadable app enabled people to buy prod-ucts, arrange home delivery, and even claim e-coupons. Within a month online sales more than doubled, and more than 50,000 peo-ple had used the app.

Even noble deployment of technology needs a creative frame, lest corporate social responsibility fail to strengthen the company's eq-uity. After the 2011 concatenation of tragedy in Fukushima, Honda, one of Japan's biggest-hearted corporations, used technology to aid rescue efforts. Twenty thousand people were missing, and rescuers were struggling to reach those in need because infrastructure was devastated. Honda analyzed data collected from its 3G network of

Internavi-equipped vehicles to identify routes that could still be used. (Internavi is a vehicle telematics service offered by Honda to drivers in Japan; it provides mobile access to traffic information and mapping services.) The company monitored highway conditions, disseminated a simple map to identify drivable roads, and then released data in an open-source format online for distribution across social media.[28] Millions benefited from Honda's largesse. But with quintessential Japanese modesty the company never drew attention to its efforts with a creative articulation of the initiative. Its efforts, beautifully consistent with the brand idea "The power of dreams," were heralded only in whispers so may have done little to enhance its brand loyalty.

DEFINING ENGAGEMENT IDEAS

Engagement ideas must be defined in concrete terms rather than as a rearticulation of the brand idea. If we define an idea too broadly, we end up scattered in the sky. Creative executions that are too broad lose focus and disintegrate once they are extended across media. On the flip side, if ideas are defined too narrowly, campaigns quickly become monotonous.

An idea should have three elements: what, how, and an invitation to participate. Defining the idea is difficult and subjective. The balance between consistency and malleability should emerge from debates both within the advertising agency and between agency and client. Once decided, the idea should be written down to ensure that it is larger than any single execution.

What. Some ideas use a long-term iconic device to epitomize the creative spirit of the brand. These devices are tangible brand assets, usually "critters" or mascots. Marlboro Country would not be the same without the Marlboro cowboy, while the "Singapore girl" embodies the gracious hospitality of Singapore Airlines. For decades

Tony the Tiger, of Kellogg's Frosted Flakes fame, has encouraged children to "Show 'em what you can do! Bring out the tiger in you!" The Pillsbury Doughboy—aka Poppin' Fresh—jumped out of ovens between 1964 and 2004. Since 1963 Ronald McDonald has taken children through the Golden Arches. It is important to note that not every engagement idea has a what. In fact most do not. Some advertising experts consider them old-fashioned, even cheesy, although Old Spice's "real man" might beg to differ. Personally I think "whats" are underused because, at the very least, they provide visual consistency, a critical element in a fractionated media universe.

How. This is the *drama* of the engagement idea. Hows are creative elements—structure, shape, tone, and concrete story elements—that make each execution true to the engagement idea. The first step in defining the how is listening to your heart. If something in the idea elicits a smile or tear, identify that element, verbalize it, and write it down. Defining the drama is a challenge even for pros. Judgment is subjective so debate is necessary.

The how usually has more than one component, and it must coalesce into a cohesive idea. Marlboro Country has been an advertising fixture for decades—a lone cowboy on horseback, lassos, sunsets, campfires, wide-open ranges, *allegro con brio* scoring for the soundtrack, and cigarettes. But how does the Marlboro man live and what is he doing? He isn't roaming around the American West but conquering the *Wild* West. If we define the how as, say, "Enjoy the freedom of Marlboro Country," the idea evaporates; it's too loose, too anodyne. Better to say, "Come to Marlboro Country. Tame the Wild West with your rugged individualism." Once those words are verbalized, extending the idea becomes easier.

The "irresistibly attractive" brand idea for Axe, the Unilever deodorant, has resulted in many successful executions. But the best of these executions boast an unexpected juxtaposition. The guys are not ordinary, they are supernerds, while the women are not merely pretty but drop-dead gorgeous. Articulate the how to capture the drama: "Experience the Axe Effect. Even geeky guys become irresistible to the most stunning goddess."

Some creative executions don't have a how and therefore aren't ideas. The "Absolut ____" vodka ads ran for decades. They integrated the brand's famous bottle in a series of print ads—Absolut Beijing, Absolut December 24, Absolut Christmas, Absolut Future, Absolut @#$$!!—to reinforce iconic ubiquity. But there was no idea. This long-running campaign was purely a series of graphic treatments, ill-suited for the engagement era and probably why Absolut introduced a three-dimensional engagement idea, "In an Absolut world," in 2007.

The invitation. The definition of an engagement idea should trigger participation that eventually leads to sales, and the range of options here is infinite. However, consumers should be invited to play with, respond to, or dive into an idea. Consumers must be asked to "come to" Marlboro country rather than admire it. The "Axe Effect" should be tried, rather than believed. A small Thai beer, Cheers, had a lovely idea crafted to increase consumption frequency: "Cheers! Let even the smallest fortune unleash a tidal wave of celebration."

Idea definition and creative use of media. As the examples on the following page illustrate, sharp definition of engagement ideas can inspire creative use of media, even a marriage of idea and media. Ideas form in unexpected ways. This is true for both conventional vehicles and ambient media—nontraditional out-of-home advertising that can be found anywhere and everywhere—that could never be considered without defining the idea.

USELESS BUZZWORDS

A few marketing expressions have passed their sell-by dates and, in my opinion, should be retired. They are no longer appropriate in an era of making brand ideas central and of media neutrality.

Brand	Category	Definition of Engagement Idea	Creative Use of Media
Nike (Hong Kong)	Marathon	"Life is a race"	Track lines placed on the subway floor
Ariel (India)	Detergent	"Stain removal so powerful, you can practically see it disappear before your eyes"	Three consecutive outdoor billboards placed along a highway. As cars drive by, the stain disappears
Saridon (China)	Pain relief	"For when pain is so strong, it feels like your head is splitting open"	A sticker of a head silhouette placed on random cracks on a wall
Monster.com (Hong Kong)	Job search website	"Don't get 'stuck' in the wrong job" (a Cantonese play on words that implies mismatch)	Street actors doing inappropriate tasks (for example, a race car driver pulling a rickshaw, an air traffic controller ushering movie patrons)
The North Face (Korea)	Outdoor apparel	"Explore Seoul. Discover adventure in unexpected corners"	Small stickers of rock climbers placed on cracks in brick walls and ledges of stone walls
Economist (UK)	Newspaper	"The 'key' to unlock your future success"	Business hotel key cards designed as a red-and-white Economist logo with the outline of an old-style keyhole in the middle
Special K (UK)	Weight-loss cereal	"Change your lines"	Straight parking space lines redrawn as curves
KIT KAT (South Africa)	Chocolate bar	"Take a break from real world tribulations"	Newspaper ad with the KIT KAT brand and its tagline, "Have a break, have a KIT KAT," in the center of an otherwise blank page

Nestle Polo's engagement idea, "a blast of winter refreshment," inspired invention of a new medium, the "Polo Snow Stamp." It was quickly created during a freak 2010 London snow storm.

Polo (UK)	Mint candy	"The flavor of winter freshness"	A stamp in the shape of a Polo mint deployed in snowfields around London after a freak storm

Traditional media. Mass media are not traditional. Nor are they old-fashioned or classic; they are timeless. Mass media have been and always will be invaluable for message consistency and awareness. Internet advertising rarely reaches broad audiences, unless its distribution is paid for. Witness the following results, for major brands:

- Burberry has only one commercial that has attracted more than one million views.
- Rolex commercials have never exceeded 250,000 views.
- Budweiser's YouTube channel displays 37 commercials, but none has exceeded one million views.
- Only five Nike ads have achieved more than one million views.

Digital and mass media are complementary. Mass media define the brand idea, while new media deepen engagement. Both are here to stay.

360-degree branding. This term, originated by the WPP group advertising agency Ogilvy & Mather, was born in the late 1990s, shortly after the digital big bang. As media options exploded, Ogilvy stressed "image consistency" at all touch points: "We want to create attention-getting messages that make a promise consistent and true to the brand's image and identity. And guiding actions, both big and small, that deliver on that brand promise. To every audience that brand has. At every brand intersection point. At all times." Today technology personalizes communications, so the advertising industry should avoid terms that smack of Big Brother. More fundamentally communications must unify top-down advertising with bottom-up consumer advocacy, the latter frequently facilitated by new technology. The 360-degree philosophy, like a donut, has a hole in the middle. The gravitational force of ideas—brand ideas and engagement ideas—forges conceptual order from chaos. When advertisers forsake conceptual craftsmanship, they are lost in a sea of bits and bytes. So the industry should reinforce the importance of conceptual unity by referring to good communications as ideacentric or media neutral.

Above- and below-the-line creative executions. These terms are not common in the United States but are widely used elsewhere. In the United States "above-the-line" is called mass media advertising. Historically agencies earned commissions for placing television and print creative executions. "Below-the-line" is called in-store collateral, and agencies use a rate card to charge for this type of material.

Around the world above-the-line creative execution typically is associated with image building. Below-the-line companies, sometimes denigrated as "bucket shops," have been regarded as poor cousins, their work scrappier and designed to trigger sales. It is time to end the industry's class divide. Above- and-below-the-line advertising are not mutually exclusive, and technology reshapes engagement with all media. Television commercials can be interactive; outdoor billboards will, sooner rather than later, be three dimensional; and point-of-sale merchandising should deepen brand engagement. Digital media such as Bluetooth, radio frequency identification, quick response codes, holographic displays, and interactive projection technology can deliver an immersive multisensory experience that both builds image and rings the cash register. Mass and one-on-one media must strengthen equity and sales. They are yin and yang, complementary and distinct, and the power of ideas should unify them.

The key visual. Clients often ask agencies to produce a key visual—that is, an illustration that encapsulates an idea and appears across a broad range of media. When this happens, the client-agency relationship is shallow. Creative execution does not appear *on* media; ideas live *through* media, and consumers engage different media in different ways. Executions should be tailored for each interaction. Creative assets can be deployed across an array of places and spaces, but those assets should be assembled differently for every engagement opportunity.

A few years ago JWT's Beijing team produced a lovely engagement idea for Nestlé ice cream. We created a "snow angel"—sexy, beautifully photogenic—and her "delicious kiss transported you to a land of magical indulgence." Each product variant corresponded to a different world. Films, including a music video, were broadcast on television and online to popular acclaim. However, even though the snow angel's image appeared on shelf talkers, refrigerator cases, bunting, and outdoor billboards, we failed to create a character that seduced. She should have engaged but instead remained aloof. She also failed to sell. It is probably not a coincidence that, in China, we no longer handle Nestlé ice cream.

TVC (television commercial). Despite the continuing importance of broadcast advertising, this phrase smacks of conventional thinking for industry insiders. Advertising agencies should say "filmic expression" instead—and then specify the medium on which it will be viewed or engaged. Screens of all shapes and sizes proliferate. In sports arenas they are more than 200 feet long. Samsung's UHDTV has a 110-inch screen, which is described as "like looking out of a window." Screens also have shrunk—on gaming consoles, mobile phones, and, imminently, watches. Screens will assume new forms, with Google Glass probably just the tip of the iceberg. Some will be interactive, swiped with an index figure or perhaps manipulated with our minds; others will be passive. The character of each screen is different: large televisions are authoritative; computers, at least during working hours, are professorial; mobile phone screens are intimate.

Most filmic expressions are broadcast and all tell stories, but they should be tailored to the dimensions of the screen on which they appear. Clients who tell advertising agencies to "make a TVC" are implicitly requesting old-school thinking. Filmic expressions broadcast on television are meticulously constructed and usually, but not always, appear in 15- or 30-second versions. Internet films, on the other hand, can be any length because online engagement is more active and involved. Online films can even be episodic, such as "Bring Happiness Home," the ten-minute minimovie PepsiCo released as part of its 2012 Chinese New Year Internet extravaganza. It was viewed more than a billion times.[29]

It is worth noting that establishing broad awareness with preroll online videos is not inexpensive. Although online ads have narrower targets than television advertising, online ads are almost as expensive on a cost-per-thousand basis.

CONCLUSION

Engagement ideas are creative expressions of the brand idea. They can be short term, long term, promotional, or thematic, but they must always invite participation—that is, behavior that leads, directly or indirectly, to sales. A brand can have one unifying engagement idea or several different ones, so long as they are all reflections of the brand idea, the long-term relationship between consumer and brand. In an era of consumer empowerment and digital liberation, creative execution must strengthen the intimacy between consumer and brand. If ideas invite consumers to opt in, the opportunity for advocacy, or active recommendation, grows. Three levels of passion enhance the odds of sparking a dynamic interaction between idea and consumer: me, we, and the world. Finally, engagement ideas should be defined to ensure consistency across a fractionated media landscape. A sharply defined idea also stimulates use of media, both conventional and those that wouldn't be considered without the idea, in more creative ways. Media and creative execution achieve a symbiotic relationship.

six

engagement planning

Once marketers have channeled a brand idea into an engagement idea, they must devise an engagement plan—a framework for weaving a brand through the fabric of consumers' lives to change consumers' behavior in a way that increases likelihood of purchase and loyalty. This approach is rooted in conventional media planning, yet digital technology has made media planning throughout a "shopping journey" anything but conventional. New platforms can enhance the intimacy between consumer and brand, prompting a reassessment of the placement of creative ideas. However, the divide between traditional and digital media is misleading; use of both is necessary to optimize engagement.

During a 2014 episode of *Mad Men,* a television series about the advertising world of the 1960s, the seventh season's starchy antagonist Jim Cutler gleefully predicts a day when emotion-led creativity, the pursuit of the show's romantic antihero Don Draper, will be an afterthought: "I know what this company should look like," he insists. "Computer services, media buys pinpointed with surgical accuracy. We can offer these services beyond our clients. It's the agency of the future."

Many believe Cutler's dystopian vision has become reality. On some levels no area of marketing is more affected by the digital revolution than the media scene, for two reasons. First, Big Data have the potential to revolutionize media buying. Irwin Gotlieb, chair of GroupM, the media arm of the communications holding company WPP, foresees a day when it will be possible to construct profiles of individual consumers by aggregating their visits to various digital platforms. The media agency will be in a position to quantify the buying potential of discrete Internet users based on previous purchase histories. It could then buy media from vendors at a lower price than the value of the space to manufacturers and make a profit on the difference. And all this happens in real time.

Second, there are now many more media than during the analog era and this has altered the balance of power between established and new media players. Twenty years ago the options were television, print, and radio. Today Facebook and Twitter are only the tip of a digital iceberg. In 2013 Publicis Group and Omnicom, the world's second- and third-largest communications holding companies, respectively, announced a historic bid to orchestrate "merger of equals" to create a behemoth approximately 50 percent bigger than WPP, the industry's number one. Some analysts saw the move as a defensive play against the likes of Google, a media giant in its own right with the financial heft to gobble up old-line holding companies. The world has evolved—and the structure of the communications industry will continue to change. (In the end, the Publicis-Omnicom marriage was called off. Culture clash, tax regime complications, and lack of a clear value proposition were the reasons most often cited to explain the break up.)[1]

In many ways, though, the essentials are the same. Consumers' decision-making process has not changed, at least not fundamentally. Neither have the principles of how marketers should connect

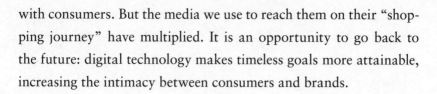

with consumers. But the media we use to reach them on their "shopping journey" have multiplied. It is an opportunity to go back to the future: digital technology makes timeless goals more attainable, increasing the intimacy between consumers and brands.

INTIMACY

Marketers have always sought to forge deep connections with consumers, and these efforts can be low tech. In China, for example, marketers spend hundreds of millions of dollars on in-store promoters. They deploy tens of thousands of "brand ambassadors" across thousands of retail outlets in hundreds of cities to engage consumers close to the point of purchase. The goal: present a human face to shoppers unfamiliar with the new products that confront them each time they enter a supermarket. In 2006 JWT and WPP purchased a majority share in Always, the largest in-store promoter management and field-marketing network in China—the ability to manage resources on a broad scale is a huge competitive advantage across the country's untamed brandscape.

New technology, however, facilitates the one-on-one connection between consumers and brands; digital media are inherently more personal. In 2013 Post Visual, a leading Korean digital creative agency, produced a billboard that allowed consumers to reach out and touch a sports idol. When people pressed their hands against the window of a Nike store, a digital image of the Olympic figure-skating champion Yuna Kim slid into the foreground. She raised her palm to touch theirs and asked, "Do you feel the passion through my fingers? It's like electricity going through my body, like floating in space." The connection was fleeting but vivid, personalizing the rush of "Just do it" release.

Another Post Visual example is the Huggies "Babbling Translator." The 2011 online campaign was a hit with parents who could upload videos of their babies prattling away, and the "Huggies

Babbling Lab" would translate the chatter into loving messages. Through technology Kimberly-Clark bridged the eternal gap between curious parents and speechless infants.

Gome, a leading consumer electronics retailer in China, used technology to transform white goods into warm emotion. Young Chinese buy their parents gifts to show respect during Lunar New Year, so winter is the best selling season for household appliances. However, China is a Confucian culture that discourages self-expression, so few say "I love you." Gome launched an in-store platform for shoppers to tell their parents how they feel without the awkwardness of a face-to-face exchange. Gome invited customers to enter a "Love Delivery Box" booth and record a message on a light sensor chip that then was inserted in an appliance box as an audio greeting card. When the parents opened their present, they heard heartfelt words, and presumably tears flowed.

Intimate connections can, of course, cross the online and offline divide. (The industry's newest buzzword is O2O, or online to offline.) Unilever's Lynx deodorant, known globally as Axe, executed one of the most celebrated campaigns of recent years in Australia. In 2005 the brand presented consumers with a faux airline, the idea underpinned by "irresistible attraction" and with the tagline "Get on. Get off." Lynx confronted perceptions that its product was "something my little brother would use" by ramping up the eroticism and building a multimedia campaign linked to a postcollegiate rite of passage: a young man's first trip abroad. The campaign rebranded a plane as the LynxJet. Risqué television and print work created broad awareness of the campaign, while videos featuring mud wrestling and pillow fights generated online buzz. Provocative signage confronted travelers at actual airline check-in counters. Faux *Mad Men*–era flight attendants, who became walking billboards, provided live "service sampling." On the streets of Australian cities, bevies of LynxJet "Mostesses" titillated passers-by with free massage coupons to encourage men to visit a campaign microsite. These on-the-ground activities resulted in more than 25,000 memberships in the Mile High Club, an online loyalty program. Traditional airline sites carried pseudo-interviews with Mostesses. The Lynx team also created a mock booking system and staged a Mostess recruitment drive on job search websites.

BEHAVIORAL CHANGE AND THE CONSUMER ENGAGEMENT SYSTEM

Participation in, or intimacy with, an engagement idea is not an end in itself. Through the creative platform, we must encourage a person to *do* something that leads to sales—learn more, buy more, use more, or tell (advocate) more. As we will now discuss at some length, the process of buying a product is often complex, the culmination of several stages that progress from awareness generation to information search to purchase and, hopefully, to repeat purchase. Each creative expression of the brand idea should be conceived with a specific behavioral objective in mind.

The success of creative is measured by its effectiveness in changing behavior through this shopper journey. And the range of actions communications can elicit varies depending on the strategic challenges a brand faces. Creative can stimulate trial of a product; encourage switching from one brand to another; increase frequency of consumption; trigger a search for more information; lift repeat purchase rates and reward loyalty; induce cross-category purchase between, say, shampoo and conditioners or tea and biscuits; inspire recommendations among friends; solicit participation in promotional activity; or incentivize upgrades to higher price tiers. Changing purchase behavior is obviously a multifaceted undertaking. Unless activities spring from a distinct brand idea and cogent engagement ideas, consumers will tune out.

During the 1970s Stephen King, the legendary J. Walter Thompson strategic planner, articulated a model of how consumers make purchasing decisions, one that remains powerful today. He dubbed it the "consumer buying cycle," a framework of six phases that constitute a consumer's journey: trigger, consideration, comparison, preference, purchase, and experience. As consumers move through these phases, their motivations vary; so should the ways marketers communicate. I have rechristened King's "buying cycle" an "engagement system." The change in nomenclature might seem cosmetic, but it's an important reminder that every point of the journey presents an opportunity to connect with—or engage—consumers. This is done through engagement ideas, creative expressions of the brand idea that invite participation. As we explore each stage in detail, we should keep three overarching points in mind:

- Each engagement system is different. They vary according to product category. High-involvement products are expensive. Decisions to purchase are complex and require a broad range of media. Consumers consciously pass through each phase with deliberation, although in a nonlinear manner as they reconsider their options. Low-involvement products have simpler purchase cycles, and shoppers frequently skip phases altogether.
- The early phases of the engagement system shape perceptions and therefore rely on mass media, albeit not exclusively. The later phases encourage purchase and rely more on one-on-one communications.
- Marketers deploy both old and new media at each stage. The media-planning process should be holistic; the perceived divide between traditional and digital vehicles is a false distinction.

High- Versus Low-Involvement Categories

No two engagement systems are identical, and each consumer's journey is unique. However, some generalizations are valid. The journeys of consumers shopping in high-involvement categories are more complex than in low-involvement ones. High-involvement categories are more important to consumers because they play a more significant role in life, which means marketers can charge higher prices relative to cost of goods. No matter how many brands of detergent boast a powerful ability to remove stains, consumers who are parents will take less care in selecting laundry powder than they will a school for their children. They will also tap a broader range of media in making the school decision. Products exist along a low- to high-involvement *continuum*. Low-involvement products can never become high-involvement ones—a cookie will never be as important as a car—but the goal of all marketing is to nudge the perceptions of a brand from a relatively lower to relatively higher point. This is done with effective positioning, imbuing functional attributes with emotional meaning. When "shining hair" evolves into "silky hair that turns heads," or "soft skin" is elevated to "soft skin he loves to touch," the wording strengthens the relationship between consumer and brand. Then manufacturers have the luxury of raising prices and therefore profit margins.

Broadly speaking, there are three types of high-involvement products: ego and identity, life advancement, and life-or-death items. These groupings are not mutually exclusive. Expensive cars both project status and open doors, particularly in emerging markets, where online car clubs are popular. Premium whiskies both suggest sophistication and lubricate business transactions.

Ego and identity goods are all about projecting status. No matter their location or culture, people crave external acknowledgment of their position in the social hierarchy. In some cultures, however, status is important. In Asia face transcends recognition and is social currency, the fuel for upward advancement. That is why Asians are the world's most avid buyers of luxury items, despite their relatively modest incomes. Even before license plate fees are considered, the cost of a mid-tier car such as Volkswagen's Golf is approximately $25,000.[2] This is approximately four times the average yearly disposable income of a resident of Shanghai or Beijing, two of China's wealthiest cities.[3] Average Chinese consumers spend lavishly on their first car because it announces their arrival in the ranks of the middle class. McKinsey & Company predicts that China could overtake the United States as the world's largest market for luxury cars by 2016,[4] despite a per capita income level approximately 20 percent of America's. In Hong Kong all top ten cars are high-end brands. Real estate is also a surrogate indicator of status. In capitals across Asia the names of apartment buildings project nobility. In Shanghai, Rich Gate offers the most expensive units in Puxi, the city's historic area, but buyers could also choose to live in Peacock Dynasty or the Gathering of All Heroes Under Heaven. The size of the diamond in their engagement ring signals who has prospects as a power couple. Activities can also be high involvement. Travel, for example, is not only experiential; exotic destinations signal worldliness, particularly in newly affluent societies. Adults in Beijing take art appreciation classes, studying everything from calligraphy to Picasso in an effort to project refinement, exude an air of intellectuality, and minimize perceptions of them as one-dimensional materialists.

Life advancement products help people realize their goals. In competitive societies they are weapons of success or investments that yield dividends. In a global knowledge-based economy, a "brand name" education is a ticket to the top and not just for Westerners. An Ivy League diploma is considered both badge and passport. When I arrived at work one morning in Shanghai, I found an ambitious woman in tears because her six-year-old daughter had failed a piano test. I asked whether her daughter enjoyed piano. She said no. I asked if she had talent. "No," the woman continued, but "if she doesn't learn structure and discipline now, she will never get into Harvard!" Since the mid-2000s US colleges and universities have seen a 43 percent increase in the number of international students, with more than 800,000 enrolled since 2013. In a recent episode of the popular sitcom *Modern Family,* the father, Phil, encourages

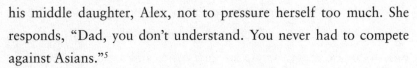

his middle daughter, Alex, not to pressure herself too much. She responds, "Dad, you don't understand. You never had to compete against Asians."[5]

The definition of *life advancement* depends on the cultural context. The advice of a financial consultant with a record for providing good information commands a premium anywhere. But people in Western countries place a higher value on retirement savings plans than do people in Confucian societies, where older parents prefer—and expect—to live with their children.

The third category of high-involvement goods, life and death purchases, is not influenced by culture. Everywhere in the world self-employed individuals carefully consider health-care programs. Expectant parents invest time in researching hospitals. Older individuals with families take life insurance seriously.

Low-involvement products are simple. They don't involve risk and are usually inexpensive; the consequences of making a wrong choice are not important. Most fast-moving consumer goods are low involvement; toilet paper and soap are extremely low involvement. Few women actively search for information about different brands of shampoo, although some offer more beauty benefits than others. For the most part people receive information passively about low-involvement products. "Lean back" media such as television, online videos, and print ads are critical for their campaigns. Digital platforms are useful but rarely dominate.

At least in some cases cultural factors affect consumers' involvement in items they use daily. In the United States and Europe, for example, expensive bathroom tissue is a significant segment of the market. Premium variants—quadruple-ply, aloe injection, and quilted finish—sell well. Asians consider such comfort benefits to be frivolous. They are less motivated than Westerners by internal or sensorial benefits, or at least Asians are not as willing to pay for them. Satisfaction, both physical and emotional, is a means to an end rather than an end in itself.

The lowest-involvement products are impulse purchases. These items don't even make it onto a shopping list. Most fulfill sensorial urges—for example, beverages, fast food, and ice cream, but they can also be eye candy, such as inexpensive toys, playful accessories, and inexpensive fashion items; they benefit from sophisticated point-of-sale media, both digital and traditional, to arouse desire. Nestlé, a company that sells a wide variety of impulse products, allocates more than 50 percent of its advertising budget to point-of-sale materials to create awareness outside the store, whet shoppers' appetite as they enter, and highlight Nestlé options near the shelf or freezer.

Beginning, Middle, End, Repeat

The early phases of the engagement system are unstructured. They focus on creating awareness of a need in life and, broadly speaking, the different ways to address that need. This happens at the category, not brand, level. The middle phases involve assessing strengths and weaknesses of competing brands and providing consumers with incentives to purchase, while the final phase reinforces postpurchase satisfaction and repeat purchase. W. Edwards Deming, the famed American statistician and lionized adviser to Japanese corporations during the postwar period, noted long ago, "Profit in business comes from repeat customers, customers that boast about your product or service, and that bring friends with them." His words ring true today: the most profitable customer is a loyal customer.

The relative importance of media type varies according to the phase of the engagement system. The three dimensions for classifying media, which are not mutually exclusive, are:

- "Lean back" versus "lean in," or passively versus actively received, media. Lean-in media *inherently* encourage consumers to engage in a brand experience, whereas lean-back media do not.
- Mass media versus one-to-one, or broadcast versus direct, media.

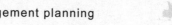

- Traditional versus new, or nondigital versus digital, media.

Lean-back, mass, and traditional media should dominate phases in which marketers seek to forge perceptions in a broad population of consumers. Television—with its sound, color, movement, and ability to break through clutter—is an indispensable tool in new markets where consumers are disoriented from an explosion of category offerings. Even in the United States, the 30-second television commercial will continue to rule despite the proliferation of smartphones and other digital devices. Manufacturers did not spend $67 billion on broadcast advertising in 2013 for sentimental reasons. Print, both magazines and newspapers, also remains indispensible for providing consumers with details that support a brand's main message.

On the other hand, as consumers move toward purchase, "lean in"—direct and digital media—should dominate. These media provide more opportunity for engagement—that is, direct interaction with a brand idea and its creative expression. Marketers have more opportunity to trigger behavioral change and increase the probability the consumer will buy a product. Advertising can encourage a limitless range of actions—from clicking through a banner ad and spending more time on a microsite to increasing consumers' frequency of washing their hair; the arsenal of tools marketers can deploy to encourage certain behavior is broad. Marketers also can use passive and analog media to trigger specific behavior during later phases—for example, by using stunning "product beauty shots" and other point-of-sale material to stimulate trial.

Digital and Traditional Media: Complementary Tools

TechCrunch.com, a leading technology news provider, keeps a close eye on how media consumption is evolving. The website shrewdly sums up the current state of play:

If you look at 2012, the combined ad spend for newspapers and magazines still outweighed that of Internet spend. If you add in radio, by 2015 they will still outweigh Internet spend. And while we talk about the rise of Internet video and streaming services like Netflix that bypass commercials, television advertising is still by far the biggest piece of the pie—40 percent in 2012, and declining by a mere half [of] a percentage point by 2015. That says a lot about why Twitter is focusing so much attention on how it plans to grow its advertising and marketing services in tandem with the TV industry.[6]

Old and new media not only will coexist but also will holistically complement each other. This is true at every stage of the engagement system, as the simple chart that follows suggests. Television and online video can generate brand awareness; Twitter feeds and print ads both facilitate product differentiation. Offline "road shows"—that is, traveling exhibitions—and online apps, games, and other creative engagement platforms can deepen brand experience. Both product review websites and *Consumer Reports* enable shoppers to compare and contrast competitors' offerings. Laminated VIP cards, snail mail loyalty clubs, or online customer relationship management programs can reinforce repeat purchases. Direct marketing—that is, maximizing an individual's contribution to profit over time—is not a new tool. In fact my first job was in the circulation department at *Time Magazine,* then at the leading edge of direct response advertising.

When will the death knell toll for traditional advertising? Never. But the continued rise of digital platforms is also inexorable. Digital platforms cannot compete with mass media in reaching tens of millions of people efficiently, at least on a cost per thousand basis; traditional vehicles can't compete with new media in deepening brand experience. New technology allows consumers to dive into an idea, play with it, debate it, share it. Digital allows flat ads to blossom into multidimensional experiences.

Phase	Role	Traditional media examples	New media examples
Trigger	Providing a real-world stimulus that raises awareness of unmet needs	N/A	N/A
Consideration	Reviewing options that can address a need, culminating in a decision to enter a product category	Mass-market television, general audience print	Banner ads, viral video, Facebook fan pages, social content and reviews, apps
Comparison	Reviewing information within a category	Consumer Reports, magazines	Corporate websites, product review sites (e.g., Yelp, Angie's List, E-pinions)
Preference	Choosing a brand based on perceived brand discriminators	Niche/cable television channels, special interest print; in-store product demonstrations	Microsites and online tools, Twitter feeds
Purchase	Paying for a product	In-store shelf-talkers	E-commerce, point-of-sale quick response codes or Bluetooth transmissions
Experience	Determining the likelihood of repeat purchase according to the degree of brand satisfaction	Direct-mail loyalty clubs	Online clubs, lifestyle communities, wearable technology

In reviewing the engagement system and the type of communication that is relevant at each stage, it is worth reiterating two points: consistency is critical, and consumers' every exposure with a brand is an opportunity for engagement. Each media exposure should be a manifestation of an engagement idea, the creative expression of the brand that invites participation.

Trigger

The trigger is the moment of awareness of an unmet need. Marketing activity rarely stimulates whatever happens outside the commercial domain. In general, marketers do not create needs—they create products that address them.

The range of triggers is broad, so categorization is difficult. Triggers can be personal habits. The buzzing of an alarm clock triggers the need to wake up and become alert. From shower massages to athletic shoes, many products are positioned as an energizing start to the day. In coffee-drinking cultures the brand that owns the morning is usually a dominant player. Since 1984, the American brand Folgers has promoted itself as "the best part of waking up." Over the years various recording artists, including Randy Travis and Aretha Franklin, have sung its jingle which is now part of popular culture.

Triggers can be physical changes to the body, often the result of aging or major life events. Noticing thinning hair triggers baldness avoidance, not to mention existential panic, in young men. When a 35-year-old woman spots her first wrinkle, she may dream of eternal youth. Landing an overseas job triggers the need to assimilate into a foreign culture. Getting married triggers many needs, from finding a place to live to financial planning. A baby also brings new needs, including finding a pediatrician, planning for the child's education, and redecorating.

The introduction of major product innovations requires deep understanding of triggers—marketers must become cultural anthropologists. In 1972 McDonald's added the Egg McMuffin to its menu, essentially creating breakfast on the go. The company must have carefully researched what its customers needed and then shaped the McDonald's breakfast experience accordingly. If the primary motivators for buying a fast-food breakfast were emotional—say, "a warm-up for working warriors"—sit-down fare would have dominated its menu. Clearly this was not the case. The Egg McMuffin, a sandwich, could be consumed while driving. The increasing prevalence of two-income families had elevated the importance of convenience in resolving a tension between good food and fast pace. By 1987 one-quarter of morning meals eaten outside the home in the United States were at McDonald's. As of 2013 breakfast fare accounted for 15 percent of the company's global revenue.[7]

The Sony Corporation invented music on the go. In 1979 it introduced a 14-ounce blue-and-silver portable music player with chunky buttons and a leather case—a streamlined design at the time. It also had a second earphone jack so two people could listen at the same time. Sony could have described the product as offering "new dimensions of privacy" or "life's soundtrack," and Sony's US division actually wanted to call it the Disco Jogger. Akio Morita, Sony's founder, wisely resisted, partially for fear of alienating older consumers. In the United States the product was originally named Soundabout and eventually was dubbed the Walkman. Sony, in quintessential Japanese fashion, had meticulously identified the triggers of needing stress relief away from home and relief from the fatigue caused by lugging bulkier cassette players. The Walkman satisfied both with its portability and headphone-optimized sound system. The Walkman opened up new horizons of personal entertainment, ones that would not have been possible without a grasp of environmental triggers.

It is worth repeating that marketers, contrary to popular perception, cannot fundamentally affect macrotrends that impact our lives both individually and collectively. But marketers can profit from these trends, harnessing waves of change to shape product offerings and communications. Given the rate at which technology now creates new needs, marketers must avoid the temptation to overly invest in quantitative—that is, observational—research at the expense of qualitative insight. We must grab every opportunity to immerse ourselves in the actual lives of consumers.

Consideration

Once consumers' awareness of a need has been triggered, they move into the "consideration phase," a review of potential product categories to meet the unmet need. Marketers sometimes refer to this consideration set as the "frame of reference," the various categories competing against one other, implicitly or explicitly. A young professional under intense pressure at work needs stress release. She has several options: go on vacation, choosing between luxurious Paris or the sun-drenched Caribbean; visit a spa; soak in a home Jacuzzi; buy a more comfortable bed; see a psychologist; indulge in a massage; drink a health tonic, and so on. A professional Shanghainese woman rides her bicycle to work and gets caught in the rain. She needs to stay dry. To accomplish that, she can invest in a new car; hire a taxi service; buy a bigger umbrella; rent an apartment closer to her office; or use a headhunter to help her find a job closer to home. Triggered needs can be simple, but the ways of satisfying them are broad.

Frames of reference constantly evolve because of innovation, which is disruptive. In the 1990s the music industry phased out the single, leaving consumers with no means to purchase individual songs. Illegal peer-to-peer file-sharing technologies initially filled this market, followed by online retailers such as iTunes and Amazon.com. This "low-cost" disruption eventually undermined the sales of physical high-cost CDs. More recently websites such as airbnb.com compete with boutique hotels to an extent few would have predicted five years ago. Mobile payment apps compete with credit cards. In China social networks such as WeChat and search engines such as Baidu sell financial services that compete directly with products offered by state-owned banks.

Innovation can reshape the competitive landscape in counterintuitive ways. Few clichés are sadder than the middle-aged man driving a hot red Porsche convertible. Men of a certain age take stock of their lives, look to the sky, ask, "Is this it?" and feel the need to relive the vigor of their earlier years. Historically the answer to a midlife crisis was a sports car. Now there is another way, one that generates more than $2 billion in sales in the United States alone. It's sildenafil citrate, popularly known as Viagra. Reframing the competitive landscape reveals a surprising truth: Viagra competes with cars. Between 2008 and 2012 the average age of sports car buyers increased by three years to 51, and the median age of a Corvette driver is now 60 plus. It is virtually impossible to draw a direct correlation between age of driver and the introduction of Viagra, but the frame of reference for middle-aged men looking for a kick has broadened in unexpected ways.

During the consideration phase marketers' media choices should reflect that consumers are at only the preliminary stage of assessing their options. Messages should not require major thought but should simply raise awareness of a brand's basic role in life. Passive vehicles such as television, online video, print, outdoor billboards, and website banner ads are appropriate. Marketers should seed these messages in locations where solutions are salient and consumers open to rethinking their frames of reference. Ratan Malli, director of strategic planning at JWT Asia Pacific, calls these "receptivity zones" and recommends use of "ambient media"—that is, placement that is surprising in real-world environments. Examples could include:

- Mouthwash trial packets placed at the bottom of paper cups in business conference rooms with a warning, "Don't let bad breath spoil first impressions"
- Whitening detergent in office elevators exhorting, "Time to rise and shine"
- Auto advertising, visible to crowded subway straphangers, that promises "sitting room only"
- Weight-reduction cereal ads on department store changing-room mirrors urging women to "alter your measurements"

Comparison

After the consumer has selected a category to resolve the trigger, the "comparison phase" begins. This phase is a review of information about different brand options within a category. Consumers want open-ended information: design, taste, provenance, technological innovation, sustainability, brand values, price, size, endorsers, and so on.

Sometimes the consumer will actively engage in comparison research—high-involvement categories such as purchasing a new car or moving to a new house require lots of comparison shopping. But research for a low-involvement product such as shampoo is more passive. The former involves a conscious decision to become more knowledgeable about a category because brand choice is important. The media the consumer is likely to use are "lean in"—active destinations, including, but not limited to, corporate websites, social networks, and product review sites such as Angie's List or Yelp.com. Search engines have become a vital link connecting consumers seeking information and businesses and brands providing information. Search marketing is a crucial discipline for advertisers. According to GroupM, the media buying and planning holding company, 60 percent of consumers use engines such as Google, Bing, and Yahoo! to initiate their comparison research, and this "represents a definite opportunity for advertising to capture the expressed intent by creating engagement in these channels in order to best position themselves for purchase."[8] Dedicated comparison websites are also rapidly emerging to aid consumers during the comparison phase.

Sources of comparative information are almost limitless and vary greatly depending on the product category. People looking for information about cars, for example, might glean impressions from *Consumer Reports* magazine, corporate websites, peer review sites, social networks, test drives, dealership events, and model-specific brochures. Broadcast media and newspaper ads—"lean-back" media—are also influential.

The digital domain is obviously critical during this phase, but many marketers seem flummoxed as to which platforms suit which categories. As a general rule marketers have three ways to digitally engage consumers with brands:

- Paid distribution guarantees your brand appears online. Paid advertising can include display advertising (banners) or paying to put your content in an existing online destination (content integration), but the biggest form of paid advertising online is search marketing on platforms like Google. According to a recent report by Adobe, a multinational computer software company, search advertising, or search engine marketing, may not be sexy, but it is still "the biggest driver of return on investment."[9] This explains why 48 percent of 2013 digital ad spending was invested in search engine advertising, a highly analytic algorithmic domain—and beyond the purview of this book. Suffice it to say, good creative execution drives search engine optimization.

- Owned sites are online destinations—corporate websites, microsites, Facebook pages, Twitter feeds—where the manufacturer is responsible for the publishing content. Owned sites are cyberstores and an influential representation of the manufacturer's brand. They are either permanent (or "evergreen") destinations that require significant investment to maintain or microsites designed for temporary purposes, including promotions or other short-term campaigns.

- Earned media mentions are user-generated content that appears on social websites and blogs in response to a brand's online and offline activities. These mentions of products are often called e-PR (public relations) and are seen as attractive because of the free exposure but are difficult to spark. Furthermore, comments can be supportive or derogatory.

Consumers visit brands' websites of their own volition. They expect up-to-date information, images, videos, and descriptions of all parts of the product offering. They value sites that make it easy to compare and find the most important information they need. These sites are expensive, costing perhaps millions of dollars per year to design and maintain. But they are extremely important in influencing the purchase of high-involvement consumer goods such as audiovisual equipment, cars, travel, couture, and financial products. In no particular order, these sites require blog or content management capability, sophisticated graphic design, multimedia functionality, social media and e-commerce capability, and ongoing technical maintenance. Smart platforms for managing digital content and license fees for software to track and analyze visitor data cost hundreds of thousands of dollars. Costs for hosting websites securely and coping with high visitor traffic from multiple countries can quickly add up to an annual investment of six figures. Upgrades to or investment in apps are in the same range.

Most lower-involvement goods cannot count on consumers' actively choosing to visit their sites. Few would spontaneously visit KIT KAT Break World or the Head & Shoulders Confidence Zone—the gravitational pull of even these strong brands just isn't powerful enough to justify the investment required for a complex evergreen site. This is where a strong brand idea with relevant engagement hooks can drive consumers' interest—an entertaining video that dramatizes taking a break, brought to you by KIT KAT—or unique content—found through a Google search that leads to the Head and Shoulders website—about how to prevent dandruff.

It is worth nothing that iconic brands, even low-involvement ones, often invest in evergreen websites. Iconic stature is achieved when a brand transcends its category benefits to represent broad, usually universal, cultural values. Pepsi owns youthful liberation, choices of the new generation. But when web surfers visit an iconic evergreen site, they go to experience multidimensional brand immersion, not to search for information or compare. Coca-Cola's site has been dubbed an e-magazine. The Coca-Cola Journey incorporates postings on everything from "52 Songs of Happiness" and "The Importance of Family Dinners" to "My Dog Gus" and a "Pictures of Happiness" photo gallery. "We designed Coca-Cola Journey to be a sharp departure from how companies use their corporate websites," explained Ashley Brown, director of digital communications and social media. "Our corporate site is our most trafficked online property, so we wanted to create an brand experience that would make this incredibly valuable digital real estate work harder for us."[10]

Preference

The "preference phase" occurs as consumers differentiate between brands and subsequently develop partiality for one. The challenge is simple: to ensure a brand is known for something that appeals to the greatest number of people possible. Given the infinite number of attributes of any brand, and the explosion of media to convey information about those attributes, simplifying messages is critical. Brand characteristics—or "reasons to believe"—should lead to the same single-minded benefit. This benefit is the unique brand offer.

Brand differentiation can be functional, rooted in tangible attributes. Until laptops eclipsed desktop computers, Dell was known for customization, Sony for multimedia compatibility, and IBM for reliability. Preference can also be based on the service experience, which is often enhanced by online technology—for example, an airline that makes searching for flights easier or a store whose e-commerce experience makes shopping more user friendly.

Alternatively marketers can distinguish their brands on an emotional level: Chanel is chic, Vivienne Westwood is rebellious, Giorgio Armani is understated, and Versace is glamorous. Many marketers, however, mistakenly assume they must choose between functional and emotional differentiation. Magic occurs when function and emotional attributes are mutually reinforced—when "white teeth" can become "bright smiles" and "smooth hair" can flow into "irresistible softness." Conceptual precision yields powerful brands that touch both head and heart.

To avoid consumer confusion, consistency in communications is imperative. This is particularly true in emerging markets, which are flooded with new products, most of which are unknown commodities. The heuristics of sorting through options to develop preference are complex, the realm of behavioral and cognitive psychology. To reach consumers in the preference phase, the marketer uses practically all media—digital and analog, passive and active, mass and one to one. Allocation of marketing funds across these vehicles depends on the nature of the category, brand familiarity, and business task. But, as I discussed earlier, low-involvement products rely heavily on mass and in-store media. Messages must sink in because consumers do not spend time thinking about them.

As consumers sift through their options, the contours of a brandscape gradually appear. The holy grail for most marketers is occupation of the high ground—or ownership of the category benefit: why most people enter a category in the first place. In the United States, an advanced marketing environment, brands have already captured most high grounds, at least in categories that do not involve information technology and where the competitive field is well established and innovation cycles are less frequent. Budweiser owns male bonding in beer, Haagen-Dazs owns sensuous indulgence in ice cream, and Hallmark owns heartfelt emotion in greeting cards. Owning the category benefit typically results in sustained dominance of market share (until category disruption occurs) and a hefty price premium. In this context all marketers aspire to brand name "verbification." If workers "Xerox the document" on a Ricoh copy machine, the former still enjoys preferential advantage. Documents are "FedExed," not "DHLed," and this makes Federal Express tantamount to "dependable overnight delivery." Google is synonymous with online search, whereas Band-Aids "heal the ouch."

While owning the high ground translates into market dominance, would-be competitors should not resign themselves to undifferentiated follower status. The definition of what constitutes a category is malleable, allowing savvy competitors the opportunity to narrow the classification, refine the market target, and elevate the benefit, perhaps even charging a higher price in the process. For decades IBM personal computers were associated with reliability and enjoyed dominant market share, particularly among businesses. Apple came along in 1998, targeted youthful creative types, designed sleek machines in candy-colored hues, introduced the iMac, and quickly became a stylish trendsetter. Depending on the country, either Colgate or Crest owns "oral care" for toothpaste, but among mature consumers Sensodyne has staked out a premium "sensitive teeth" position. In Asia Rejoice owns "soft and smooth," but Head & Shoulders owns dandruff curative, a therapeutic benefit that commands a higher price. Ecology-minded consumers, meanwhile, go to the Body Shop, now part of the L'Oréal group.

Purchase

The product that people prefer is not necessarily the product they buy. The in-store environment is a bazaar in which hearts and minds can wander, seduced by competitors' promotions, packaging, and sampling. OgilvyAction, an arm of the advertising agency Ogilvy & Mather, conducted global research into unplanned in-store brand switching. According to the study, "Even when shoppers have planned which category they will buy from, the decision on which brand to buy is left until inside the store for 28 percent of shoppers. On top of this, a further 1 in 10 shoppers will switch brands inside the store. . . . Marketers must activate their brands in-store or shoppers will switch."[11]

Marketing to shoppers—known as "shopper marketing" by marketing professionals—and activation are critical. Shopper marketing is a collaborative process for the manufacturer and retailer, which conduct joint marketing planning, based largely on the shopper's journey and intercategory dynamics. The goal is to encourage behavior that results in purchase. Activation brings these plans to life by using prestore, in-store, in-aisle, and postpurchase marketing media. It is important to note that not every activation activity takes place in the store—but all activation must lead to sales. Activation is "last-mile marketing," a science in and of itself.

Effective shopper marketing both reinforces brand equity and enhances the retailer's profit. For example, Procter & Gamble's Gillette installed "men's zones"—aisles specifically tailored for men's grooming products—in partnership with the H-E-B supermarket in Texas. Blue low-rider lights glowed from the floor while speeding cars flashed by on flat-screen TVs. Shoppers could browse more than 530 individual items, with Gillette products featured prominently although not exclusively. The behavioral goal was straightforward: to encourage cross-category purchase between, say, shaving cream and skin moisturizer, and for the consumer to upgrade from lower- to higher-margin products.

It is also important to note that shopper marketing has evolved to address the dynamics of e-commerce, a topic beyond the scope of this book. Suffice it to say, the digital shelf needs to present brands in a way that both encourages shoppers to close the sale and maximizes retailer profitability. Furthermore, regardless of whether brands build their own online stores or partner with retailers such as Amazon and networks like Taobao, brands should design their online presence around a vivid brand idea. Digital real estate need not be chaotic bazaars. Effective "virtual merchandising" streamlines choice.

In bricks-and-mortar stores brands deploy both traditional and new media, as is the case for all engagement stages. Shelf talkers, wobblers, end-of-aisle displays, and in-store television are invaluable tools that pop. They call attention to a new product or offer. However, digital media such as Bluetooth, radio frequency identification, quick response codes, holographic displays, and interactive projection technology are increasingly used for deepening brand engagement close to point of purchase. They can deliver an immersive multisensory experience to drive in-store traffic to the sales register—or they can do more basic things such as provide information. Sephora, a cosmetics brand, uses live Twitter feeds on countertop screens that display live peer-to-peer product reviews, both positive and negative. In a digital world there is nowhere to hide.

Despite the plethora of activation options, a fundamental truth remains: all marketing communication should build long-term brand equity. Every activation effort should be consistent with the brand idea and rooted in an engagement idea. Activation that offers a discount without deepening a preexisting relationship degrades affinity. An end-of-aisle display of inexpensive candy bars merely decreases revenues. In the Philippines Kraft created recipe centers in supermarkets to reinforce its position as "Mom's partner in the kitchen." Consumers were entitled to discounts if they bought three or more items to make a meal; in the process Kraft dominated end-of-aisle displays and gained in-store visibility.

Better still are activation activities with a clear engagement idea. Unilever's Rexona, a deodorant targeted at teenagers, has long positioned itself as "cool protection." In the Philippines the brand stimulated back-to-school sales with its "Funk" campaign. Road shows at malls around the country drew students; to qualify for coupons they rapped the "First Day Funk," a call to raise their arms with confidence and "salute the prof" on the first day of school. Rexona used short text messages to spread the music, lyrics, and promotions, as well as the timing and address of "Funk Fest" concerts, dance competitions, and other live events. After the activation campaign Rexona's share in the Philippines was the highest of any market in the world, with sales revenue increasing more than 25 percent over the previous quarter. Even small activation campaigns can be memorable if they spring from an engagement idea. Philadelphia Cream Cheese, another Kraft brand, had promoters dressed as angels and walking on stilts offering product samples outside British supermarkets. The brand's long-standing idea: "With a creamy taste this heavenly, even an angel like you can't resist."

Experience

The final phase in the consumer engagement system refers to the degree of satisfaction a brand creates among buyers, which in turn determines the likelihood of repeat purchase. Happy customers are loyal customers, and loyal customers are profitable customers.

Most so-called loyalty clubs are not profitable because they offer nothing more than discounts competitors can match. They are un-differentiated. According to Colloquy, a loyalty marketing company, the United States had 2.6 billion loyalty program memberships in 2012, a 27 percent increase since 2010. Its "loyalty census" further revealed the average household belongs to 22 different programs, although fewer than half had been activated. The report noted, "Cookie-cutter programs can confuse and numb consumers. If a consumer joins three programs in a specific retail category, for instance, and all three programs offer the same value proposition, why would that consumer choose a specific outlet for any reasons other than price and convenience?"[12] A 2013 study by Deloitte, a professional services company, highlighted low levels of customer loyalty toward airlines, despite the widespread prevalence of frequent flyer programs. Adam Weissenberg, head of the firm's travel, hospitality, and leisure division, noted, "Airlines should approach any effort to improve loyalty programs as a customized exercise. One size most certainly does not fit all."[13]

A brand generates affinity when its role in life expands over time. Johnny Walker's tagline, "Keep walking," is an invitation to explore new dimensions of personal identity. Red Label sponsors nighttime parties at which young adults cultivate their social selves, while Blue Label holds exclusive "whiskey appreciation summits" at which men extend their professional networks. Apple used to sell elegant computer technology; today it curates a streamlined digital ecosystem. Haier, the largest appliance manufacturer in China, is known as much for 24-hour service as a broad product range. Airlines must lift their product from transportation to comprehensive travel management. Even Bayer's Elevit, a multivitamin tablet consumed by pregnant women, can evolve from nutritional supplement to a holistic prenatal adviser.

Technology enhances the postpurchase experience that brands can deliver to consumers. Real-time marketing platforms can collect data about what consumers have purchased, considered, or reviewed and then respond in a timely way. However, most of these applications are still pretty basic. Personalization feels algorithmic. For example, Amazon keeps customers updated on their shopping orders and then suggests other purchases. Kimberly-Clark delivers written content to moms who buy Huggies diapers; the material is based on a baby's age and offers tips that match a child's development needs at a given point in time.

Media vehicles for generating loyalty must be able to personalize both the message and the offer. As a result loyalty marketing is direct marketing that comprises one-to-one communications, as well as a series of tailored offers and acceptances that leads to purchase. A clever direct mail piece won't cut it. Customer relationship management (CRM) is a long-term dialog between manufacturer and consumers that maximizes an individual's contribution to long-term profit. This is achieved through sophisticated database management, cross selling, and promotion of product upgrades across several purchase cycles.

Direct marketing can be online, offline, or a combination. The true divide between digital and direct marketing comes down to one simple economic fact: cost per incremental online contact is effectively zero. Once you have set up an e-mail program and a website, each e-mail or page view costs you tenths of a penny. Traditional direct marketing starts with good list selection. Given the cost of paper, printing, and postage, the cost of each piece of direct mail delivered is exponentially higher. Traditional direct marketers carefully select their target audience for maximum potential response. They "cut a list"—a small subset of the prospect universe—by eliminating great swathes of the population that are less likely to respond to an offer. Digital CRM, on the other hand, starts with creating an inspired offer, and this can be presented to any individual whom marketers have permission to contact. Predictive Big Data applications compile comprehensive lists from virtual communities or user profiles. Digital marketers have no economic reason not to contact everyone; the only penalty for overmailing is an increase in opt-outs. So segmentation is invaluable online for gleaning guidance for how to structure an offer and maximize content appeal among different clusters of consumers.

MOBILE TECHNOLOGY: OMNIPRESENT DELIVERANCE?

It is difficult to overstate the transformative role mobile technology has had in the lives of consumers. For many in the emerging world, their mobile phone is the only device they own, the only portal to a digital universe of apps and other services. According to ComScore, a leading digital analytics firm, more than 50 percent of searches in the United States take place on mobile devices. But marketers have yet to invest significant advertising dollars in mobile. In 2011, for example, American consumers spent 20 percent of "digital time" engaging with their phones. But, according to digital guru Mary Meeker, only 4 percent of advertising spending is allocated to mobile media.[14] Given the omnipresence of the mobile device in consumers' lives, the contrast between the theoretical central role of mobile in any communications strategy and the limited spending behind the device demands an explanation.

An easy answer is screen size. Few relish squinting to read a banner ad on a two-by-four-inch space. Creative material must be created with a "mobile first" mentality—that is, designed with a small screen and clumsy thumbs in mind. But perhaps the aversion to allocating significant budget to mobile is driven by more than technical limitations. Mobile phones are more than "just another screen." We have a uniquely intimate relationship with our phones. They accompany us everywhere. People are resistant to invasive mobile messages. Marketers must ensure communications surpass a high threshold of personal relevance. Context is king. As a result, users will be most receptive to mobile advertising that touches the heart or the head by (a) connecting people to their passions through a rewarding creative idea that dimensionalizes the brand idea, and (b) facilitating the purchase of salient products throughout the purchase cycle.

Mobile technologies took Nike from an aspirational to an enablement brand. Their suite of services helps consumers live their "Just do it" ambition by joining the Nike+ community. In the words of Stefan Olander, Nike's vice president of digital sport, "It's an emotional connection to myself, and my achievement, and my friends. We've now created an entire ecosystem of services that complement the product."[15] Mondelez' Stride, the chewing gum known as "ridiculously long-lasting,"[16] achieved perfect synergy between product benefit and gaming thrills by launching a mobile game, Gumulon. Players could "chew [all the way to] the future."[17]

Technological friction also must be overcome if mobile advertisers hope to avoid alienating consumers with push notifications during the purchase process, particularly closer to the point of purchase. If and when that day comes, mobile communications will become a fundamental part of the marketing mix. Many predict each of us will soon have a "digital fingerprint," an aggregation and analysis of all our digital and physical (location-based) behavior. Brands will be able "harvest" information on a minute-to-minute basis and design a mobile experience. Without necessarily knowing individual identities, marketers will be able to home in on interests and target messages accordingly through a meticulously designed mobile journey. The following chart has been adapted by a presentation delivered by Joseph Webb, the head of digital at TNS, a market research company. It neatly illustrates that consumer pull can be utilized to optimize, and lower resistance to, mobile communications.

Engagement System Phase	Goal	Mobile Activation
Trigger	Drive impulse	Targeted offer through coupons, other location-based communications
Comparison	Offer more information about more products	Find products, check availability, on-line catalog, in-store comparison
Preference	Improve point-of-sale interaction	Bar or QR code-generated product immersion
Purchase	Increase purchase amount ("size of basket")	Social interaction, mobile "show rooming," mobile loyalty

It should go without saying that all mobile advertising should reflect a well-established brand idea. Relevance is one hurdle. Confusion will also alienate. The most intimate of devices can deepen, or detract from, a long-term relationship between consumer and brand. McDonald's "McGreetings" gave Hong Kongers the chance to personalize lunar New Year's messages to friends and family through an augmented reality enabled mobile app. At the same time, the brand breathed life into the "I'm loving it" proposition.

CONCLUSION

The engagement plan weaves a brand message through the fabric of consumers' lives. The consumer engagement system outlines how consumers make decisions in different areas and how these lead to brand loyalty. The system is a cycle, with six discrete, but not necessarily sequential, phases: trigger, consideration, comparison, preference, purchase, and experience. The types of media consumers use vary according to where they are in the buying cycle, whether products are high or low involvement, and the buyers' familiarity with category options. Digital media facilitate deep engagement with brands, an intimacy that has been the goal of marketers since the dawn of branding. But digital media have not eclipsed mass media. New and traditional media should work synergistically, clearly defining brand propositions while forging a dynamic relationship between consumer and brands.

Technology has the capacity to humanize engagement. Digital media are inherently intimate, and creative ideas channeled through technology are experiences, not messages. They touch the heart and empower people. Ideas turn transactions into relationships. The lynchpin of loyalty, now and forever, remains a distinct brand idea rooted in insight into consumer behavior and brought to life by compelling engagement ideas—online, they are often called content, a topic to which we now turn—that invite participation.

seven

creativity 2.0

The Rules of Online Content

The worlds of online and offline creativity are not parallel universes. Both require message consistency born of a clear brand idea that underpins engagement between consumer and brand. But digital creative execution, usually called "content," must be designed to accommodate the imperatives of an era of consumer pull. Digital platforms ask consumers to take immediate action; content must provide concrete benefits while answering an urgent question: "What's in it for me?" Digital technology is interactive and more intimate than "lean back" media. So marketers must avoid overtly commercial sales pitches. Brands should harness "people power"—that is, the voices of like-minded netizens—to strengthen authenticity and deepen advocacy.

The previous chapter illustrated how engagement ideas, always conceived to trigger behavioral change, are woven through the fabric of consumers' lives as they progress along a shopper's journey and path to purchase. I also made the point that, at each stage, both digital and analog media can be deployed to encourage desired behavior. "Traditional" and "new" methods of communication do not exist in separate universes. But there *are* important differences between digital and "top down" creative.

First, digital advertising is sometimes called "liquid content" because it can appear practically anywhere. The number of digital platforms is multiplying yearly. Marketers no longer control when, where, and how people come into contact with creative. The fractionated nature of digital content can lead to disjointed messaging. Inconsistency across digital channels is a lost opportunity. Since 2013, Singapore Airlines has been running a campaign, "The Lengths We Go To," featuring the iconic "Singapore Girl" originally introduced in the 1970s. On YouTube and other video platforms, beautiful films dramatize dedication to providing the best possible travel experience, a message consistent with the company's long-standing premium position. However, linkage to the campaign is missing from content on the brand's website and other digital real estate. Users are confronted with retail specials and destination offers as well as an undifferentiated online booking process. At several points, the chance to remind consumers of Singapore Airline's uniqueness is missed. Instead, customers are engaged on only a transactional level, the same as with any other airline.

Instead, each piece of content should be approached purposely and reinforce a consistent theme. Red Bull, the performance-enhancing energy drink that targets active youth, focuses all assets on extreme sports and a high-octane lifestyle. These include "mountain climbing bulletins," real-time video feeds of skydiver Felix Baumgartner's "Mission to the Edge of Space," and coverage of two Formula One racing teams, Red Bull and Toro Rosso. In 2013, Red Bull's YouTube channel was the most viewed of any brand, with more than 2.9 million viewers.[1]

Second, digital creative is actively digested. New levels of consumer empowerment and the inherent "connectivity" of digital media require a clear call to action. Surfers make conscious decisions whether or not to engage with—or click on—content. In cyber space, consumer pull—the ability of creative to elicit active participation— is king. As such, all content must answer the question: What's in it for me? For example, in pragmatic China, "instructive" content— complete with course completion certificates—is motivating. Nike's online community of female fitness fans can perfect aerobic skills through a series of "signature moves" videos. Whatever the audience's needs, the creative must be rewarding enough to "opt into." Here are nine ways to do this:

1. Let "people power" enhance authenticity.
2. Let content create value exchange—that is, something useful in exchange for consumers' attention.
3. For message amplification, wrap value in creative execution.
4. Develop inherently social content.
5. Produce "snackable" content to entice deeper engagement.
6. Align content with the path to purchase.
7. Reduce waste by targeting.
8. Ensure content is discoverable.
9. Use data to optimize creative execution.

Just a quick glance at this list suggests digital creative execution does not exist in a parallel universe. Many of the issues I have raised in this book—the importance of insight, the unifying power of brand ideas, and the power of clear creative ideas—are as critical online as they are offline.

1. LET "PEOPLE POWER" ENHANCE AUTHENTICITY

The litmus test of content effectiveness is whether it is interesting enough to be shared. Creative that smacks of commercialism tends not to spread. Content branding should be relatively unobtrusive. In Chapter 3, we talked about Banco Popular, the Puerto Rican bank that encourages citizens to "move forward." The financial institution hit the zeitgeist's bull's-eye with a campaign featuring a popular reinterpretation of the song "I Do Nothing," which also happened to win a Grand Prix at the 2012 Cannes advertising festival.

Jaime Rosado, JWT's Puerto Rico-based regional creative director, explained to me his approach to ensuring genuineness:

> Most brands are already creating relevant content for their consumers. But, in reality, they often need to overcome the perception it's nothing more than advertising disguised as entertainment. That's why I think the brands that will succeed are the ones willing to make partnerships with media players that already have a strong reputation for delivering content to consumers. Banco Popular could have created an original song in order to convince Puerto Ricans to be more productive, but it wouldn't have had the same effect. Changing an already well-known song, and having the same group that made it famous in the first place record it again, was the key to success for this perfect example of content campaign. The partnership with El Gran Combo de Puerto Rico gave credibility and honesty to the bank's content.

In 2014, Banco Popular went one step further. It harnessed people power to maximize authenticity of its creative content. The bank orchestrated a social campaign featuring dozens of ordinary people that also spurred the island to "move forward." Small business owners were invited to promote their products and services. To ensure consistent executional standards, the bank built a full-fledged production studio. From a dread-locked cycler who "sells the best bike brands" to a woman in clown garb who "puts on the best kiddie shows," people got their message out. More than 140 short films and a series of fifty print ads, each adopting the same visual style and storytelling format, were produced within a week. They were

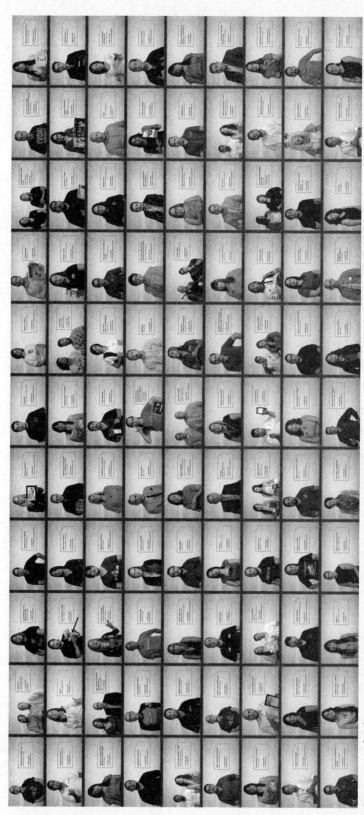

Banco Popular harnessed "people power" to maximize authenticity of its creative content. In an era of growing consumer cynicism, marketers must ensure that their communications, particularly online content, are not perceived as overtly commercial.

then placed on the bank's social media platforms and eventually on broadcast media.

The Puerto Rico Tourism Company earned street cred by using the voices of real people to dramatize the allure of travel destinations. On TripAdvisor, a travel website, traveler reviews were transformed into beautiful short movies narrated by local icons including actor Jimmy Smits and golf pro Chi-Chi Rodriguez. Because the films provided a fresh user experience, buzz spread. Within only three months, they had been viewed three million times and featured in a variety of blogs and leisure publications. Puerto Rico Tourism's social campaign also reminds us of the importance of advocacy; it's not what you say about yourself that counts, but what others say about you.

With a population of only 3.6 million, Puerto Rico is small. But these two cases convey important lessons. In an era of growing brand cynicism and resistance to commercial intrusion, content that harnesses real voices is powerful. But marketers must still make sure they don't lose control of their message. Puerto Rico Tourism, not an unruly blogosphere, carefully selected relevant testimonials and then enlivened them with evocative filmic and musical treatment. Banco Popular constructed a studio so all ads had the same look and feel. Skillful "meme-making" resolves the conflict between top-down message clarity and bottom-up authenticity.

2. LET CONTENT CREATE VALUE EXCHANGE

Back in 2005, Craig Davis, former chief creative officer of JWT Worldwide, produced *Hold My Skateboard While I Kiss Your Girlfriend*, a book that describes the firm's creative approach for staff and clients. The title, a bit confusing even to some advertising people, hints that technology is liberating because it leads to more lifestyle choices. People therefore expect more from brands and demand, "What's in it for me?" Content therefore cannot interrupt—it must *be* what people are interested in. This begs a basic question: What are people interested in? On the most basic level, consumers want information, and that is why they embrace sites that provide it. In China, for example, Johnson & Johnson places content on its Baby Center portal, a natural destination for new mothers. L'Oréal Paris partnered with YouTube to create Destination Beauty, an online resource for teenage girls new to style and dating. The site "not only scopes out the hottest make-up and hair trends for you but also teaches you how to recreate them . . . See a video of one of *Seventeen* magazine's 'Beauty Smarties' showing you how to apply Rihanna's own cover look!"

Deeper value, however, is rooted in insight. Marketers should address fundamental motivations for behavior that spring from unresolved conflicts. Nike+ digital assets and online events such as the Big Gym Throw Down address the tension between the solitary nature of running and the need for collective benchmarks. Knorr, a food and beverage brand owned by Unilever, has introduced the What's for Dinner? website, a destination for busy mothers who lack time but want to express love through home-cooked meals. Founders of small and medium-sized enterprises value both independence and being connected with their counterparts. That is why Singtel, Singapore's largest telecommunications operator, has built myBusiness, an online platform that promotes itself as "the island's largest online SME community." A strong content ecosystem includes myBusiness workshops, data backup message boards, one-office app stores, and video tutorials.

3. FOR MESSAGE AMPLIFICATION, WRAP VALUE IN CREATIVE EXECUTION

Marketers are excited about digital media because it enables them to target their advertising precisely and measure advertising's effectiveness in real time, but sometimes marketers forget about the power of creative execution to maximize the impact of their message. This is unfortunate but understandable. *Digital* is a fat word. It encompasses a broad range of disciplines, some detached from the craftsmanship of ideas that is associated with long-term brand equity—that is, the emotional attachment to brands. The technical engineering skills required to build a platform, optimize users' experience, and design customer relationship management (CRM) programs are linear, analytic, and "left brain." On the other hand, the creativity required for coming up with microsite campaigns, managing an online community, and developing content is lateral, conceptual, and "right brain." Hard-core digital experts do not adapt well to the environment of an advertising agency. As a result their output often lacks a strong creative idea.

It is an obvious observation, but this must stop. Even sophisticated CRM programs should be expressed through engaging ideas. However, few powerful examples spring to mind. Marketers are nonetheless making progress in combining functional messages and new product news with stimulating creative executions. In 2013 Maybelline introduced a new mascara with an interactive sleuth film built around the "hypnotic eyes" of a beautiful spy. Billed as a "Falsies film," the movie had a provocative title, "The Girl with the Big Eyes." Her secret is revealed as "revolutionary dual-ended mascara for 360° all around lash glam," followed by a quick "get it" call-to-action.

Oriental Princess, Thailand's leading mass-market cosmetics brand, produced a similar initiative, an interactive murder mystery called "If Looks Could Kill." The campaign rested on the insight that, for Asian women, beauty is a weapon. In a four-part interactive online miniseries, six femmes fatale, each representing a different makeup set, were suspected of pushing an innocent man to his death. Within a week 250,000 users signed up on Facebook to solve the crime. By watching the four-part miniseries, participants could connect clues to earn discounts. And when each suspect was interrogated, participants had the option of clicking on a how-to-get-the-look video tutorial providing skin-type analysis and application tips. Within two months sales were up more than 40 percent.

To promote its catalog of soft furnishings Ikea, the Swedish home furnishings retailer, produced a series of videos featuring kittens—the real celebrities of YouTube—doing adorable things on

Oriental Princess, a leading Thai cosmetics brand, developed "if looks could kill," an engagement idea that fused technology, cut-through creative, and feminine empowerment.

bedspreads and cushions (needless to say, these videos went viral). Shameless manipulation? Perhaps. But at least cat cuteness was woven into a relevant proposition, "Home. It's how it makes you feel," and a beautiful tagline, "Happy inside."

4. DEVELOP INHERENTLY SOCIAL CONTENT

Content that people share helps build word of mouth and, it is hoped, brand advocacy—that is, peer-to-peer recommendations. No surefire formula for determining what goes viral exists, but content that *surprises* seems to work. As part of its 2005 "Real Beauty" campaign, Dove soap produced two online videos. "Evolution" depicted a plane Jane model who was transformed into a perfect specimen through image manipulation, and the film generated more than six million hits. "Mother and Daughters," an exploration of the negative impact of external beauty standards on young girls, was viewed 500,000 times. According to Millward Brown, an advertising effectiveness research company, the films were equally inspiring, but "Evolution" was almost six times more unexpected.

The challenge marketers face is developing unexpected creative executions that also strengthen brand equity. Here are two examples of how *not* to do it. Tampax, a tampon brand, used extreme humor in a 2013 Russian ad, with a woman in the ocean devoured by a shark. The ad, which may have been a spoof, was perhaps funny to men but not to women who probably resented the association of periods with violent death. Ikea, today one of the most adept players in digital space, released a 2002 video in France that opened with a man seducing a woman on his couch; she ends up dead with a fork stuck in her back. The punch line: "Keep tidy." Crude gags do not reinforce brand loyalty.

Online content should reinforce a brand idea, the long-term relationship between consumer and brand. In 2013 Heineken developed a surprising campaign, "Departure Roulette," that showed travelers in an airport deciding whether to drop everything and fly to an exotic destination. The campaign reinforced Heineken's "Open Your World" platform while whetting people's appetite for the next episode. Equally popular was a series of ads called "Evian Babies" that has run since 2009. Infants dance with the skill of professionals and in mirrors as reflections of adults' younger selves. Rooted in Evian's long-standing claim of purity, the commercials also capture the brand's "Live young" brand idea.

What-if scenarios are surprising. Burger King's "Whopper Freakout," discussed in chapter 6, asked, "What if we took away America's number-one burger for a day?" The answer: both regret and anger. The fast-food chain also conducted an experiment by offering a free Whopper as an incentive to "unfriend" someone on Facebook. And in 2008 actors posing as reporters traveled to far-flung destinations to find "Whopper Virgins" and observe their reactions when tasting the sandwich for the first time. Coca-Cola's viral "Vending Machine" video also falls into the what-if category. Viewers became voyeurs by observing the disorientation of students who expected a Coke but received free goodies instead.

Brands also use topicality to improve the odds that their videos will go viral. Notable examples include:

- Nokia's tweeting "Thanks Apple! ☺ Imitation is the best form of flattery!" during the 2013 debut of Apple's candy-colored iPhone 5c series. Since 2011 Nokia had positioned its high-end Lumia as a colorful alternative to Apple and Samsung.
- OREO's tweeting "Power out? No problem. You can still dunk in the dark" immediately after a blackout at the 2013 Super Bowl.
- Deutsche Telekom's release of the "T-Mobile Royal Wedding" dance video to celebrate the 2013 marriage of Prince William and Catherine Middleton. With the help of several royal look-alikes, the brand dramatized its tagline, "Life is for sharing," in a larger-than-life way.

5. PRODUCE "SNACKABLE" CONTENT
TO ENTICE DEEPER ENGAGEMENT

Snackable content is bite-sized chunks of information that an audience can quickly consume and that the marketer hopes will lead to extended immersion in richer content. Glenn Engler, CEO of the Digital Influence Group, a digital marketing agency with social media at its core, explains, "Is the huge Hershey's bar too much? Here are some bite-sized candies . . . Is the big bag of cookies too filling? Here are 100-calorie packages." Engler's description is frivolous, but then he gets to the point: "[Snackable content] drives trial—and, as a parallel, engagement" and is usually inexpensively produced, often in episodic formats that mobile phone users find to be friendly.

Tablespoon.com, General Mills's online recipe portal, leverages short-form content to tempt Internet users to spend more time on the main site. Users find 30-second videos with simple recipes, with titles ranging from "Brown, Sticky or Jasmine? Pick the Right Rice!" to "How to Roll a Spring Roll." The recipes use General Mills's products as ingredients. In China the Ford Motor Company made 24 short talk-show episodes hosted by Cheng Cheng, a fictional character. Each was filmed inside a Ford Focus, now China's best-selling auto nameplate, with the car's features incorporated in the program. For example, Cheng used its SYNC voice control to change radio stations, set off on long drives to emphasize the car's fuel efficiency, and brought along three beefy guests to highlight its backseat legroom. Ford distributed the content on Chinese Twitter-like social networks. Invitations to visit the permanent Focus site appeared only at the close of each episode.

Again, entertainment value is important, so branding in snackable content should not be too conspicuous. In the words of Sun Tzu, the sixth-century BC Chinese general and author of *The Art of War,* an ancient book on military strategy: "Men can see these tactics whereby I conquer, but what none can see is the strategy out of which victory is evolved." Or, as the old saying goes, "You catch more flies with honey than you do with vinegar."

6. ALIGN CONTENT WITH THE PATH TO PURCHASE

Throughout the buying cycle the distinction between digital and nondigital media is artificial. As discussed at length in the previous chapter, marketers should use both at every stage, although the interactive nature of the online world means that digital creative execution has a more direct impact on consumers' behavior. So it bears repeating: Every piece of content should have a clearly defined purpose based on the shopper's journey. Every piece of content should lead to the next, creating a virtual cycle of "excite, demonstrate, and select." Image-driven creative execution deepens brand engagement in a specific market target, with subsequent content narrowing the consumer's choice and leading to purchase.

Intel is an "ingredient brand" because it is sold only as a component of other brands' products. Despite limited direct sales to consumers, Intel has built a content ecosystem to deepen its brand engagement among indifferent young professionals who influence but do not make IT decisions. It is important to note that each piece of creative execution reinforces Intel's brand idea, "Intel inside," an association of internal substance with external performance on both technological and human levels. Initiatives include social films such as "The Beauty Inside" and "The Power Inside" starring actors Topher Grace and Harvey Keitel, respectively; a series of viral videos that explores the deeper meaning of the tattoos of the Chinese badminton icon Lin Dan; a "Creators Project" to support artists who use technology to push their boundaries of creative expression; and a curated magazine, *iQ*, that adds another dimension to the Intel brand story.

Ikea boasts a content ecosystem that spans the entire shopper journey. To introduce its 2010 "Small Spaces" campaign, it distributed an online video on social media. Demonstrations of how to make "more out of less" sparked consideration of Ikea as the answer to cramped rooms. The film's voiceover led to a call for action: "Small ideas can transform a small space into a generous space. Does a living room really need a sofa? There. We just created a whole wall for storage. And, by adding a love seat, a cozy little nest for two. Now you can do what you want. Together. To make the most of the space you've got, all you need is an open mind . . . It's about finding and using hidden space and choosing furniture that does more than one thing. And it works. And it's not about waiting. It's about doing it today." The video, which more than four million people viewed, included links to an online catalog of space-saving products. Virtual reality apps allowed people to see different decorating and furnishing options, and they could use Ikea's e-commerce site to buy the items they chose.

The buying dynamics of various categories are different so marketers focus their content strategy on different phases of the buying cycle. Johnson & Johnson, for example, provides information to pregnant women and new mothers through social media at times when they are particularly receptive to baby care messages. The company also operates the high-traffic and subtly branded J&J Baby Center. Kraft Foods reinforces consumers' prepurchase preference with a mobile iKraft recipe app—although both Kraft and its competitor General Mills have failed to fuse their branded content with an evocative, and differentiating, brand idea. The airline KLM uses Facebook as a CRM tool to reinforce postpurchase satisfaction by providing personalized responses to 85 percent of all customer queries. In 2009 the consumer electronics retailer Best Buy set a standard for "marketing as a service" to increase the likelihood of repeat purchases. Within a year its "Twelpforce" customer response platform, hosted on Twitter, had responded to nearly 28,000 customer inquiries and enlisted 2,600 employees to share their knowledge. Both KLM and Best Buy's postpurchase efforts would have been even stronger with a creative idea.

Content should complete the loop of the buying cycle. For example, Nike Free, a line of shoes that allows natural foot movement, used creative executions targeting several stages: an online film featuring the tennis star Roger Federer to generate excitement; a two-minute demonstration video to educate consumers about product features; and an e-commerce microsite to convert desire into sales. Likewise, Mercedes-Benz introduced its "magic body control" suspension with a quirky video to generate awareness, a stylish video featuring a German engineer demonstrating on-road responsiveness, and a website with three-dimensional product display through which consumers could also schedule test drives.

7. REDUCE WASTE BY TARGETING

One of the most powerful aspects of online marketing is the ability to target specific demographic or behavioral segments of the market. Too often marketers waste money with content that attracts inappropriate users. In an era of consumer pull, content is like cheese in a mousetrap. Because the cheese, usually an incentive or an experience, can be expensive, marketers must offer the content to carefully defined individuals. This is particularly true for specialized categories and niche segments of the market.

Marketers often celebrate high response without considering what type of consumer should actually engage a specific type of content. For example, in 2012 Microsoft produced several entertaining videos that went viral and featured specific Windows 8 product benefits. Executions included a makeup application contest ("beautiful and fast"); a musician who plays piano while playing Ping-Pong ("work and play"); and an elaborate watermelon sculpture carved with a finger ("the magic of touch"). From a pull perspective these films were successful; one attracted more than five million unpaid views. From a targeting perspective, however, results were less impressive. The YouTube audience was skewed toward people older than 40 rather than early adopters of new technology.

Two problems usually drive misfires. First is the basic issue of content that does not appeal to the right demographic segment. Sofy, the Japanese feminine hygiene brand, used such incentives as a free Apple iPad to draw viewers to Weibo, a Chinese social network. However, 60 percent of the viewers were men. Second, content distribution plans are often poorly conceived. The afore-mentioned Windows 8 videos did not use Facebook, a platform that would have enhanced engagement with the under-30 set. MyBusiness, the portal owned by SingTel, the Singapore telecom-munications giant, is an example of best practice—content was compelling for SME (small and medium-sized enterprise) owners and only SME owners. Likewise, the Nike+ ecosystem draws only serious runners. Depth of engagement, not breadth of viewership, determines success.

Reduction of waste also has a longitudinal dimension. While content should be exposed to only *relevant* individuals—say, run-ners for Nike+ or young women for Sofy—it is worth noting that content is most relevant at particular points in time. Windows 8 should define its target as "people who want to buy a computer," which would in turn help define both content creation (for example, demos that compare and contrast different operating system brands) and touch points (that is, media near the point of purchase). HSBC Premier, an investment service, could distribute content based on, say, the dates fixed deposits mature.

8. ENSURE CONTENT IS DISCOVERABLE

Content will not be effective if consumers do not know it exists or are unable to find it, and broad awareness is difficult to achieve with "unpaid" online media. Although television commercials are often repurposed as online videos, only five Nike commercials have gener-ated more than one million hits, and only two have had more than five million hits. Coca-Cola, a deft online marketer, has produced only four commercials with more than five million views.

Without a search engine optimization strategy, branded content will be a tree falling in a forest when no one is around. No one will see it. Banners ads, the "print" of digital, are an expensive way to lead consumers to online destinations, but new technologies have impressive customization capabilities to ensure creative executions appear only on relevant web pages. For example, if KIT KAT wants to attract viewers to an "ideas for your coffee break" microsite, its banner ad could appear only on leisure and entertainment portals. By tracking users' Internet protocol addresses, marketers can also target specific geographic regions.

Pay per click refers to a small ad that appears on the "sponsored links" section of search results leading Internet users to content. Google's AdWords program is the leader in this space, with Yahoo! and MSN in second and third place, respectively. Many methods are available to optimize "paid search," usually by carefully selecting key words and updating those selections based on specific creative elements of new branded content. "Organic" (sometimes called "natural") results constitute the remainder of what a search engine produces, with listings based on keywords and relevant content found on a website. By specifically tailoring these elements on its website, a company can identify particular audiences, without the expense required for pay per click.

One final basic—but often overlooked—point about discoverability: content should appear only where consumers are receptive to any given message. For example, during 2010 Fisher Price, the manufacturer of educational toys for infants, placed only 47 percent of its content on online forums, with the remainder distributed through Twitter and Facebook. Despite the broad reach of these social media sites, they were ineffective platforms because mothers with kids rarely went to either one to talk about toys. Marketers should also pay attention to the timing of content distribution on any vehicle. Facebook video posts are skewed toward the middle of week and evening, but viewer engagement rates are significantly higher on weekends and during the afternoon.

9. USE DATA TO OPTIMIZE CREATIVE EXECUTIONS

The basics of producing creative material—rooted in relevant insight into consumer behavior and posted where consumers will be receptive to the ads—have not changed as a result of the popularity of digital media. Even using data to optimize creative content is not new. For decades direct marketers have made creative decisions based on "test versus control" experiments in which they adjust their "offer packs" based on the response rates. In the digital era, however, data have turbocharged content optimization. By using real-time analytics programs integrated into social sites such as Facebook, Twitter, and YouTube, marketers can pinpoint the precise elements of banner ads that correlate with increases in response rate.

Every content manager needs a data dashboard to visually represent the effectiveness of content in triggering behavioral change. The content manager then can modify creative execution according to what is and is not working. Content is typically assessed according to two variables: depth of engagement and effectiveness in eliciting desired behavior. The former is measured by such indexes as time spent on site and "bounce rates"—that is, how many people click to a site but leave quickly. The latter is based on whether users move to the next phase of the buying cycle or, in the words of direct marketers, the "purchase funnel." These indexes can be anything from test drive sign-up rates to microsite click-through rates. If engagement and behavior scores do not meet benchmarks, the creative execution is modified. Enhancements include product presentation, for example, side versus front shot; "call to action" copy, such as "try now" versus "discover more"; and "call to action" button presentation, for example, placement at the top or bottom of the screen. Design improvements are usually implemented incrementally, even granularly. Over time, however, the look and feel of advertising can evolve significantly when based on data that fuel a virtuous cycle of "test, learn, and apply" content optimization.

Before

After

Engagement with digital media is measurable. The constant feedback loop that highlights exceptional elements that elicit consumer response and those that do not should lead to creative that evolves over time, as in the case of these "before" and "after" Ford Motor Company digital assets.

TWITTER IS NOT A STRATEGY: WRAP UP

Digital creative execution must evolve. The online world offers infinite destinations, each of which competes with brand advertising. Digital creative execution must evolve. The online world offers infinite destinations, each of which competes with brand advertising. Content has to harness "people power" to avoid overt commercialism and provide value in exchange for their attention. Ideas have to earn consumers' participation. And marketers must become more disciplined to ensure people are even exposed to content. But the digital revolution does not mean marketers should throw away their belief in the value of great creative ideas: creative execution should still reflect a deep understanding of consumers' motivations and be expressed through ideas that intrigue.

In this slim volume I have tried serve a dollop of reassurance to those who may be disoriented by a tidal wave of change. The balance of power between manufacturers and consumers has been upended. Most concretely, *Twitter Is Not a Strategy* offers a paradigm based on four interconnected fundamentals: insight into consumer behavior, the brand idea, engagement ideas, and the engagement plan. By marrying the conceptual craftsmanship of a clear and effective top-down message and the dynamism of bottom-up consumer engagement, marketers attain the freedom in a framework required for strong brand equity and deep loyalty.

I have made a couple broad points, more than once, throughout the book. First, the barriers between traditional and new media are artificial. They must be deconstructed. Throughout all phases of the shopper's journey, both analog and digital channels are critical in defining a brand and providing incentive for consumers to remain loyal to it.

Second, engagement is more than a digital connection between manufacturers and consumers. The latest digital totem or the hottest Silicon Valley data application must not seduce marketers.

Loyalty is rooted in a long-term relationship between people and brands they love. It is born as a "brand idea"—a two-way commitment, long term and dynamic—that provides conceptual unity across an ever-changing marketing landscape, expressed as engagement ideas people want to spend time with. Engaging creative ideas, today or forever, are the source of high price premiums and margins.

Despite new technological possibilities, science must not replace belief. Let's resist the temptation to bow to algorithmic salvation. When process and data overtake inspiration and creativity, marketers are adrift. Function turns people's heads, and emotion moves their hearts. Great marketers have always understood this. They always will.

It will be easier to raise advertising's game if we have enough self-possession to embrace the timelessness of marketing. Marketers have always been consumer advocates; they will always be idea masters. And that's not just reassuring—it is something to be proud of.

notes

INTRODUCTION: BACK TO THE FUTURE

1. Emily Steel, "Algorithms Threaten to End 'Mad Men' Era of TV ads," *Financial Times,* May 13, 2013, http://www.ft.com/cms/s/0/43dde58c -baf5-11e2-b289-00144feab7de.html#axzz338BNkGO0 (accessed May 29, 2014).
2. Alison Griswold, "Big Data Can Help Marketers Unlock up to $200 Billion," *Business Insider,* November 22, 2013, http://www.businessinsider .com/big-data-can-boost-marketing-roi-2013-11#ixzz338CzhzZ2 (accessed May 29, 2014).

CHAPTER 1: NEW WORLD DISORDER

1. The editors of Advertising Age, *Procter & Gamble: The House that Ivory Built* (Lincolnwood, Illinois: NTC Business Books, 1989), 11.
2. "History of CocaCola," Coca-cola.co.uk, n.d., http://www.coca-cola.co .uk/about-us/history-of-coca-cola-1905-1918.html (accessed May 29, 2014) and "Who Designed the Distinctive Coca-Cola Bottle?" Coca-cola .co.uk, n.d., http://www.coca-cola.co.uk/faq/heritage/who-designed-the -distinctive-coca-cola-bottle.html (accessed May 29, 2014).
3. Susan Strasser, *Satisfaction Guaranteed: the Making of the American Mass Market* (New York: Pantheon Books, 1989), 47.
4. "TV Basics," *Television Bureau of Advertising,* June 2012, www.tvb.org /media/file/TV_Basics.pdf (accessed May 29, 2014).
5. "1950s TV Turns on America," *Advertising Age,* March 28, 2005, http:// adage.com/article/75-years-of-ideas/1950s-tv-turns-america/102703/ (accessed May 28, 2014).
6. Ibid.
7. "Global Entertainment and Media Outlook 2013–2017," Pricewater-houseCoopers, n.d., http://www.pwc.com/gx/en/global-entertainment -media-outlook/segment-insights/tv-advertising.jhtml (accessed May 29, 2014).
8. Greg Jarboe, "Super Bowl 2013 Ads: Budweiser's 'Brotherhood' Wins the Big Game," Searchenginewatch.com, February 4, 2013, http://search enginewatch.com/article/2241339/Super-Bowl-2013-Ads-Budweisers -Brotherhood-Wins-the-Big-Game (accessed June 4, 2014).
9. Tom Morton, "The Ads of Super Bowl 2014: A Popularity Contest with Puppies," *Guardian,* February 3, 2014, http://www.theguardian.com

/sport/2014/feb/03/super-bowl-commercials-ads-review-puppies (accessed May 28, 2014).

10. Owen Gibson, "Internet Means End for Media Barons, Says Murdoch," *Guardian,* March 14, 2006, http://www.theguardian.com/media/2006 /mar/14/newmedia.studentmediaawards (accessed April 9, 2014).

11. Jacob Poushter, "Which Developing Nation Leads on Mobile Payments? Kenya," *Fact Tank* (blog), *Pew Research Center,* February 18, 2014, http://www.pewresearch.org/fact-tank/2014/02/18/which-developing -nation-leads-on-mobile-payments-kenya/.

12. Simon Kemp, "Social, Digital and Mobile in Asia," *We Are Social* (blog), *We Are Social,* October 23, 2012, http://wearesocial.net/blog/2012/10 /social-digital-mobile-asia/ (accessed May 28, 2014).

13. Sharon Jayson, "Study: More Than a Third of New Marriages Start Online," *USA TODAY,* June 3, 2013, http://www.usatoday.com/story/news /nation/2013/06/03/online-dating-marriage/2377961/ (accessed May 28, 2014).

14. Yasmine Ryan, "How Tunisia's Revolution Began," *Al Jazeera,* January 26, 2011, http://www.aljazeera.com/indepth/features/2011/01/2011 126121815985483.html (accessed May 28, 2014).

15. Sam Gustin, "Social Media Sparked, Accelerated Egypt's Revolutionary Fire," *Wired,* February 11, 2011, http://www.wired.com/2011/02/egypts -revolutionary-fire/ (accessed May 28, 2014).

16. David Smith, "How TV Ads Are Taking the Net by Storm," *Observer,* February 15, 2009, http://www.theguardian.com/media/2009/feb/15/tv -ads-internet (accessed April 9, 2014).

17. Ibid.

18. Kevin Ashton, "That 'Internet of Things' Thing," *rfidjournal.com,* June 22, 2009, http://www.rfidjournal.com/articles/view?4986 (accessed June 28, 2014)

19. Jack Neff, "K-C: 'We Don't Believe in Digital Marketing . . . [But] Marketing in a Digital World,'" *Advertising Age,* March 21, 2012, http:// adage.com/article/cmo-strategy/kimberly-clark-elevates-clive-sirkin-top -marketing-post/233451/ (accessed June 2, 2014).

20. Jonah Bloom, "Jim Stengel Exhorts 4A's: 'It's Not About Telling and Selling,'" *Advertising Age,* March 01, 2007, http://adage.com/article /special-report-4asmedia07/jim-stengel-exhorts-4a-s-telling-selling/11 5259/ (accessed May 28, 2014).

21. Claire Cain Miller, "Flash-Sale Site Shifts Its Model," *The New York Times,* August 14, 2011, http://www.nytimes.com/2011/08/15/business /flash-sale-site-turns-to-more-traditional-retail-models.html?pagewanted =all&_r=0 (accessed May 29, 2014).

CHAPTER 2: THE VALUE OF STRONG BRANDS

1. Alex Wynick, "iPhone 5S and 5C Launch: Teenager Noah Green Is First Person in UK to Own Gold iPhone 5S," *Mirror,* September 20, 2013, http://www.mirror.co.uk/news/technology-science/technology/iphone-5s -5c-launch-noah-2287362#ixzz3307f67MB (accessed May 28, 2014).

2. "BrandZ Top 100 Most Valuable Global Brands 2013," WPP, May 2013, p. 6, http://www.wpp.com/~/media/Reading-Room/BrandZ/brandz_2013 _top_100_report_may13.pdf.

3. J. Joško Brakus, Bernd H. Schmitt, and Lia Zarantonello, "Brand Experience: What Is It? How Is It Measured? Does It Affect Loyalty?," *Journal of Marketing,* vol. 73 (May 2009): 52–68.

4. Ray Aguilera, Roberto Baldwin, Paul Curthoys, Florence Ion, Susie Ochs, and Nic Vargus, "50 Reasons We Love Apple," *Mac\Life,* April 11, 2011, http://www.maclife.com/article/features/50_reasons_we_love_apple?page=0,4 (accessed June 4, 2014).

5. "Why Do People Love Harley Davidson Motorcycles?" online discussion, n.d., https://answers.yahoo.com/question/index?qid=20080821193852AAXJQAb (accessed June 4, 2014).

6. "LinkedIn's Most InDemand Employers," n.d., http://talent.linkedin.com/indemand/ (accessed May 28, 2014).

7. "Building Brands for the Discerning Consumer," Deloitte.com, n.d., http://www.deloitte.com/view/en_US/us/Industries/consumer-products/d2dd4ac3b6dad310VgnVCM2000003356f70aRCRD.htm (accessed May 28, 2014).

8. "This Time It's Personal: From Consumer to Co-creator," *Ernst and Young,* 2012, http://www.ey.com/Publication/vwLUAssets/This_time_it_is_personal_-_from_consumer_to_co-creator_2012/$FILE/Consumer barometer_V9a.pdf (accessed May 28, 2014).

9. Jube Shiver Jr., "Grand Met Agrees to Buy Pillsbury for $5.7 Billion," *Los Angeles Times,* December 19, 1988, http://articles.latimes.com/1988-12-19/news/mn-457_1_grand-met (accessed May 28, 2014).

10. John M. Murphy, *Brand Strategy* (Cambridge: Director Books in association with the Institute of Directors, 1990), 152–153.

11. Jan Lindemann, "Brand Valuation," in *Brands and Branding,* The Economist Series, ed. Rita Clifton and John Simmons with Sameena Ahmad et al. (Princeton, NJ: Bloomberg Press, 2003), 28–29.

12. Robert D. Buzzell and Bradley T. Gale, *The PIMS Principles: Linking Strategy to Performance* (New York: The Free Press, 1987), 8.

13. Nigel Hollis, "What Price a Strong Brand?," *Millward Brown's POV,* June 2007, http://www.millwardbrown.com/Libraries/MB_POV_Downloads/MillwardBrown_POV_PriceStrongBrand.sflb.ashx (accessed May 2, 2014).

14. "Value-D Balancing Desire and Price for Brand Success," *Millward Brown,* February 2011, http://www.wpp.com/wpp/marketing/brandz/valued/ (accessed May 29, 2014).

15. Michael V. Marn, Eric V. Roegner, and Craig C. Zawada, "The Power of Pricing," *McKinsey Quarterly,* February 2003, http://www.mckinsey.com/insights/marketing_sales/the_power_of_pricing (accessed April 9, 2014).

16. Jon Miller and David Muir, *The Business of Brands* (Chichester: John Wiley & Sons, 2004), 61.

17. Spencer E. Ante and Will Connors, "In the Smartphone Race, Money Talks for Samsung," *The Wall Street Journal,* March 12, 2013, http://online.wsj.com/news/articles/SB10001424127887324096404578356651577771618 (accessed May 29, 2014).

18. Ibid.

CHAPTER 3: INSIGHT INTO CONSUMER BEHAVIOR

1. "Health, United States, 2012," National Center for Health Statistics, www.cdc.gov/nchs/data/hus/hus12.pdf (accessed June 4, 2014).

2. Paula Span, "They Still Don't Want to Live With You," *The New Old Age* (blog), *The New York Times,* June 20, 2012, http://newoldage.blogs .nytimes.com/2012/06/20/they-still-dont-want-to-live-with-you/? _php=true&_type=blogs&_php=true&_type=blogs&_php=true& _type=blogs&_r=2& (accessed May 29, 2014).
3. "Dr Pepper "/1" Campaign Spotlights Real People with Real One-of-a-Kind Stories," *Teletrader.com,* December 28, 2012, http://www.tele trader.com/news/details/19418414?culture=en-GB&ts=1401351016389 (accessed May 29, 2014).
4. Sylvia Ann Hewlett and Ripa Rashid, "Talent in China: A Legion of Ambitious, Qualified Women," *HBR Blog Network* (blog), *Harvard Business Review,* March 17, 2011, http://blogs.hbr.org/2011/03/talent-in-china-a -legion-of-am/ (accessed May 29, 2014).
5. Beth Greenfield, "The World's Richest Countries," *Forbes,* February 22, 2012, http://www.forbes.com/sites/bethgreenfield/2012/02/22/the -worlds-richest-countries/ (accessed May 29, 2014).
6. "Global Index of Religiosity and Atheism,' WIN-Gallup International, 2012, www.wingia.com/web/files/news/14/file/14.pdf (accessed May 29, 2014).
7. "Pakistani Youth Sentiment Survey: Time For Change," *JWT Pakistan,* December 5, 2012, http://www.jwt.com/en/pakistan/thinking/atimefor change/ (accessed May 29, 2014).
8. "The Pulse of Singapore," YouTube video, 2:20, posted by Channelocbc, November 15, 2012, http://www.youtube.com/watch?v=0hEOa8EHrVA.
9. Vinay Dixit, Max Magni, Ian St-Maurice, Claudia Suessmuth-Dyckerhoff, and Hsinhsin Tsai, "2008 Annual Chinese Consumer Survey," *McKinsey,* n.d., http://csi.mckinsey.com/~/media/Extranets/Consumer Shopper In sights/Reports/2008/2008_ANNUAL_CHINESE_CONSUMER_SUR VEY.ashx (accessed May 29, 2014).
10. Neil MacFarquhar, "Banks Making Big Profits From Tiny Loans," *The New York Times,* April 13, 2010, http://www.nytimes.com/2010/04/14 /world/14microfinance.html?pagewanted=all&_r=0 (accessed June 2, 2014).

CHAPTER 4: THE BRAND IDEA

1. Andrew Maia, "The Lego Story: More than just a toy brand," (blog), *CoreBrand.com,* August 14, 2012, http://www.corebrand.com/news -views/blog/613-the-lego-story (accessed June 28, 2014).
2. "JWT's Bob Jeffrey Advocates for the Primacy of the Brand; At Next Big Idea Conference, Chairman and CEO Explores 21st-Century Brand Building and the Dumbing Down of Brands in Keynote Address," *PR Newswire,* n.d., http://www.prnewswire.com/news-releases /jwts-bob-jeffrey-advocates-for-the-primacy-of-the-brand-at-next-big -idea-conference-chairman-and-ceo-explores-21st-century-brand-build ing-and-the-dumbing-down-of-brands-in-keynote-address-58956817 .html (accessed May 29, 2014).
3. Maurice Saatchi, "The Strange Death of Modern Advertising," *Financial Times,* June 22, 2006, http://www.ft.com/cms/s/0/abd93fe6-018a-11db -af16-0000779e2340.html#axzz330xX82sZ (accessed May 28, 2014).

4. Enid Tsui and Henny Sender, "TPG Steps in to Restructure Li Ning," *Financial Times,* July 5, 2012, http://www.ft.com/intl/cms/s/0/92481b96-c67e-11e1-943a-00144feabdc0.html#axzz32stN5qxK (accessed June 3, 2014).

5. "Nielsen: 50% of Global Consumers Surveyed Willing to Pay More for Goods, Services from Socially Responsible Companies, Up from 2011," Nielsen press release, August 6, 2013, http://www.nielsen.com/us/en/press-room/2013/nielsen-50-percent-of-global consumers-surveyed-will ing-to-pay-more-fo.html (accessed May 28, 2014).

6. Saj-Nicole Joni, "Beware the Hidden Traps in Cause Marketing," *Forbes,* October 20, 2011, http://www.forbes.com/sites/forbesleadershipforum/2011/10/20/beware-the-hidden-traps-in-cause-marketing/ (accessed June 3, 2014).

7. Zara Stone, "The K-Pop Plastic Surgery Obsession," *The Atlantic,* May 24, 2013, http://www.theatlantic.com/health/archive/2013/05/the-k-pop-plastic-surgery-obsession/276215/ (accessed June 3, 2014).

8. "Safeguard. Empowering Mothers over the World to Protect Their Families' Health with Trusted Germ Protection, Day in and Day out," Pg.com, n.d., http://www.pg.com/en_US/brands/global_beauty/safeguard.shtml (accessed June 3, 2014).

9. Adidas Group, "Pushing Boundaries. Adidas Group Annual Report 2012," http://www.adidas-group.com/media/filer_public/2013/07/31/gb_2012_en.pdf (accessed May 28, 2014).

10. Adidas Group, "Pushing Boundaries. Nine Months Report January–September 2013," http://www.adidas-group.com/media/filer_public/2013/11/07/q3_2013_en.pdf (accessed May 28, 2014).

11. Cherry Lu Cui, Mickey Fang Xu, and Jeff Kao, "China's Beer Industry: Breaking the Growth Bottleneck," *Accenture Institute for High Performance,* October 4, 2012, http://www.accenture.com/us-en/pages/insight-china-beer-industry-breaking-growth-bottleneck.aspx (accessed May 28, 2014).

12. "China Beer Consumption Hits the 50 billion Litre Mark for First Time in 2011," Mintel press release, June 13, 2012, http://www.mintel.com/press-centre/food-and-drink/china-beer-consumption-hits-the-50-bil lion-litre-mark-for-first-time-in-2011 (accessed May 28, 2014).

13. "The Milk and Dairy Market in China," *KPMG,* June 6, 2008, http://www.kpmg.com/cn/en/issuesandinsights/articlespublications/pages/milk-dairy-mkt-china-200806.aspx (accessed May 28, 2014).

14. "Air Transport, Passengers Carried," Worldbank.org, n.d., http://data.worldbank.org/indicator/IS.AIR.PSGR/countries?display=graph (accessed May 28, 2014).

15. Mary Jane Credeur and Mary Schlangenstein, "Airlines Fight for First- and Business-Class Passengers," *Bloomberg Businessweek,* May 30, 2013, http://www.businessweek.com/articles/2013-05-30/airlines-fight-for-first-and-business-class-passengers (accessed May 29, 2014).

CHAPTER 5: ENGAGEMENT IDEAS

1. Roland T. Rust and Richard W. Oliver, "The Death of Advertising," *Journal of Advertising,* Volume XXIII, Number 4 (December 1994): 71-77.

2. Becky Ebenkamp, "CLIO: 'Advertising Agencies Are Dead,' Says Exec," *AdWeek,* May 14, 2009, http://www.adweek.com/news/advertising-branding/clio-advertising-agencies-are-dead-says-exec-112284 (accessed May 28, 2014).

3. Bill Lee, "Marketing Is Dead," *HBR Blog Network* (blog), *Harvard Business Review,* August 9, 2012, http://blogs.hbr.org/2012/08/marketing-is-dead/ (accessed May 28, 2014).

4. Stefan Olander and Ajaz Ahmed, "A Public Announcement: Advertising Is Over," *Wired.co.uk,* May 18, 2012, http://www.wired.co.uk/magazine/archive/2012/06/ideas-bank/a-public-announcement-advertising-is-over (accessed May 28, 2014).

5. JWT, "Rising from the Grave—Advertising Is Alive and More Creative Than Ever," *JWT News* (blog), *JWT.com,* October 1, 2012, http://www.jwt.com/blog/jwt_news/death-of-advertising/#sthash.Kogi62on.dpuf (accessed May 29, 2014).

6. Guy Murphy, "How Brands Are Built in the Digital Age: The Opt-in Age of Brands," *Admap,* December 2013, http://sodapi.files.wordpress.com/2013/12/how_brands_are_built_in_the_digital_age_the_optin_age_of_brands.pdf.(accessed June 28, 2014)

7. Ibid.

8. Celia Garforth, "It's what's on the inside that counts: a heart-to-heart model of brand building in the digital age," *Admap Prize 2014,* n.d. (accessed June 28, 2014)

9. "Bruce Lee: The Lost Interview (Filmed in 1971)," YouTube video, 24:36, posted by Movies, Books & Fun, http://www.youtube.com/watch?v=PFQ7UxUdIH8.

10. Jack Neff, "How Much Old Spice Body Wash Has the Old Spice Guy Sold?" *Advertising Age,* July 26, 2010, http://adage.com/article/news/spice-body-wash-spice-guy-sold/145096/ (accessed June 3, 2014).

11. Jacques Bughin, Jonathan Doogan, and Ole Jørgen Vetvik, "A New Way to Measure Word-of-Mouth Marketing," *McKinsey Quarterly,* April 2010, http://www.mckinsey.com/insights/marketing_sales/a_new_way_to_measure_word-of-mouth_marketing (accessed May 28, 2014).

12. "Beyond the Dashboard: The Correlation between Online Advocacy and Offline Sales," *MotiveQuest,* n.d., http://motivequest.com/wp-content/uploads/2013/03/The-Dashboard2.pdf (accessed May 29, 2014).

13. "Volkswagen: Building the People's Car—Case Study," YouTube video, 2:13, posted by Brand News, June 30, 2013, http://www.youtube.com/watch?v=2sDmROr1Xjk.

14. Alice Vincent, "China's Internet Rehabs Highlighted by Web Junkie Documentary," *The Telegraph,* January 23, 2014, http://www.telegraph.co.uk/culture/film/film-news/10591750/Chinas-internet-rehabs-highlighted-by-Web-Junkie-documentary.html (accessed May 29, 2014).

15. Nick Parish, "Projector's Koichiro Tanaka Explains the UNIQLOCK," *Advertising Age,* April 03, 2008, http://adage.com/article/behind-the-work/projector-s-koichiro-tanaka-explains-uniqlock/126141/ (accessed May 29, 2014).

16. "APG Creative Strategy Awards—Axe 'Wake-up Service' by BBH Singapore," *Campaign,* August 11, 2009, http://www.campaignlive.co.uk/news/926148/ (accessed May 29, 2014).

17. "JWT Vintage—Wilkinson Sword 'Fight for Kisses' by JWT Paris—2007," YouTube video, 4:02, posted by JWTMENA, October 24, 2011, http://www.youtube.com/watch?v=8gblZDqA3vU (accessed May 28, 2014).

18. Thomas Crampton, "Harry Hui: How Pepsi Engages China's Youth," *Thomascrampton.com*, October 16, 2007, http://www.thomascrampton.com/media/harry-hui-how-pepsi-engages-chinas-youth/ (accessed June 3, 2014).

19. "Durex Fundawear—The technology [OFFICIAL]," YouTube video, 1:55, posted by Durex Australia, April 17, 2013, http://www.youtube.com/watch?v=T6vul95hwOY (accessed May 29, 2014).

20. "Cannes Winners 2013: Durexperiment Fundawear," *Havaspr.com*, n.d., http://havaspr.com/?page_id=1404 (accessed June 4, 2014).

21. "IAB Awards 2012 winner—Pedigree Adoption Drive," *Marketing*, August 21, 2012, http://www.marketingmag.com.au/case-studies/iab-awards-2012-winner-pedigree-adoption-drive-18048/#.U47eUnaG7eE (accessed June 4, 2014).

22. "She Runs the Night," Nikeinc.com, May 16, 2012, http://nikeinc.com/news/she-runs-the-night-sydney (accessed May 29, 2014).

23. "Canon 'Photochains' Case Study," YouTube video, 3:35, posted by Leo Burnett, June 22, 2010, http://www.youtube.com/watch?v=wS1dO8ydngE.

24. "Kiwis to Be Stitched Up by Adidas," *Campaign Brief*, July 17, 2008, http://www.campaignbrief.com/nz/2008/07/kiwis-to-be-stitched-up-by-adi.html (accessed June 4, 2014).

25. "Pepsi Refresh Project Opens Online Site for Idea Submissions," Pepsico.com, January 13, 2010, http://www.pepsico.com/PressRelease/Pepsi-Refresh-Project-Opens-Online-Site-for-Idea-Submissions01132010.html (accessed May 29, 2014).

26. "R K Misra Journeys from Village to Lead India," *The Times of India*, February 10, 2008, http://timesofindia.indiatimes.com/india/R-K-Misra-journeys-from-village-to-Lead-India-/articleshow/2770280.cms?referral=PM (accessed June 4, 2014).

27. "Tesco Builds Virtual Shops for Korean Commuters," *The Telegraph*, June 27, 2011, http://www.telegraph.co.uk/technology/mobile-phones/8601147/Tesco-builds-virtual-shops-for-Korean-commuters.html (accessed June 4, 2014).

28. "Connecting Lifelines," *Spikes.asia*, n.d., http://www.spikes.asia/winners/2012/promo/entry.cfm?entryid=1421&award=99&order=0&direction=1 (accessed June 4, 2014).

29. "M13. Online Marketing," Digitalasiafestival.com, n.d., http://www.digitalasiafestival.com/winner/m13-online-marketing/the-shortlist (accessed June 4, 2014).

CHAPTER 6: ENGAGEMENT PLANNING

1. Dana Mattioli, Ruth Bender, and Suzanne Vranica, "Omnicom and Publicis Call Off $35 Billion Merger," *The Wall Street Journal*, May 9, 2014, http://online.wsj.com/news/articles/SB10001424052702304655304579550422060704330 (accessed June 3, 2014).

2. "Cost of Living in China," Numbeo.com, n.d., http://www.numbeo.com/cost-of-living/country_result.jsp?country=China (accessed June 3, 2014).

3. Wang Yanlin, "Shanghai Residents Still Top of Income Table," *Shanghai Daily.com*, January 26, 2013, http://www.shanghaidaily.com/Business /economy/Shanghai-residents-still-top-of-income-table/shdaily.shtml (accessed June 3, 2014).

4. Erwin Gabardi, Theodore Huang, and Sha Sha, "Getting to Know China's Premium-Car Market," *McKinsey Quarterly,* June 2013, http://www .mckinsey.com/insights/asia-pacific/getting_to_know_chinas_premium -car_market (accessed May 29, 2014).

5. *Modern Family.* Season 5, Episode no. 12, aired on January 15, 2014 on ABC. Directed by James Bagdonas.

6. Ingrid Lunden, "Digital Ads Will Be 22% of All U.S. Ad Spend in 2013, Mobile Ads 3.7%; Total Global Ad Spend in 2013 $503B," *TechCrunch .com,* September 30, 2013, http://techcrunch.com/2013/09/30/digital -ads-will-be-22-of-all-u-s-ad-spend-in-2013-mobile-ads-3-7-total-gobal -ad-spend-in-2013-503b-says-zenithoptimedia/ (accessed June 3, 2014).

7. "The Birth of the Egg McMuffin," Aboutmcdonalds.com, n.d., http:// www.aboutmcdonalds.com/mcd/our_company/amazing_stories/food /the_birth_of_the_egg_mcmuffin.html (accessed June 3, 2014).

8. "The Virtuous Circle," *GroupM Search,* February 2011, http://www.wpp .com/~/media/sharedwpp/readingroom/digital/groupm_search_the _virtuous_circle_feb11.pdf (accessed May 29, 2014).

9. Sid Shah, "Adobe Releases First Global Digital Advertising Update for Q1 2012," *Digital Marketing Blog* (blog), *Adobe.com*, April 11, 2012, http:// blogs.adobe.com/digitalmarketing/digital-marketing/adobe-releases -first-global-digital-advertising-update-for-q1-2012/.

10. "Coca-Cola Invites the World to Join Its New Journey," Coca-cola company.com, November 12, 2012, http://www.coca-colacompany.com /press-center/press-releases/coca-cola-invites-the-world-to-join-its-new -journey (accessed May 29, 2014).

11. "Shopper Decisions Made In-store by OgilvyAction," WPP Consumer Insights, n.d., http://www.wpp.com/wpp/marketing/consumerinsights/shop per-decisions-made-instore/.(accessed June 28, 2014)

12. Jeff Berry, "Bulking Up: The 2013 COLLOQUY Loyalty Census," *COL-LOQUY,* June 2013, http://www.colloquy.com/files/2013-COLLOQUY -Census-Talk-White-Paper.pdf (accessed May 29, 2014).

13. Adam Weissenberg and Jonathan Holdowsky, "Rising Above the Clouds," *Deloitte,* n.d., http://www.deloitte.com/assets/Dcom-UnitedStates/Local Assets/Documents/THL/us_thl_rising_above_the_clouds_POV_080813 .pdf (accessed May 29, 2014).

14. Mary Meeker, "Internet Trends 2014—Code Conference," *Kpcb.com,* May 28, 2014, http://www.kpcb.com/internet-trends. (accessed June 28, 2014)

15. Tim Nudd, "How Nike+ Made 'Just Do It' Obsolete," *Adweek,* June 20, 2012, http://www.adweek.com/news/advertising-branding/how-nike -made-just-do-it-obsolete-141252 (accessed June 28, 2014)

16. "Stride, The Ridiculously Long Lasting Gum, Introduces Stride Spark— A New Gum With B Vitamins," Mondelezinternational.com, February 10, 2011, http://global.mondelezinternational.com/mediacenter/country -press-releases/us/2011/us_pr_02102011b.aspx (accessed June 28, 2014)

17. "CHEW THE FUTURE! Introducing Gumulon," Welcome to optimism (weblog), *Wieden + Kennedy London,* June 20, 2013, http://wklondon

.typepad.com/welcome_to_optimism/2013/06/chew-the-future-introduc
ing-gumulon.html (accessed June 28, 2014).

CHAPTER 7: CREATIVITY 2.0

1. Zoe Fox, "The 10 Biggest Brands on YouTube," *Mashable.com,* October
   30, 2013, http://mashable.com/2013/10/30/youtube-biggest-brands/ (accessed June 28, 2014).

index

360-degree branding, 185
360-degree marketing, 155
4As Media Conference and Trade
    Show, 31

above- and below-the-line creative
    executions, 185–86
Absolut, 104, 182
Accenture, 142
Adidas, 108–10, 129–31, 174
Adobe, 207
Advertising Week, 154
Agassi, Andre, 117
Ahmed, Ajaz, 154
airlines, 101–2, 144–46, 180,
    192–93, 210, 215, 222, 234
Al Jazeera, 24
algorithms, 1–2, 30, 207, 215, 241
Ali, Rafat, 25
Alibaba Group, 150
Allergycast, 2
American Airlines, 102, 145
American Dream, 64, 109
Angie's List, 201, 206
Anheuser-Busch In-Bev, 142
Anta, 96, 109–12
Apple
    brand cynicism and, 43–44
    brand idea, 95, 135, 137
    brand strength, 39–43
    composite products, 82
    consumer engagement, 211, 215
    differentiation, 109, 135, 211
    loyalty of customers, 37–39, 47–48
    market share, 53, 131
    Nokia and, 231
    price and, 49

success, 38–39
    targeting and, 236
    technological innovation, 135
    "Think Different" campaign,
        40–41, 95, 135
Apple Jacks, 16–18
AppsFlyer, 29
Arab Spring, 24
Arby's, 158
Ariel, 183
Armani, 109, 150, 210
Ashton, Kevin, 29
ASIMO, 125
Australia, 8, 43–44, 55, 79, 166,
    171–74, 192
authenticity, 5, 9, 14, 221, 223–26
Axe, 6, 8, 170, 181–82, 192
    see also Lynx

B&Q, 85
Banco Popular, 75, 223–26
Barbie, 79, 122
Bass Brewery, 14
Bayer, 215
Beckham, David, 130
Best Buy, 234
Big Brother (TV show), 27
Big Data, 1, 188, 214
Bing, 206
blogs, 9, 23, 27, 61, 92, 106, 134,
    154, 165–66, 169, 208, 226
BMW, 11, 32, 39, 106, 109, 116
Body Shop, 37, 82, 209
Bouazizi, Mohamed, 24
bottom-up engagement, 4–5, 11, 16,
    25–28, 30, 185, 226, 240
Bouras, Tricia, 64

Boyd, Michael, 145
BP, 123
branding
  brand characteristics, 96
  brand experience, 93, 157, 198, 200, 209
  brand extension, 46, 146–50
  brand stewards, 33, 132
  history of, 12–16
BrandZ Top 100 Strong Brands, 45–46
Branson, Richard, 146
brevity, 98
bricks-and-mortar stores, 22, 45, 179, 213
British Airways, 145
Brown, Ashley, 209
Brown, Josie, 166
Bryant, Kobe, 116, 173
Buddhism, 6, 61, 68, 71
Budweiser, 184, 211
Buick, 150
Burberry, 184
Burger King, 162, 164, 231
business-to-business (B2B), 149
buzzwords, 1, 182–84, 192

Cadbury, 26–27, 100–2
Canadean, 44
Cannes advertising festival, 58, 92, 125, 134, 170, 179, 224
Canon, 8, 141, 174
Carnegie Mellon University, 29
Carter, Majora, 175
Cartier, 50, 70
Cathay Pacific, 145
Chanel, 210
Cheng Cheng, 232
Cheng, Wendy, 23
China
  brand ideas and, 130, 132
  branding and, 12, 43, 87–89, 99, 149, 215, 223, 227, 232–33, 236
  consumer behavior, 6, 22–24, 55, 57–58, 196
  CSR and, 124
  culture, 70–72, 74, 77–80
  disruption and, 141–43
  engagement and, 31, 60, 165, 167–68, 170–71
  "face" and, 70–71

imagery and, 186–87
individualism and, 63, 65–67
insight and, 53–54
internationalism and, 108, 110–13, 116–19
intimacy and, 191–92
lian ziji, 96
loyalty and, 165
megabrands and, 77–80
Mont Blanc and, 70–71
Nike and, 20
pricing and, 50
product truth and, 100
secularism, 69
social media and, 21–22, 205
trend arbitrage and, 83–85
value justification and, 81–82
Chunlan, 79, 149
cloud hosting, 30
Coca-Cola, 7, 15–16, 35, 45, 49, 99, 104, 133, 209, 231, 236
Colgate, 211
Colloquy, 214
colors, 15, 104, 122, 155, 199, 211, 231
ComScore, 51, 217
Confucianism, 6, 61, 63, 65–67, 71–72, 77, 110, 132, 192, 197
conglomerate brands, 79
consistency, 2–3, 5–7, 13–15, 31–32, 36, 42, 44, 48–52, 88, 91, 99, 106, 108, 115, 124, 129, 132, 137, 143–44, 155, 169, 174, 176, 180, 185, 213, 222, 224
Consumer Reports, 200, 207
contextual rationalism, 85–86
cookies (food), 162–63, 195, 232
cookies (Internet), 1
core equities, 103
corporate social responsibility (CSR), 122–24, 147, 172
creative execution, 7–10, 88, 90, 92, 116, 130, 133, 143, 155–56, 159–60, 179–80, 182, 185–88, 207, 221, 223, 227–30, 233, 235, 237–40
Crest, 211
cross-category competition, 85
Cultures and Organizations: Software of the Mind (Hofstede), 62

customer relationship management (CRM), 1, 30, 113, 165, 216, 228, 234

Daley, Tom, 130
Danone, 82
Datura, 28
Davis, Baron, 108
Davis, Craig, 226
De Beers, 74, 115, 118, 135–36
Dean, James, 64
Deloitte, 43, 215
Delta Airlines, 146
Deng Xiaoping, 110
Deutsche Telekom, 231
developing countries, 43, 48, 71, 78–82, 85, 113
Diesel, 64
differentiation, 2, 6–7, 12, 14–15, 57, 86, 88–90, 97–102, 109, 113–14, 140–41, 144–46, 151, 200, 209, 214, 220, 234
disruptions, 2, 25, 137–46, 204, 211
  changes to business environment, 144–46
  changes to competitive set, 142–44
  technological upheaval, 137–42
Double A, 102
Dove, 7, 55, 102–3, 123–24, 175, 230
Downy, 79
Dr Pepper, 65
Dru, Jean-Marie, 137
Dumex, 113
Durex, 171–72

earned media mentions, 208
e-commerce, 1, 22, 33–34, 113, 149, 179, 201, 208, 210, 212, 234–35
Economist, 183
ego goods, 195–96
Egypt, 12, 25, 136–37
Einstein, Albert, 58
Elevit, 215
Eloqua, 30
E-Mart, 179
Enfantbon, 113
engagement
  advocacy and, 162–77
  "be water," 158–61
  common interests, 171–74
  defining, 180–82
  engaging e-influencers, 166–77
  individuals, 168–71
  opting in and, 156–58
  overview, 153–56
  ROI and, 165–66
  useless buzzwords and, 182–87
  with technology vs. ideas, 177–80
  worldwide, 174–76
Ermenegildo Zegna, 150
Ernst & Young, 43
Evian, 82

Facebook, 9, 21–22, 24–25, 43, 92, 105–6, 150, 154, 162, 165, 172–73, 190, 201, 207, 228, 231, 234, 236–38
Fakka, 137
filial piety, 65
Fisher Price, 85, 237
flash sales, 36
FlightTrack, 146
focus groups, 76
Folgers, 202
Ford, 147–48, 232, 239
Friesland Dairy, 113–15
Friso, 113
Frosted Flakes, 181
frugal innovation, 82–83
Fry, Stephen, 27
Fujifilm, 137, 141
Fukushima disaster, 179

Garforth, Celia, 157
Garnett, Kevin, 112
Gate Guru, 146
General Electric, 149
General Mills, 232, 234
General Motors, 109, 147, 150
Gillette, 212
Gilt.com, 34
Gini coefficient, 110
globalization, 14, 61, 95
GoDaddy, 19
Gome, 192
Google, 19, 34, 38, 42, 94, 98, 105–6, 157, 187, 190, 206–7, 209, 211, 237
Gotlieb, Irwin, 190
Grace, Topher, 233
Green Giant, 18

Green, Noah, 37–38, 44
GroupM, 190, 206
Gucci, 84

H-E-B supermarket, 212
Häagen-Dazs, 50, 211
Haier, 215
Harbin, 142
Harley-Davidson, 42, 106
HBO, 39, 60–61
Head & Shoulders, 208, 211
Heineken, 230–31
Heinz, 14
high-involvement, 48, 194–97, 206,
    208
Hilton, Perez, 27
Hofstede, Geert, 62–63
Hold My Skateboard While I Kiss
    Your Girlfriend (Davis), 226
Homeplus, 177, 179
Honda, 107, 125–30, 150, 179–80
Hong Kong, 63, 65–68, 72, 196, 219
HSBC, 96–97, 150, 236
Huggies, 191, 215
Hui, Harry, 171

IBM, 210–11
identity goods, 195–96
illegal DVDs, 23, 51
image consistency, 185
India, 18, 43, 61, 66, 80, 82, 119,
    133, 143, 149, 176–78
individualism, 6, 61, 63–67, 73, 77,
    85, 110, 116, 119, 122, 129,
    173, 181
Indonesia, 18, 55, 61, 68, 71–72, 88,
    166
Industrial Revolution, 4, 12–13, 47,
    91
innovative communications, 133–34
Instagram, 22, 92, 173
intangible assets, 106–7
Intel, 140, 233
Interbrand, 45
internationalization, 107, 116
intimacy, 191–93, 219
iPad, 82, 135, 236
    see also Apple
iPhone, 37–38, 40, 51, 141, 231
iQ magazine, 233
Ivory soap, 14–15, 91

Japan, 8, 21, 34, 61, 67–68, 78–79,
    83, 87–88, 90, 94, 100, 107,
    129, 137, 159–61, 169–70,
    179–80, 198, 203, 236
Jeffrey, Bob, 95
Jetblue, 101–2, 146
Jiayuan.com, 23
jingles, 17–19, 65, 106, 154, 202
Jobs, Steve, 40, 95
Johnny Walker, 215
Johnson & Johnson, 2, 7, 14, 47–48,
    99, 106, 227, 234
Joni, Saj-Nicole, 123
J.P. Morgan, 45
juken, 159–61
JWT, 4, 8, 33, 68–70, 87–88, 95,
    105, 119, 154–56, 159–60, 166,
    186, 191, 193–94, 205, 224, 226

Kano, 33
Kantar Media, 18, 51
Keillor, Garrison, 127
Keitel, Harvey, 233
Kellogg, 13, 17, 80, 83–84, 181
Kerouac, Jack, 64
key opinion leaders (KOLs), 166–67
key visual, 186
Khan, Shahruhk, 176
Kia, 107
kiasu, 66
Kim Jin-goon, 109
Kimberly-Clark, 31, 115, 119,
    121–22, 192, 215
King, Stephen, 193–94
KIT KAT, 105, 159–61, 183, 208–9,
    237
Kleenex, 115, 119, 121–22
KLM, 234
Knight, Bob, 95
Kodak, 137–39
KPMG, 143
Kraft, 79, 102, 106, 162, 213–14,
    234
kyosei philosophy, 174

Lao Shan, 143
"lean back" 197–99, 207, 221
"lean in," 156, 198–99, 206
Lee, Bill, 154
Lee, Bruce, 159
Lee Kuan Yew, 67

LEGO, 93–94
Lemon, Keith, 130
"Let It Out" campaign, 119–21
Levi Strauss, 14, 64, 109
Li Ning, 108–9, 111, 113
Li Yuchun, 23–24
life advancement, 195–97
Lin Dan, 233
Lincoln, Abraham, 58
LinkedIn, 22, 42
Lipton Tea, 14, 148
Liu Xiang, 118, 143
logos, 104–5
long-term orientation, 63
L'Oréal, 80, 211, 227
Louis Vuitton, 84
low-involvement products, 48, 134,
    194–97, 206, 209–10, 219
loyalty
    bottom-up communication and,
      25–26
    brand cynicism and, 43–44
    brand experience and, 93,
      214–15
    brand ideas and, 95, 146, 151
    branding and, 3–6, 148
    cause marketing and, 123–24
    differentiation and, 99
    engagement and, 156, 164–65,
      180, 189, 193, 198–200
    human truths and, 58
    price and, 55
    programs, 145–46
    strong brands and, 37–43, 47–49
    technology and, 33, 35
Lumia, 141, 231
luxury brands, 32–34, 49, 73, 84,
    101, 148, 150, 195–96
LVMH, 84
Lynx, 192–93
    see also Axe

MacDonald, Matt, 154
Mad Men, 1, 189–90, 192
Magnolia, 79
Malli, Ratan, 205
Mao Zedong, 74, 110
Marlboro, 180–82
Mars brand, 172
masculinity, 63
Maslow, Abraham, 55–58

mass media, 17, 19, 88, 92, 165,
    184–85, 194, 198–200, 219
Mattel, 79, 82, 85, 122
Maxus Global, 33
McCartney, Stella, 130
McCaw, Richie, 175
McDonald's, 34, 45, 105, 137, 162,
    181, 203, 219
McKinsey & Company, 47, 50, 78,
    164, 196
Mead Johnson, 83, 113
Meeker, Mary, 217
megabrands, 78–80
Meiji, 113
Mengniu, 143–44
Mercedes-Benz, 32–33, 106, 109,
    235
Messi, Lionel, 130
Microsoft, 43, 49, 82, 106, 109,
    149–50, 235
Millward Brown, 45, 48–49, 230
Mishra, R.K., 177
Mizone, 82
mobile banking, 21
Modern Family, 196
Moir, Ben, 172
Monster.com, 183
Mont Blanc, 50, 70–71
Morita, Akio, 203
Motive Quest, 164
MSN, 27, 150, 237
Mubarak, Hosni, 25
multinational brands, 80, 92, 113,
    150
Murdoch, Rupert, 21
Murphy, Guy, 156–57
Mustafa, Isaiah, 133–34, 164
MySpace, 21

NBA, 108, 112
Nestlé, 14, 45, 80–81, 105, 113, 149,
    159–61, 184, 186, 198
Next Big Idea Conference, 95
Nielsen, 17, 43, 122
Nike, 6, 8, 19–20, 39, 48, 73, 95,
    104, 108–10, 116–18, 129, 131,
    134–35, 138, 158, 166, 172–73,
    183–84, 191, 217, 223, 227,
    235–36
Nikon, 140–41
Nokia, 80–82, 109, 141, 231

North Face, 2, 183
Nvidia, 141

OCBC Bank, 72
Ogilvy & Mather, 155, 185, 212
Olander, Stefan, 154, 217
Old Spice, 133–34, 137, 164, 181
Olympics, 58, 108, 112, 116, 118,
    130, 143, 173, 191
Omnicom, 190
OMO detergent, 59–60
online to offline (O2O), 192
opting-in, 8, 156, 158, 168, 188,
    223, 240
OREO, 162–63, 231
Oriental Princess, 228
Oscar Mayer, 106
Outbrain, 29
owned sites, 207–8

packaging, 15, 104, 114–15, 122,
    138, 171, 212
paid distribution, 207
PaidContent, 25
Pakistan, 68–69, 124, 133
Panasonic, 94
Pancasila, 71
passive loyalists, 47
Pedigree, 172
"people power," 9, 221, 223–26
Pepsi, 171, 175, 191, 209
Perry, Katy, 130, 166
Philadelphia Cream Cheese, 102,
    214
Philippines, 38, 78–79, 124, 133,
    213–14
Pillsbury, 45, 181
Pinterest, 22, 92
Playtex, 64–65
Polo (candy), 184
Post Visual, 191
power distance index, 62
PricewaterhouseCoopers, 18
Primo, 30
Pringles, 79
Procter & Gamble, 14, 31, 57,
    75, 77–79, 82, 88, 100, 124,
    133–34, 147, 212
product families, 147
Publicis Worldwide, 2, 190
Puerto Rico, 75, 224, 226

"pull," 9, 156, 208, 218, 221, 223,
    235
pushing, 26, 28–29

Qantas, 145
Quaker Oats, 14
Qualcomm, 141
quantitative rationalism, 30
quick response (QR) codes, 179, 218

"Real Beauty" campaign, 123–24,
    175, 230
real estate, 196
real-time marketing, 28, 215
Red Bull, 222
Refaeli, Bar, 19
Rexona, 213–14
road shows, 200, 214
Robinson, Kane, 33
Rodriguez, Chi-Chi, 226
Rolex, 34, 84, 96, 184
Rolston, Lee, 26–27
Roper Reports, 78
Rosado, Jaime, 224

Saatchi, Maurice, 98, 106
Safeguard, 57, 78, 124
Salsabella, Ollie, 166
Sampras, 117
Samsung, 51, 79, 107, 109, 187, 231
Saridon, 183
Schick Williamson, 170
Schultz, Howard, 82
self-actualization, 56–58, 117, 172
Shaklee Corporation, 84
Shell, 150
shopper marketing, 212
Silverpop, 30
Singapore, 23, 59–60, 66–67, 72–73,
    105, 108, 227, 236
Singapore Airlines, 180, 222
SingTel, 227, 236
Sirkin, Clive, 31
siSense, 28
smartphones, 8, 11, 21, 39, 51, 61,
    82, 141, 158, 172, 179, 199
SME (small and medium-sized
    enterprise), 227, 236
Smits, Jimmy, 226
"snackable" content, 9, 223, 232–33
Snow, 142–43, 184

social networks, 2, 4, 8–9, 19, 22, 24, 34, 92, 149, 165, 173, 205–7, 232, 236
Sofy, 87–90, 100, 236
sonic devices, 106
Sony, 94, 203, 210
Special K, 84, 183
Stamminger, Erich, 130
Starbucks, 11, 39, 50, 82
Stengel, Jim, 33
Sukarno, 71
Sun Tzu, 232
Sunsilk, 100
Super Bowl, 7, 18–19, 156, 231
symbols, 104–5

taglines, 58, 60, 70, 89, 91, 96, 105–6, 112, 125, 138, 144, 175, 183, 192, 215, 231–31
Taiwan, 31, 63, 65, 67–68, 74, 84, 88
Tampax, 230
Tan, Jooheng, 59–60
Tan, Paulk, 166
Tanaka, Koichiro, 169
tangible brand assets, 104–6
Taobao, 149, 213
targeting, 9, 28–29, 76–77, 85, 88–89, 110, 129, 137, 141, 143, 147–48, 150–51, 167, 187, 211, 213, 216, 218, 222–23, 227, 233, 235–37
Tata Group, 149
TBWA, 2, 137
TechCrunch.com, 199
television commercial (TVC), 186–87
Tesco, 177
Thailand, 6, 61, 68, 71–72, 74–75, 88, 102, 182, 192, 213, 227–29
Thompson, J. Walter, 3
see also JWT
Tiffany, 104
Times of India, 176–78
Tingyi Holding Corporation, 84
TNS, 218
top-down marketing, 4–5, 16–20, 26, 30, 67, 93, 185, 222, 240
TPG, 109
trademarks, 14–16, 45, 70, 142
traditional media, 16, 85, 154, 184–85, 199–200, 221

Trailhead, 2
trend arbitrage, 83–84
TripAdvisor, 226
Tsingtao, 99, 142–43
Tumblr, 65
Twitter, 9, 19, 21, 24–25, 35–36, 63, 67, 97, 107–8, 156, 168, 192, 202–3, 209, 215, 234, 236, 239–40, 242
Tylenol, 48

Ubimo, 28
uncertainty avoidance index, 63
Unicharm, 87–90, 100
Unilever, 43, 58–59, 77, 100, 102–3, 123, 170, 181
Uniqlo, 33, 169–70
unique brand offer (UBO), 7, 90, 96, 99, 101
United Kingdom, 14, 26, 32, 37, 43, 62, 66, 79, 121, 130, 140

value
  brand idea and, 91
  cause marketing and, 124
  consumer behavior and, 54, 64, 72
  contextual rationalism and, 85
  customer engagement and, 37–39, 156–57, 190
  internationalism and, 107
  justification, 80–82
  loyalty and, 47
  price and, 49–50
  strong brands and, 39–45
Vancl, 171
Versace, 210
Vesper, Leslie, 65
Victoria's Secret, 106
Vivienne Westwood, 99
Vodafone, 136–37
Vogue, 72
Volkswagen, 19, 167, 195

Webb, Joseph, 218
WeChat, 150, 154, 205
Weibo, 236
Weissenberg, Adam, 215
Wendy's, 162
West, Kanye, 27
What's App, 150
Whisper, 88, 100

Wieden + Kennedy, 20, 104, 125, 129, 164
Wild West, 12, 64, 181
Williams, Andy, 128
Williams, Pharrell, 158
WIN-Gallup, 67–68
Wired magazine, 25, 154
World Cup, 130
WorldMate, 146
WPP, 45–46, 185, 190–91
Wrigley, 82
Wu, Andrew, 84
Wyeth, 113

X Factor, 27

Xbox, 82
Xerox, 211

Yahoo, 42, 206, 237
Yelp.com, 201, 206
Yili, 143–44
YouDrive, 32
YouTube, 19, 65, 119, 123, 133–34, 170–72, 184, 222, 227–28, 235, 238
Yuna Kim, 191

Zazoo, 58
Zegna, 109, 150